MARRIED
to
PARADISE

One Woman's Courageous
Journey of Intuition, Passion,
and Purpose to Build an
Eco Lodge in the
Rainforest

LANA WEDMORE

with Lesley S. King

Virginia

Published in the United States by WriteLife Publishing
(an imprint of Boutique of Quality Books Publishing Company, Inc.)
www.writelife.com

Printed in the United States of America

978-1-60808-232-2 (p)
978-1-60808-233-9 (e)

Library of Congress Control Number: 2020933075

Book design by Robin Krauss, www.bookformatters.com
Cover design by Rebecca Lown, www.rebeccalowndesign.com

First editor: Michelle Booth
Second editor: Olivia Swenson

To my mother for teaching me about respect and values; my father for teaching me about philosophy and astrology; and my stepfather for teaching me to be courageous and to work hard for what you want in this life. To everyone who has been a part of my life, thank you for all of your love and support.

INTRODUCTION

Married to Paradise first germinated within the lush and airy space of the Rancho Grande, or great room, at Luna Lodge. There, I sit with guests and friends during meals and we share our stories. These stories are rich, full of the flesh and bones and heartbeats of our lives. We travel into whole worlds of existence that span the globe.

My stories come from more than thirty years of living within the wilds of the Costa Rican rainforest. I tell of when a boa constrictor nearly squeezed my dog to death. I tell of how a white hawk once cast his glorious shadow across my body while I lay in *Savasana*, and so became my friend and guide. But most importantly, I tell of how, by following my intuition and overcoming great odds, I built my life's dream: a lodge nestled in the middle of a rainforest, and how through this experience, I found my true home.

After relating my stories, guests would look at me in awe, and then exclaim, "Lana, you have to write a book. You have to record this tale for the world to read. It is important and it will help people." For years I listened to this response, from hundreds of people, but I was so busy with the lodge and with projects that I'm passionate about, such as preserving the rainforest, saving sea turtles, and preventing fish farming in our area, that I never ventured into writing.

One day, when yet another guest at the lodge told me he thought I should write a book, I told him my life was so complicated that I wouldn't even know where to focus a book. He said a lovely thing that remained with me: "Write it all." There was such freedom in that notion. It was as though the sky opened and I was flying with my friend the white hawk.

One morning shortly after that, I awoke and said to myself, "I'm writing a book!"

A decade before, a journalist had come to the lodge to write an article for *La Vie Claire*, a magazine adorned with rich photos and published out of the U.S. She wrote of her experience on the Osa Peninsula including a detailed account of the liberating time she had at Luna Lodge. She introduced me in the article as a magical Shaman who talked with the forest's animals, always reaching for my highest dreams and inspiring others to do the same. She captured the true essence of Luna Lodge; I loved the article so much I kept a copy of it in the Rancho Grande for guests to read.

The day I decided to write this book, I called the journalist who wrote that article, Lesley S. King. We hadn't spoken in a decade but she said she had thought of me over the years, and had wondered if I would ever want to write a book. I told her I sensed it was time for this project because of what I was going through. My boyfriend of twelve years and I had just broken up, so I had more space to focus.

As we began the writing process, I could see the Divine's hand in it. I realized how much I needed to give myself love and attention. After so many years of giving to the community, to the lodge, and to my boyfriend, I had forgotten about myself. Writing *Married to Paradise* became a way for me to heal. I thought I was here on this earth to help protect the rainforest, but now I know that I'm here to do that, and more; I'm here to help people become more aware of their need to heal themselves. Now I know my mission is to heal myself, to help heal others, and to heal Pachamama, Mother Earth.

As Lesley and I recorded the beginnings of this creation, we went all the way back to my childhood and my struggles and accomplishments as a young adult, and the experiences that shaped me and gave me the courage to meet the momentous challenges of building a lodge in the rainforest. Through this process, an interesting thing occurred, which often happens when we open up to a new experience in our lives. As my outer life came onto the page, my inner life began to swell with the power of a tsunami. Suddenly, my spiritual path gained momentum. I had pursued spirituality for many years through yoga and study with many inspiring teachers who came to Luna Lodge, but this felt like a crucial new beginning. Revelations came to me daily about my family, my work, my past, and future. The revelations about my past helped heal some deep wounds. Most notably, my sister and I had been estranged for a decade, and through the great surge of love I was experiencing, we reconciled. During this time I also became a Forest Bathing Guide and a Reiki Master.

Everything happens in the Divine's perfect time. When I built Luna Lodge I was being guided, but I didn't know it. I achieved my dream by listening to my intuition, and that fundamental idea threads throughout this book. My soul was guiding me, and I knew that I had to build this place, and I had to be in this place to feel this deep, healing love.

These days, I'm traveling a lot. I speak and raise money for the White Hawk Foundation, whose mandate is to set aside rainforest to preserve it. I also speak about healing within, and the value of doing forest bathing. This work helps me see how much the world needs a book like *Married to Paradise*. People are ready to return to the more elemental part of themselves, to get in touch with their senses and with the love that each one has within.

After my travels in a world that can be chaotic and extroverted, I always return to the rainforest. This sumptuous place throbbing with life calls me back, and I know that I am blessed to have this way of reconnecting with myself. We each have our ways, though in our busyness, it's easy to ignore them. This book, I hope, will serve as a reminder to many to come back into themselves, into the tastes, sounds, and sensations of life, the sensuality that can be such a gift every day if we only open to the now and pay attention.

My father used to quote Ralph Waldo Emerson to me: "Do the thing and you will have the power." In writing this book, we took a step and then another. It took two years to write it, and then we set out to find a publisher. We were graced with an excellent one, that offers a lot of support throughout the process of birthing a book into the world. Now *Married to Paradise* has manifested, with a stunning cover and an inspiring story. Through taking one step, whole new worlds opened to me. That's what I did when I built the lodge, too. I stepped in and took action. This story inspired new beginnings for me. I hope it will do the same for you.

PART I

SNAKE

SHEDDING SKIN: DEATH AND REBIRTH

CHAPTER 1

"I am fearless in the face of all challenges," I say to myself as I shove both feet against the floor of the pickup, trying in vain to slow us down, even though I'm not driving. My '72 Chevy, pulling a horse trailer holding my future, hurtles toward a cliff edge some two hundred yards ahead. An hour ago, I took a break from driving, so my friend Greg Smith is at the wheel. My heart pounds and my hands shake while he pumps the brakes to no avail.

Again I say, even louder, "I am fearless in the face of all challenges," an affirmation I often use to start my day. I repeat it over and over. My heart settles for a moment but then accelerates again. This situation may take more than my affirmations to restore my inner peace.

It's our second week of traveling on a month-long journey from Colorado to Costa Rica. We're descending into Panajachel, one of many villages bordering Lake Atitlán in Guatemala. The paved road slopes steeply as it winds down to the lake, the asphalt ending at a drop-off where landslides have washed away any shoulder, leaving a precipice that plunges hundreds of feet into dense brush. A switchback looms before us, and at this speed we will not be able to complete the turn but will instead launch off the side.

My boyfriend, Fabio Mendez, lies on a mattress in the truck bed, protected from the elements only by a nylon cover. A *Tico*, or Costa Rican by birth, he felt confident he could drink the water anywhere along our journey through Central America, so he drank straight from the tap as we made our way through Mexico. The rest of our group stuck to bottled water.

Raised by fiercely independent gold miners, he tends to follow his own counsel. Much of the time he wears a machete strapped to his hip, and he likes to catch *fer-de-lance* snakes, Costa Rica's most venomous, between his fingers. But now he is weak with traveler's diarrhea, and as we careen around these turns, I imagine his insides swishing from side to side, his stomach heaving with each bump.

Still racing toward the big switchback, we pick up yet more speed, the horse trailer behind us wobbling on its axles. I reach for the door handle. I could open the door and jump out. But I stop myself. Like most situations, the only way out of this is to get through it.

"What do we do?" I yell, taking deep breaths to calm myself.

"Lana, I don't know." Greg continues to frantically pump the brakes, but still nothing happens. Usually a calm man, his red face and shaking hands reveal a whole other part of him. In the back, Fabio is likely oblivious to the danger we're in.

Before it even begins, the dream I have nursed for a decade might end: building my own lodge and welcoming travelers to my piece of paradise in Costa Rica; sharing with them the lushness, wildness, and freedom I have found on the remote Osa Peninsula, where nature rules. When I'm there, my senses awaken, my heart opens, and I merge with the moist air, the symphony of rain and waterfalls, and the chorus of birdsong.

The horse trailer with no brakes of its own swerves madly behind us. All my careful plans are in jeopardy: the grand thatched-roof restaurant with a deck looking out over rainforest canopy to the Pacific Ocean; the bungalows with porches where guests can completely soak in the forest's beauty and the soft, humid air; the healthy food and outdoor yoga classes that will enable a feeling of lightness and communion with nature and themselves. And then my utmost aspiration: to protect my animal friends.

Here, above the stunning sapphire of Lake Atitlán, backed by mighty volcanoes, I call out to the Universe and to all the forces that have guided my life leading up to this moment: *Please help us.* But I get no sign and feel no safer.

Less than a minute has passed since we realized our brakes were gone, and now we near the switchback that will kill my dream. *The dream might kill me. The dream might kill us all.*

Greg yells, "Hold on. I have a plan."

I tighten my seat belt and wrap my fingers around the armrest as we come to the corner. Greg cranks the steering wheel hard to the right, away from a waterfall streaming down the hillside and toward the edge of the cliff. "What are you doing?" I scream.

He doesn't answer as he holds the wheel in a white-knuckled grip.

The pickup lurches, causing the seat belt to cut into my shoulder and waist. I look back to see the trailer racing toward my door. Metal squeals as the trailer strains on the hitch ball and we jerk, and jerk again, so strongly that my head whips forward and my chin hits my chest before the truck screeches to a halt. Brilliantly, Greg turned the truck so sharply that the trailer jack-knifed, forming a V shape with our vehicle—a makeshift brake.

The stench of burning rubber swirls in through the window, and I let out a breath that I have held for who knows how long. My whole body is wet with sweat and my mind is numb. I gaze off the edge of the cliff to see rocks and pebbles, dislodged from our sudden stop, falling and falling until they disappear into brush. Greg and I look at each other.

"That was amazing," I say to him. "Thank you. You saved us."

Our friends who are traveling with us in another truck pull up behind the trailer, jump out, and rush forward, asking questions. I let Greg field them as I hurry to check on Fabio. He clambers out of the back of the truck, still green in the face.

"*Lana, ¿qué pasó? ¿Qué está pasando?*" he demands, desperate to know what is happening. He scans the scene and looks over the cliff edge.

My voice shaking, I tell him about the horror we just escaped. His dark eyes grow wide, and he pulls me into a hug. I let him hold me, comforted by his familiar salty scent.

In this moment, I have no idea what my future holds. All I know is that we are safe, and my dream lives on.

Now I am even more determined to make it real.

CHAPTER 2

An astrologer once told me that my task in this life is to dive down into the lush world of the feminine to develop the softer traits in me and to bring them to others. This is the gift Costa Rica gives me: the lush, moist, and uninhibited influence that I so crave and that is needed to balance modern life.

However, before I made my decision to live in Costa Rica full time, I had to shed a whole world of ideas about who I was and what my life would look like. Those strong influences were at work even before I was born.

My parents met in college and fell in love, both ambitious intellectuals. However, Mom left college with Dad to move to South Dakota to take care of his family's Hereford cattle ranch when his father no longer could. She and Dad both taught Sunday School at the local Baptist church, Mom working with kids and Dad with adults. Mom was aware of Dad's fondness for one of his students, Diane Dodge, an alluring married woman twenty years his senior. But since they mostly saw each other at church, Mom set aside her suspicions.

My father's father had affairs, and my dad, too, was unfaithful to my mother. Dad had low self-esteem, possibly because his father never praised him, instead constantly commended his brother, who became a successful attorney. Dad was intellectual and an impressive orator, traits not valued in his South Dakota ranching family. He also sought a lot of female attention. My mother, too, was philosophical, and she admits they connected more intellectually than physically.

When Mom was five months pregnant with me, she and my father traveled to Denver with Diane Dodge and her husband, Ed. The big event was a touring production of the musical *Hello Dolly*, which they intended to see on the last night. The day of the performance, they all lounged around the hotel pool. My dad and Diane were in the water, very close, talking and laughing. My mother and Ed watched them from lounge chairs on the side. Mom thought she saw them touching underwater but couldn't be sure.

Mom's belly was large with her pregnancy, and she tended to get hot and then her ankles would swell, so she decided to go up to the room to get out of the sun. Ed accompanied her. When they looked off the balcony attached to my parents' room, Dad and Diane were hugging in the water below, her arms wrapped around his neck. His hands clutched the wet hair on her nape.

Before long Dad and Diane came up to the room. Mom turned to look at them through the open sliding glass doors. They stood dripping, with towels around them and big smiles—not even guilty ones—on their faces.

"We had so much fun in the pool, we wanted to see if it's all right if we finish this in bed," Diane said, her cheeks glowing with arousal. It was as though she was asking permission from my mom, who sat stunned.

Diane headed toward the door to their adjoining room. Dad took a step to follow her.

Mom felt a stone in her stomach, where at that very moment I was growing. The life she had previously enjoyed had become a weight. She stood and grabbed the balcony railing. "I think I'm going to jump," she said, and she meant it. So much despair weighed on her heart in that moment that she was prepared to fall five stories and take both of our lives.

Ed came to her. "You're going to be okay, Willie," he said. He held her as she cried into his shoulder.

Dad didn't go out on the balcony. But he didn't follow Diane into the adjoining bedroom either.

My mother let go of Ed's kind embrace and stepped inside, the refrigerated air waking her from her miserable trance. Ed followed, took his wife's hand, and forcefully led her to their room. When they were gone, Mom looked at Dad's smug expression below hair slicked back from his face. She went into the bathroom and locked the door.

She took a shower, spreading her fingers over her belly while the hot water poured down her back. When she was clean and dry, she came out. As evening cast shadows over the bed, with its faux-wood headboard and matching side tables, she put on makeup and her best dress, while Dad showered, pulled on his slacks and shirt, tied his tie, and laced his shoes.

They met Ed and Diane in the lobby and went to see *Hello Dolly*.

I've heard that incidents like this can affect a child in the womb, and sometimes I wonder how it, as well as my father's infidelity in general, affected me.

In 1961, I was born in Rapid City, South Dakota, and lived with a family accustomed to the hard work of managing thousands of acres of ranch land. When I was a little girl my grandfather took me up on a mesa with a 360-degree view. He pointed all around us and said, "As far as you can see, this is our ranch." As great as it was to have that much land, because of it, ours was a family that never stopped moving, and I took on that tendency. It has been my greatest attribute and my biggest challenge because I don't stop and evaluate my choices. Instead, I plunge into the next adventure.

I was the first granddaughter in our family, and so I was special to everyone, especially my grandparents. When I was two years old, my parents brought my new sister home from the hospital and introduced her as Janice Kathryn. I patted her plump little face and called her Jani, and she has gone by that name ever since. Jani had encephalitis, which is an inflammation of the brain, causing irritability, poor appetite, and fever. My parents were definitely stretched. Add to that the pressure of living five hundred yards from my father's parents, who always pushed for more work from us all.

Mom told Jani and me that we were each other's greatest gift, and I believed her. We were inseparable, so much so that people would run our names together. Lana and Jani became Lanajani. We played tag outside on the grass and board games inside on the carpet. Mom taught us not to come "tattling" to her, but instead to settle our differences ourselves, and so we did.

Life on the ranch taught me to be tough. When I was four years old, I went with my grandfather to check on our cattle, and when we returned, he dropped me off at our ranch house. I stepped through the back door that led to the kitchen. Suddenly, a menacing sound filled the room, and in the corner just paces from me, I saw a rattlesnake coiled in a ray of sun. I turned, ran outside, and screamed. My mother and our hired hand came running. Once they knew what had happened, she directed him to get a shovel and kill the snake, which he did.

As we grew up, my father continued seeing Diane Dodge. One time I was running through the choir room at church and I ran into something hard behind the curtain. When I pulled the fabric aside, I found my father kissing Mrs. Dodge. I was little, but I knew something terribly wrong was happening. Dad would also take me over to Diane's house. Her daughters would babysit me while Dad and Diane retreated to a guest bedroom.

When I was five years old and Jani three, Mom couldn't take his infidelity anymore. She was still friends with Ed, Diane's husband, and he told her that the affair was never going to stop. He said she should leave so she could take care of her young girls, so she took us from the ranch to live in Rapid City, South Dakota. The move was hard on me, mostly because I was so accustomed to spending my days outside. Suddenly, we were living in the middle of a city.

Unfortunately for my mom, the move did not end the conflict with my father. One time my dad came to the house and they fought in the living room. Jani and I hid under the coffee table and watched him plead with her to come back to the ranch so we could be a family again. His voice was pure agony, with a tinny, desperate tone. The failure of his marriage sealed his father's negative view of him, as it disgraced the whole church-going family.

When Mom refused to comply, he grabbed her long hair and wrenched her toward him until she screamed. I embraced Jani and we trembled under the table, huddling together as I tried to protect her. It was after this incident that Mom initiated divorce proceedings.

Six months later, Mom, Jani, and I moved to Fort Collins, Colorado, where we lived with my mother's brother and our cousins. Jani and I went to day care while Mom returned to Colorado State University to work as a teaching assistant and to complete a master's degree in English.

CHAPTER 3

At a young age, I learned to work hard, and this ethic has stayed with me. After we moved to Fort Collins, my mom started seeing Don Ihrke, who she knew from Rapid City. He, too, had moved west. Early on, Don pushed me to be strong and to try hard. When I was seven years old he took the three of us to Horsetooth Reservoir near Fort Collins. He wanted to teach us girls to water-ski, but we couldn't even swim well. In his boat, he strapped orange, puffy lifejackets on us. He picked me up and threw me off the side into the lake and then did the same with Jani. The water was icy cold. Neither of us had spent much time swimming while growing up in South Dakota, and we immediately started crying.

I screamed at my mom to help us, but she just sat on the cushion in the boat. Don was a new boyfriend, so she may have wanted to impress him by not interfering. Jani and I kicked and paddled as best we could to the side of the boat and scraped our nails on the fiberglass, trying to climb back in. Jani's little lips were blue, and so were my fingers. Finally, Don relented and pulled us back in.

We didn't water-ski that day.

Within a few years, Mom and Don married and secured teaching positions at Western State College in Gunnison, Colorado, a sweet community in the southwestern part of the state along the Gunnison River. Suddenly, I became the middle child, since my new stepfather had a twelve-year-old daughter, Devi. I started school with a new name, Lana Ihrke. My mother and stepfather wanted to present a pure front. They wanted the world to believe they were a nuclear family, perfect parents with three little blue-eyed, blond-haired girls. This was just the beginning of many lies that played out in my life while growing up.

We stayed in faculty housing at the college. Twenty-five other children lived in the complex and shared with us the whole campus as our playground. My castle was the library, with lion statues twice my size at the entrance. Though I couldn't go inside, I found all kinds of nooks to hide in and pretend I was on safari and other adventures. I also found an ally in my elementary school teacher, who adored me in a grandmotherly way, and so I engaged deeply with learning.

My parents bought property along the Gunnison River, and we began building the house where I would grow up. It was a big undertaking. There was a spacious dining and living room upstairs with a huge stone fireplace that my parents planned to be the center of family and community. Downstairs, the family room filled nearly the whole floor, with a pool table and another massive rock fireplace.

The three of us girls helped with the construction. On weekends, we put on jeans and hiking boots and went out to the Taylor and Slate Rivers where the whole family loaded rocks—big ones that we could barely lift—into a pick-up and trailer. At the Taylor River, we excavated rocks from a landslide, so we had to gather them and carry them down the steep grade to the cart—arduous work. At the Slate River, we gathered gorgeous Crested Butte slate, a blackish-gray stone with minerals that make it shine. Once the truck and trailer were full, we would sit along the riverbank, with craggy peaks high above us, and eat turkey sandwiches and watermelon that my mother prepared. Then we would drive to the homesite and unload. The rocks were used to adorn our fireplaces and the exterior facing of the house.

We also sanded and painted the house's wood trim and inner accents. We crawled on our hands and knees to level the ground for planting the garden and dug the trenches to lay the underground sprinkler system. I grew to love the feeling of dirt in my palms, especially from leveling the ground for our yard. When you put your hands in dirt, it is like serotonin. It makes you happy. The more time I could spend outside in the dirt, the happier I was.

Even after the house was completed, my stepfather would always send me outside to rake the yard or do a landscaping project. Whether he intended to torture me or test me, or just knew I would do a good job, what really happened was I fell in love with nature. I basked in the sun on my face and the breeze blowing across my skin. I adored the cottontails that hopped by and the magpies that squawked and swooped down from the trees. I even grew to love rocks because of all those that we moved. I'd rub my hands over the surface of them, feeling their roughness and strength.

As I grew older Don gave me the most physically demanding tasks, like chopping wood and feeding the horses. I liked being the strong kid. When we would snow ski with him, he would push me to stay on the mountain all day and ski the toughest runs. My whole life he pressed me to be the best that I could ever be, physically and mentally.

Jani and I still saw our father. He adored us. Even though we only saw him about twice a year after he and Mom divorced, Jani, he, and I made a great team. He moved to Denver and taught at the University of Denver. He never seemed to age, outside or inside. He was medium height and blond with eyes the color of blue ice, and he exuded an energy that empowered those around him. As I grew older I came to appreciate him more, and he me.

When we were kids, Dad enjoyed taking Jani and me to Elitch Gardens in Denver, an amusement park, theater, and botanic garden, where we would play games and ride scary rides. Jani's favorite was the frightening Mister Twister roller coaster built of wood that seemed to sway while the cars ran along the tracks. One time he took us to see the play *Man of La Mancha*, the story of Don Quixote de la Mancha and his determination to revive chivalry and bring justice to the world.

I sat in the theater as this tall, bearded man raced across the stage with knightly courage. Goosebumps rose on my skin as he attacked goals with quixotic determination. And of course there was his imaginary love, Dulcinea, who he did it all for. I wanted to be Dulcinea, with her black bouffant and notable cleavage.

That day I vowed that I would be beautiful like Dulcinea, but more importantly, I would be brave and determined like Don Quixote. I would tilt my sword at the most formidable windmills and let nothing stop me.

CHAPTER 4

Even as a young girl, animals were crucial to my well-being. I could sit in the dirt for hours and watch ants crawl around their hill, industriously working, or lizards doing pushups. I could hold a horned toad until it grew still in the warmth of my palm. It would cling to me when I tried to put it back down. In the river outside our house in Gunnison I would watch minnows flit among the rocks, and trout leap to catch mayflies and splash back into the water.

When I was in junior high school, my parents bought a pair of Arabian horses, a mother and son. We named the mother Rasha Amigo, and she was my mom's horse. We named mine, a two-year-old ready to be trained, Handy Amigo. When summer started I'd ride my bike a mile every day to where Handy was boarding with a trainer, Sharon Sanders. I'd had horses all my life. My first was when I was five years old on our ranch in South Dakota. His name was Thumper, and as well as riding him, I could walk underneath him, and even stand on top of him.

We started teaching Handy simple things. I'd learned over the years that every time you interact with a horse you're teaching him something, whether you intend to or not, so I did my best to be awake when I was with Handy and not impart bad habits. We started with brushing him, getting him used to being touched all over—even across his rump and down his legs. We moved onto leading, teaching him to respect my space while I respected his. Then we drove him in a circular corral, using the crack of a whip and my voice to coax him into a trot and canter.

Next, we put on a hackamore bridle and began the process of placing first a blanket on his back and then a saddle. This took weeks of patience. Then we cinched the saddle. I rubbed between his eyes and under his jaw to calm him. "Handy," I said, "it's okay. It's just a cinch. It won't hurt you." So he stopped rolling his eyes and jigging his hooves and stood still.

The first time I climbed in the saddle atop Handy, I talked to him in my sweetest voice, and he seemed happy to have me on his back. My fluttery heart calmed as we made our way easily around the arena, and he even dropped his head a bit, a sign that he was relaxing. When I coaxed him into a trot, he twitched his tail, and when I nudged him into a canter, he bucked up his hind end just a little, but soon he calmed down. I came to see that he was spirited, at times dancing sideways when he was excited. I loved that part of him.

After a few weeks of working in the arena, it was time to head out on a trail. The trainer, her husband, their little son, and I rode through an open meadow into the foothills. We came to a ghost town from the mining days in the 1800s. As we entered it, Handy stayed calm, though his ears pointed back toward me, a sign he wasn't fully happy. Along the dusty main road we passed dilapidated wooden buildings and a deep hole lined with sandstone, which once was a well. By this time I was tired and hot, and I could feel that Handy was too, so we turned back.

Just as we left the town, a deerfly landed on Handy's ear and he threw his head up. The fly flew off and buzzed toward me, and I swatted it away. If you've ever been bitten by one, you know how much it stings. I could hear it buzzing and looked back, trying to locate it. Right when I saw it on Handy's flank, Handy kicked his legs up, and I went flying. The fly must have bitten him. I landed in a sagebrush and everything went black.

I awoke to a feeling of wetness on my cheek. I opened my eyes to find Handy licking me, his eyes focused intently on mine, his breath sweet. I reached up and massaged his nose, which he loved. My trainer was off her horse, squatting next to me, making sure I was okay. When I told her I was, she said, "Oh my gosh, incredible," visibly impressed by the horse's tenderness.

Over the coming years, I rode Handy in the Cattlemen's Days and 4th of July Parade in Gunnison. I also competed in, and sometimes won, competitions in showmanship and conformation. Through my teens he was my best friend. Most of all, Handy taught me the value of not just appreciating animals but connecting with them. They are souls just like humans, and you really can communicate with them.

Growing up, my mother and stepfather did everything they could to provide opportunities for Jani, me, and our stepsister, Devi, to be outdoors. We had season passes at Crested Butte Mountain so we could spend our winter days on the slopes. In the summer we had horses to ride, and we took pack trips into the wilderness where we learned to camp, to understand the night sky, and to commune with nature. We also rafted the Gunnison River in our backyard. When I was twelve years old I learned to captain our raft, which is where you bark out commands to your "crew," who paddle the boat around obstacles and over waves, with your paddle serving as the rudder to position the boat.

When we did these activities, my stepfather constantly exhorted us to get our guts up. As many faults as he may have had, he knew that we were powerful beings, and he and my mother did their best to help us manifest strength and courage.

Just days before entering eighth grade, when I was thirteen, I became feverish and listless. The day I was to start school, a Tuesday, I vomited all morning. The next day my mother took me to the doctor, who gave me antibiotics for strep throat, but my condition only got worse. My mother told me to get dressed, and she drove me sixty miles west to Montrose to see another doctor. The trip was agony; with every bump my belly hurt as though a fire had ignited in it. When we arrived, we found the doctor was not in, so my mom rushed me to the ER.

They kept me overnight while performing a series of tests. The next day, my parents picked me up, and, on the recommendation of the doctor, drove me to Denver. During the four-hour trip, my stepfather sped through the mountains. My mother, in the back seat with me, fed me ice chips and wiped my brow with a wet cloth. I writhed in a state of pain and delirium. My fever shot so high, I barely knew where I was.

At the Denver Children's Hospital, six doctors surrounded my bed at 9:00 p.m. and notified us that I had ruptured my appendix, and for five days the bile had been eating my large intestine. They said I could not survive surgery because I was too weak. They would work to build my strength and operate as soon as they could. They sent my parents to a hotel to rest.

At 7:00 a.m., I entered surgery, with a 50 percent chance of survival. The operation took eight hours. When I woke up, my parents were there standing on either side of the bed.

That night in the hospital, I opened my eyes to the green, gloomy light of the intensive care unit. I had tubes coming out of my stomach and IVs on both of my arms. A tall African American nurse stood by my bed looking down at me. "Honey," she said, "we know what's going on with you."

I was relieved to hear this, as it had been a long, painful five days.

She came closer, her glistening eyes staring at me. "You have an angel looking over you," she said. I smiled, so happy that the doctors knew what was wrong and grateful for that sweet angel—and for this one by my bed too.

My mother and stepfather stayed in Denver for the next three weeks and visited me daily in the ICU as I fought to live. Even though my father was living in Denver at the time, my mother didn't tell him I was there.

Word got back to my school about my condition, and the teachers and students stretched an adding-machine roll of paper along the halls at the school. Everyone signed. Once I got strong enough, I sat in bed with the roll flowing over the sheets and read every inscription and encouragement, my body tingling from so much love. The students also voted me Best Girl in School, a high honor.

My mother loves to tell the story of what I said to her once I had recovered. We sat at our cozy breakfast nook in Gunnison, and I said, "Mama, you know when I opened my eyes and saw my bed surrounded by all those white coats, and saw you crying as they talked to you, I knew I might die. So, I had a talk with God. I told him that if he needed another angel, I was ready, but I hoped he didn't, as there were a lot of things I wanted to do."

CHAPTER 5

One winter morning when I was a teenager, Don had a bizarre idea. At breakfast in our little nook, he leaned across the table and said to me, "Lana, you want to go water-skiing?"

"When?" I asked.

"On January first," he said. "We'll be the first ones to ever ski Blue Mesa in the winter."

Blue Mesa Reservoir, Colorado's largest human-made lake, sits outside Gunnison. It's a stunning body of water, set below green hills in summer. But now there would be ice on it. At our house, the windows were covered with frost, and icicles hung from the roof. I sat there in my flannel pajamas eating my oatmeal and tried to imagine climbing into the water.

Tentatively, I nodded. If he thought I could, I would do it. A part of me wanted to yell, "No way!" But another part wanted badly to live up to any expectation he had of me.

At dawn two days later, on January 1, 1980, we loaded up our slalom skis and life jackets, put gas in our outboard motorboat, and headed to the lake. Jani wanted nothing to do with it, so she went snow skiing with friends. At first Mom hated the idea and said she wouldn't participate, but after helping us load up that morning, she jumped in the truck with us. My best friend Amanda Olsen volunteered to ride in the boat and act as a spotter.

At dawn the lake was serene, a deep blue—almost black—and it spread below hills under a completely clear azure sky. The rim of ice bordering the lake crunched when we put the boat in the water, and Don and Amanda climbed in. Don fired up the motor. I pulled off my parka and jeans and stood there wearing only a bathing suit, the icy air enveloping my body. As quickly as I could, I pulled on a wetsuit and life vest. I eased my foot into the front binding of the ski, and stood at the edge of the water, hoping I could succeed with a dry launch, rather than submerging myself in the relentless cold. Nodding at Don and Amanda, I held onto the water-ski rope handle as he trolled the boat out until the line was taut.

I glanced at my mom, who stood onshore a few feet away from me, and she smiled and nodded, assuring me I was ready, even though I wasn't fully convinced.

I took a deep breath and yelled, "Hit it!"

Don gunned the engine, and tension jerked into the rope. Suddenly, I was moving on the water. I inserted my back foot into the rubber sleeve and flew across the glassy surface. All my fear left, and even the cold seemed to dissipate as I carved turns. I crossed the wake and cruised along the side of the boat and then cut back, picking up speed so I flew off the wake on my way back across. When I landed, the cold water felt hard, and it threw me for an instant. I almost lost my balance, but I regained it, and took a deep breath.

If I were to fall, I would be in trouble.

While he drove the boat, Don gave me a big thumbs-up. I felt a fiery elation within, the tantalizing excitement of pleasing him. We came close to shore where people had gathered, all of them near Mom who waved and took pictures. A photographer from the local paper trained his lens on me, and I gave him a big smile.

After a few circles, Amanda pointed toward shore. I nodded. When the boat came in close, I let go of the rope and shot right in, stopping just at the shoreline. I stepped out of the ski and Mom wrapped a towel around me.

Suddenly, the freezing breeze made my ears hurt like an ice-cream headache.

"I'm so proud of you!" Mom said. "You should have heard it. While you skied, the boat wake hit the ice and made a sound like church chimes."

Smiling, I hugged her. I got dressed and then climbed in the boat to drive while Don skied. When we finished, he hugged me and said, "You did great, Lana!" I was proud of myself and excited when the whole town learned of our feat, our photo appearing on the front page of the *Gunnison Country Times*.

When I was in high school, I was a cheerleader, I played volleyball, I was homecoming queen, and at the end of my junior year the students elected me president of the Gunnison High School student body, the highest honor I could imagine. In May before my senior year, I went to a leadership conference for student council members in Denver and then a weeklong training at Colorado State University in Fort Collins. I thrived in this environment. About three hundred of us were learning how to be leaders: how to be organized, how to deal with conflict, and how to inspire our fellow students.

The most challenging moment for me was when I gave a speech in front of those three hundred students. I was running for the position of secretary of the Colorado State Leadership Council. I tend to get nervous about public speaking, but I have always been able to put the fear aside because I focus on being myself. What I say comes from my heart. And that day, as I stood on the stage in the Colorado State University conference room, I did just that. With near blinding lights shining in my eyes, and all those students looking up at me, I took a deep breath and talked about

my honesty and transparency, and most of all what a hard worker
I was. I addressed the crowd in the same way I talk to anyone. I
relaxed, and the words flowed. The audience laughed at my jokes
and sighed over my challenges. Afterward they gave enthusiastic
applause.

They elected me secretary, an honor that so thrilled me, I walked
on air for days. After that experience, the president of the Colorado
Student Leadership Council program, Mark Von Braun, wrote me
a letter. In it he said, "I'll always respect your trusting nature and
your love of people." All these years later, I still strive to live up to
what he saw in me.

In June of that same summer, the three of us elected to represent
Colorado flew to Orlando, Florida, to the National Leadership
Council Conference. The head of the conference was a notable
motivational speaker at the time named Dr. Earl Reum. He was
funny and charismatic and, best of all, from Denver, so he and I had
a real connection. Urging us to "dream big" to change the world, he
inspired me to own my power as a leader not only of my school, but
of my life. We attended workshops that helped us learn to respect
each other and to communicate better, and we played trust games.
One of my favorites was falling back into a fellow student's arms.

When I returned home, Mom and Jani and I were in the kitchen
making dinner and I was telling them about the conference. I told
them how Dr. Reum said we needed to have a dream and to set
goals, and that every decision we made from that day forward
should point us in that direction.

Mom said that she had always dreamed of going to Europe.

"Well, Mom," I said. "If you don't get there it is your own fault.
Just make a commitment to yourself and do it."

She looked at me wide-eyed. Clearly, I had become more assertive through my experience in Florida. She strode into the study
where Don was watching TV. Jani and I looked at each other as we

overheard her saying that they should go to Europe in two years after Jani graduated from high school. We were sure he would say, "No way."

We tip-toed to the door to hear his response.

"That sounds like a great idea," he said.

Two years later, in January, after Jani was settled in college, they left for three months to travel all over Europe.

CHAPTER 6

My family was very conservative. It seemed a miracle when I was sixteen and my parents let me go on my first date. It was with Tommy Martinez, a boy from nearby Crested Butte whose father was an Eastern Airlines pilot. Tommy took me to the finest restaurant in Crested Butte and told me to order anything I wanted. We ate steak and lobster, and chocolate mousse for dessert. We talked about how we were both adventurous Sagittarians—our birthdays were only a day apart. I learned that Tommy loved fine clothes, sailing, and traveling.

After we finished eating, he pulled out a silver necklace inlaid with my birthstone, turquoise, and handed it across the table to me. My eyes grew teary from the attention and the thrill of such a personal gift. When he drove me back, we were so full we were sick, so he pulled over, and we started laughing and we laughed and laughed. This set the tone for our relationship.

After my freshman year in college, when I was twenty years old, Tommy Martinez and I spent a summer in Bar Harbor, Maine, a quaint village set on Mount Desert Island near Acadia National Park. By this time Tommy and I were truly in love. I adored this Latin man who radiated a joy that attracted fun people.

In Maine, we lived on a twenty-six-foot Morgan sailboat named *Spanish Gold* in a harbor filled with old wooden fishing and lobster boats. The sailboat, owned by Tommy, his dad, and a partner, was romantic, with a big bed and everything we needed to live and play.

Just off the harbor, we waited tables at the Vagabond, a two-story restaurant with a deck always full of revelers.

At the end of the summer Tommy and I intended to sail *Spanish Gold* from Maine to Florida so that Tommy's dad and partner could cruise the Caribbean islands during the winter. Neither Tommy nor I had ever done such a trip and we were excited. When I was a kid, my stepdad taught me to sail a small boat in Colorado, and how to judge the weather, so I knew enough to get by. In Maine each week, I learned more and more when Tommy and I took the boat out for leisure sailing. I was also fit and capable from all the time I'd spent hiking, skiing, and riding horses. I loved the rigor of sailing, and I sensed I was learning an important skill. Someday I hoped to sail on exotic seas, most notably in Australia, where I dreamed of traveling.

In preparation for our trip down the East Coast, we spent summer nights on deck with candle lanterns reading books about strategies. We plotted our course, carefully choosing the ports where we would dock and the towns we would explore. We were partners and lovers, but we were also friends, and we had a fabulous time together as we planned the trip.

One bright, sunny day in September, just as the first nip of cold bit the mornings in Bar Harbor, we weighed anchor. The boat's sails quickly filled with wind and we were moving south. Tommy and I stood on deck and waved goodbye to our home for the summer.

Just a few days out, we began hearing about a storm with hurricane-force winds blowing up from the south.

"What do we do?" I asked Tommy, and he looked at me blankly. Though we could see shore, the coastline appeared small from where we were, and we didn't have a planned stop nearby. We had intended to sail a long way this day, into the evening. Suddenly, we had to change plans. We checked the charts and scanned the shore. Already we were feeling the precursor to the storm; erratic winds lashed at the sails making them billow and collapse and flap around and billow again, slowing our progress. We settled on Marblehead, Massachusetts.

We sailed as fast as the wind would carry us and were beyond relieved when we saw the harbor tucked into a little bay. We spent the night battened down below deck while the boat writhed in the wind and rain. When the storm was so loud Tommy and I had to yell to hear each other, fear struck my heart. *What am I doing? If we had not made port, we would have died. What if we hit another storm and don't make it in?* In the pale cabin light Tommy must have seen my fear because he took me in his arms and hugged me. We lay on the bed and held each other through the night.

Several days later, the storm had mostly cleared, so we headed south again. I took a deep breath and willed myself to be calm, hoping we would not face another gale like that one. That night we anchored in Newport, Rhode Island, which was stunning, the town built right down to the edge of the harbor, church steeples towering above the hills. Sailing towns have a unique energy because sailors tend to be wild and fun, and they love to tell stories. We met some of these salty characters in the local bars and listened intently to their tales of the sea.

We sailed along the coast of Long Island headed to Montauk, but another storm blew in, with rain lashing the sails. The tides were against us, so we turned on the motor. It hummed along fine for a while, but then sputtered and died. We started it up again, and again it faltered. We had to change course. For a few hours we fought the wind that seemed intent on pushing us out into the vast Atlantic. My mind raced about what to do. *What if we can't make it to shore? What if we are carried out to sea and lose our direction?* The Atlantic is so huge that sometimes boats simply disappear there.

While Tommy held tight to the helm, I reefed the sails, and our sputtering motor carried us landward consistently enough to reach a little inlet we saw on the map along West Hampton Beach. We made it to the mouth of it, and our motor chugged along enough to get us past the sandy beaches to a cluster of houses inland set along a boardwalk. There, after several days of asking around, we found a mechanic who fixed the motor.

Our next stop was Sandy Hook, New Jersey, where we anchored to take an afternoon trip into New York City. We had both been there before, but still, the skyscrapers and the busy sidewalks thrilled us. Like true tourists we visited the Statue of Liberty, climbing all the way up into the torch, which people were allowed to do back then. From there we could see up the coast where we had just sailed, and down the coast where we were headed. We held hands, and I felt the wind in my hair and the joy of this grand adventure. After New York, we visited Atlantic City, where we played blackjack, and lost and won and lost again.

As we headed farther down the coast we savored the wildlife at Cape May National Wildlife Refuge. We watched sandhill cranes and Canada geese perform their graceful antics. Ocean City, Chesapeake Bay, Cape Charles—all these stops inspired us with their beauty and unique coastal ambiance.

We'd read about the challenge of sailing around Cape Hatteras and knew of the six hundred wrecks that had occurred over the years along a string of barrier islands called the Outer Banks of North Carolina. The route has shifting offshore sandbars called Diamond Shoals, two strong currents, and a geographic position that attracts low-pressure systems. Since we had never sailed in such challenging conditions, we were determined to avoid this passage.

We chose to sail through the Intercoastal Waterway, which kept us inside North Carolina's barrier islands. Though beautiful, this sailing tended toward the mundane, but we used the time to catch our breath, knowing we were headed for the biggest challenge yet. We stopped in a bay at Morehead City and visited Beaufort's Front

Street, admiring the historic brick buildings with stately facades, and farther along, the antebellum mansions. We also perused the North Carolina Maritime Museum.

Tommy's dad, Jack, flew in to meet us in Morehead. The next leg would take us completely offshore as we made a straight shot for Florida. Jack didn't want us to risk sailing on our own, and he wanted to experience the journey for the adventure of it—and the bragging rights. We spent five days on this passage out on the open water with no land in sight, just the Atlantic stretching to infinity. During these days as Tommy and I unfurled the sails and felt the wind and sun on our faces, I had the first glimpse in my life of pure freedom.

This leg of the trip, we worked four-hour watches, which allowed the other crew members to rest. One evening during my shift, I stood at the helm while Tommy and Jack relaxed below. As I watched the orange ball of the sun melt into the ocean, my heart swelled with the beauty. All the pressure of my life began washing away, especially the drive to be perfect for my parents. It disappeared among the waves as they went *whoosh, whoosh* against the bow. Dusk settled in, stars appeared, and soon the moon rose. My mind emptied completely of any worry and anxiety. For the first time, I knew who I was and where I wanted to go. I savored the power of being at the helm. I could tack the sailboat of my own life how I wanted. I could set my own course.

My relationship with Tommy had grown over these days, and we became quite loving with each other. As we drew near to Florida, his dad began talking of taking Tommy down to Mazatlán, Mexico, for a few weeks. I knew I needed to complete my education. That mandate rested deep in my heart since my mother always insisted that I finish college before making a serious commitment to a man, especially marriage.

This was the beginning of a theme in my life. I tended to fall in love and then feel pressure because the love conflicted with my own dreams of where I wanted my life to go. Through the years, I started to listen to and feel in my heart that part of me that wanted a deeper, more fulfilling experience in life, and I call it my intuition. It is a quiet voice and sensation, so it's easy to miss. But out in the serenity of the ocean, the message spoke as clear as a radio signal. When the Florida coast came into view, I knew I needed to part from Tommy and return to college.

We didn't meet any storms on this leg, but we did experience some huge swells. I must admit I was happy when, in the middle of the night, we sailed into an inlet at Stuart, Florida. We set anchor and went to sleep, relieved to be safely ensconced in the little bay. We didn't know it, but as we came in we were checking the wrong tide tables. Through the night, the tide went out, and when we awoke the next morning we were stuck on a sandbar.

People eating breakfast on restaurant patios along the boardwalk pointed at us and laughed, and we hung our heads in humiliation. Ultimately, all we could do was laugh along with them. We climbed down off the boat onto the sandbar and walked over to one of the restaurants, where we ordered Bloody Marys and breakfast. Along with the observers, we toasted to our folly as we waited for the tide to come back in.

Tommy's mom and dad rented a house on the inlet for us all. We stayed there for two months, basking in the sun on the beaches and sailing the warm Florida waters. During that time, I received word that I had been accepted to attend Colorado State University in Fort Collins, so in January I would be transferring from Fort Lewis College. I was excited to be on that big campus, farther away from home. Though the existence would be less free than what I experienced this summer, I knew I had to heed my mom's imperative that I finish college before getting married. I also had some strong interests I wanted to pursue, mainly art and Spanish language, both of which I knew would serve the adventurous future I saw for myself.

I was deeply sad to say goodbye to Tommy. We had been together four years, but I felt a new part of my life calling and wanted to see where it would lead me.

CHAPTER 7

When I returned to Colorado, I really didn't want to see my mom and stepdad. On my trip I had experienced such a sense of independence, especially on that open ocean when I tasted pure freedom. The idea of being back under the iron thumb of my parents, and especially my stepfather, weakened my heart. So I went to stay with my dad in Denver and to pick up my car at his apartment. It warmed my heart to see him again, to sit and talk philosophy with him. A few days later I drove to Gunnison to stay with my childhood friend, Trisha.

I arrived in Gunnison and went straight to the little bar where Trisha waitressed. After she finished her shift, we hung out there and partied with another friend, Sandra. I was agitated about being back. So many emotions swirling within me: happiness to see my friends, sadness to have parted from Tommy, and then a whole rush of confusion about being back among all the memories of my hometown. So we drank and drank, Stolichnaya mostly. When we left, all three of us crammed in the front of Sandra's Ford Pinto. We had no business being on the road, and none of us put on a seat belt.

I wanted to go dancing, so we headed north on Colorado 135 to Crested Butte. Snow began falling heavily, and the roads quickly iced. As we made our way along the highway, the visibility dropped to nearly zero, so we couldn't even see the stripes along the edges of the road. Suddenly, a huge pickup truck careened toward us, sliding on the ice. It sideswiped us, shoving us over the side of the road. We flew off, and so did the pickup, and then my world went black.

It was well below freezing and after midnight, so no one was on the road. We lay there in the wrecked car, as did the pickup driver in his vehicle, for hours—unable to move, or so I heard. I had hit my head on the rearview mirror and smashed my heel under the seat and was unconscious. Trisha and Sandra lay awake but delirious with the pain of their injuries.

Hours later, when the police got to us, we were nearly frozen to death. In some ways the cold helped us, because it iced our wounds and slowed the bleeding.

The next morning, when I returned to consciousness in the hospital, I looked over at Trisha in the bed next to mine. Her arm had a cast on it and the side of her face was bandaged. "Wow, you don't look too good," I said to her.

"You don't either," she replied.

It hurt to laugh.

Sandra was okay too, though she had hurt her back and had a concussion. The man driving the truck was only bruised.

One of the nurses had called my stepsister, Devi, for me, and she came, cooing over my bandaged head and wanting all the details. After filling her in, I insisted that she not tell our parents. But when she left, she immediately called them. The police classified the crash as a DUI, so we were all in trouble. My parents came, full of concern for my welfare—and our family's reputation.

A day later, despite all their hope against it, an article about the drunken wreck appeared in the *Gunnison Country Times*. It talked mostly about the crash and about the trouble that Sandra, as the driver, was in. Still, my parents were mortified that my name appeared. When they next visited they didn't mention it, but there was a strained air as they sat on the edges of their chairs and spoke little. I was so delirious they didn't even attempt to reprimand me.

In the coming days, the doctors found water on my brain, so my parents rushed me to a more sophisticated hospital in Grand

Junction. The doctors there put me into a coma for four days to rest my brain. When I woke, I faded in and out of a bizarre delirium for another week. Once I woke completely and the pain in my foot lessened, I became restless, wanting to move my body. By the time I got out, the trouble we were all in had faded away. A judge gave Sandra a harsh warning but let her go without penalty.

I will never forget when my mom and stepdad walked into the hospital room the day after the accident. The look on their faces was compassionate, but what I really saw was complete disappointment. I had always been their shining star: high school president, homecoming queen, excellent student, and now here I was involved in a DUI. I couldn't even look at them. Mom sat on the edge of the bed while Don stood at the foot, and I just kept staring at my hands. But then I felt a spark of rebellion in my heart, and I looked at them both straight on, challenging them.

Why do I always have to be so good?

I had never experienced teenage rebellion, and here I was twenty years old and all I wanted was to break that sugar-sweet identity to pieces so that I could finally be free to live my own life. I wanted to find out who I was, and to live that, instead of always working to please this scholarly duo, who had goals very different from my own. I didn't even know what my own goals were. So as challenging as this time was for me, it caused a break that ultimately allowed me to make my own choices.

CHAPTER 8

Because he was so philosophical, my dad and I often had deep intellectual conversations late into the night. He read a great deal and had books all over his house. Plato, Aristotle, and Kant were some of his favorite philosophers. He would talk about their theories and draw diagrams on notebook paper to help me understand. Astrology also intrigued him, and he would give me readings, which ignited my interest in the arts. He gave me a copy of Linda Goodman's *Sun Signs*, which I adored.

Dad told me many things about myself. One day he trained his big blue eyes on me and said, "Lana, as a Sagittarian you have incredible power. Use it well. Create from your heart."

He sat me down at his kitchen table one evening and poured each of us two fingers of whiskey. He lifted his glass in a toast and took a sip. Then he looked at my glass. I picked it up and sipped the dark liquid. It burned my throat, but I took a deep breath and sipped again.

"Good," he said. "Wherever you go in the world, if you sit down to whiskey with people, you will become friends."

This has proven true for me.

Most importantly my dad supported my ideas. He would never say no to them, which has helped me honor them as well.

During the second semester of my sophomore year, a boyfriend and I headed to Costa Rica to attend Spanish language school. As we walked the beaches and swam in the warm surf, the sensual freedom of a tropical vacation filled my body. All my life before then felt robotic, mechanical, emotionless. But there, my skin leapt to life, so I truly felt the breeze and rain and sun. It was as though I was having fabulous sex with the entire Universe, and it lasted for months. When the wheels of the jet lifted off the tarmac en route back to the United States, I swore I would make that feeling my life.

When I was a junior in college at the University of Colorado, I returned to Costa Rica for a semester that turned into a year. I lived with a family in Santa Ana, a village separated by a mountain from the capital city of San José. As I attended classes at the University of Costa Rica, I grew to view Santa Ana as my home. I rode my racing bike that I brought from home in order to exercise my legs because of my car accident and another biking accident I had experienced. Part of my goal in coming south to a warm climate was to heal and get strong again.

Biking also proved to be a great way to meet people because it made me so visible. I biked to the market, a little stall along a narrow street, where I bought avocados, pineapples, mangos, and vegetables. I rode to dinner and to see friends. People waved at me and stopped to chat. I got to know the whole town.

One night while out at one of my favorite nightspots, I danced with a handsome, curly haired soccer player for Saprissa, a Costa Rican national team. Our sensual salsa sparked passion between us, and so began our romance. The coming months were full of excitement and drama, and I loved it. Oscar Rodriquez and I danced into the nights, hiked, and rode bikes together. One weekend we took a trip to the coast at Tamarindo. There we swam in the ocean, got sticky feeding each other pineapple by hand, and at night made love on the beach. We even talked of marrying. I can still feel the salty, sunny, luscious thrill of those days when I first fell in love with Costa Rica.

The first job I ever had was waiting tables, and this gave me my first sense that I wanted to work in tourism. I loved the community of a restaurant, everyone pulling together. But most of all, I loved to serve people, to make them happy. Slowly this morphed into the idea that I wanted to have my own establishment.

That notion congealed into a more vivid dream during my time studying in Costa Rica. My mom and stepfather came to visit, and I took them to Manuel Antonio National Park. With a pristine beach, few people, and even fewer hotels and cars, it felt like paradise. However, since there were not many taxis, we had to walk back from the beach to the hotel each day, sticky and sweaty. One day, we paused to watch a legion of leafcutter ants cross the path. I squatted down to observe their strong bodies as they hefted leaves twenty times their weight. I pointed and said, "Look at them!"

Uncomfortable from the heat, Mom and Don only glanced down. "Let's keep moving," Don said.

We started up again. I walked in my bikini, enjoying the sun on my skin and the warmth of the pale sand between my toes. Suddenly an image flashed in my mind of me presiding over a lodge in the Manuel Antonio area. In my imagination, I stood on a veranda and greeted guests, inviting them to share with me the breathtaking view of the ocean and beach.

On that day with Mom and Don, I turned around, put my hands on my hips and said, "I'm going to have a hotel here in Costa Rica."

Mom blinked and cocked her head. "All right then," she said. She knew that when I set my mind to something, I pursued it relentlessly.

That weekend we started looking for property, and we found a reasonably priced locale right above the beach with vast views of the Pacific. The prospect of buying it, building a lodge, and hosting guests there excited me so much I couldn't stop my mind from planning.

However, as we looked into the purchase, we learned that the property didn't have water—not a well, nor a municipal hook-up since there was no municipal system. I spent a sleepless night trying to solve this problem in my mind.

By morning I knew I had to let it go. But the dream had been planted.

CHAPTER 9

One of my greatest adventures was Operation Raleigh. News of the program came to me in early 1984 when I was still attending the University of Costa Rica. Immediately I knew it was for me. Britain's Prince Charles and explorer John Blashford-Snell launched this scientific, archaeological, and service adventure. The aim of Raleigh was to help young people develop leadership skills and inspire them with the kind of pioneer spirit expressed by British poet and explorer Sir Walter Raleigh, who was instrumental in the British colonization of North America.

All my friends in Colorado were planning trips to Europe after they graduated from college, but I longed to go to Australia. I was drawn to the vastness of the country and to all the natural beauty there. In May of 1984, when I returned to Fort Collins, Colorado, from Costa Rica, I applied to Operation Raleigh. My application included an essay about why I wanted to participate.

I wrote about my love of nature, adventure, and giving back to my community. It must have been convincing because I was chosen out of a field of some five hundred other applicants. The organizers called to tell me I'd made the first cut and would go to a camp in Houston, Texas, for the next stage. They sent me a list of things I needed that included a sleeping bag, rain gear, hiking boots, and a backpack. They didn't tell me what I'd be doing.

I flew to Houston, a bit nervous since I had no idea what to expect. The first afternoon, we met the other participants, about fifty of us in all. The organizers paired each of us with a partner and told us to ready our gear. They took us to a flat area where we hiked through a landscape of marsh grass and mangrove bordering broad lagoons. As we walked, raindrops began to splatter the water and then the full roar of a downpour drenched us as we pulled on our rain gear. The deluge didn't stop. We had lunch that day but no dinner in the night. Without mountains or other landmarks to help with directions, I felt lost.

I love to wear shorts whenever I can, but there were so many mosquitos, biting flies, and ticks, I had to put on long pants and douse myself with insect repellent. We kept walking and walking, and even though we were miserable, I never complained because I knew the organizers were testing us. So I just got my guts up and stuck it out.

After sunset the two leaders stopped us. They were both named Mark and were both tall. One was blond and blue eyed, and the other was dark haired with brown eyes. They told us to pitch our tents. We did, in the pouring rain. I climbed in with my partner, a guy I had hoped to get to know during the hike, but with all the rain and exhaustion, we had barely spoken. We tried to sleep, but we were soaking wet and hungry, and the rain pounded on the tent like thunder.

I fell asleep, probably because I was exhausted. About four hours later, in the middle of the night, we woke to voices yelling, "Get up! Get up! It's time to go." The two Marks explained that the rain was making the place where we were dangerous due to flooding, so we had to get out. We packed up all our soaking gear and started tromping through the rain. At dawn we arrived at a meadow, and thankfully, the rain stopped. The Marks broke us into groups of six and said, "Here's some food." I was so hungry I couldn't wait. But they only gave us a coconut, a live rabbit in a cage, and a loaf of white bread. I hated white bread but was grateful for it anyway.

We had no matches, so we all looked at each other and shook our heads, wondering what we were going to do. Since I'm a vegetarian and I love animals, I didn't want to kill the rabbit. We tried to open the coconut but couldn't without a machete. My group decided to only eat the white bread.

Next the Marks told us to march to a lake, where we played a game. They gave each team an envelope with a number of clues typed on paper. The clues would lead us to places where we could find real food. By this time, we were weak with hunger. We read through the clues and realized one indicated that we had to get across the lake. Just down the shore, we found a canoe but it didn't have a paddle. Our teamwork skills came into play as we all searched and found the collapsed paddle hidden under one of the seats.

While the other team members worked on more clues, my teammate and I traded turns paddling across the lake. To our delight we found, on the far shore in the marsh grass, a jar of peanut butter. Unfortunately, we had to wait until we returned to the rest of the group to open it.

Even though this was a grueling experience, I thrived in this part of the adventure. I love people and I'm easygoing, so I enjoyed working in a team. The Marks would come around to make sure we were okay. They would also watch to see who had the leadership skills the program required.

When you're under real stress like that, at some point you just let loose. After our team ate the peanut butter with our hands, we started laughing because it was all over our fingers and faces and on our shirts. We were still hungry, but it didn't matter much.

That night we built a fire and sat around and talked, and I felt a deep admiration for these people who I had been with the past few days. We slept in our tents again that night, and mercifully no rain fell.

The next day our march was long and hard. We were still tired and hungry, and the organizers wanted us that way to see how we functioned under duress, how we related to people, and if we could get along and be of service. One Operation Raleigh group in Peru got caught in a remote place and went five days without food, so the organizers were seeing who could cut it. One guy in our group complained a lot and cared little about the team, but the rest of us took the trip in stride and got along well.

The last day, we hiked back to where the whole journey had started. The sun came out, and it warmed my back as I hugged my new pals goodbye. The Marks said we would be notified within three weeks about whether or not we made it into the final group.

Shortly after I returned to Fort Collins where I was attending Colorado State University, I received a letter from England. I held the thick cream-colored paper in my hands, feeling the weight of its contents. I wanted this adventure so badly. Taking the envelope out on the deck of the apartment where I lived, I sat down and looked out at the jagged peaks of the Rocky Mountains. I took a deep breath, stuck my finger in the fold, and ripped it open. It was from Colonel John Blashford-Snell, and it said that I had been accepted to the program. I leapt in the air and yelled, "Yes!"

Later, I learned that out of the six people on my team, four got on the expedition. Of course, the one who was uncooperative didn't make it.

I had my choice between the land-based phases, which were in Nicaragua and Australia, or sailing on a seventy-two-foot-square rigger from Australia to New Zealand and back. I was grateful for my experience sailing with my family and with Tommy, and I loved to sail, so I chose the sailing adventure. Still, I wasn't sure which one they would put me on. One day, I got a call from blond Mark saying I was going to Australia to sail the tall ship *Zebu*. I was so elated I barely slept that night.

Because this adventure was a volunteer aid project, I had to raise $5,000 to participate. I knew that this was important to my life and that it would teach me things I couldn't learn anywhere else. To save money for the trip, I committed to spending the next eighteen months doing any work I could find.

CHAPTER 10

I completed another quarter at the University of Colorado in the spring. After it ended, I headed to Costa Rica for the month of May. Though my father and Jani said the trip would interfere with finding a good summer job, I still had to go. I wanted to see Oscar and bask in the moist warmth of my favorite country. When I returned to Fort Collins to make money and complete my last two quarters of college, I did not want to be there. I wanted to be in Costa Rica, but I set aside my desire and faced reality.

While I had been in Costa Rica, Jani had landed a lucrative job in a posh restaurant downtown and was making lots of money working lunch and dinner shifts. When I returned in June, I immediately regretted postponing my job hunt. In addition, I went back to the apartment that Jani and I shared only to find that her boyfriend was sleeping with her in our bedroom, so I was relegated to the couch.

A few days later, Jani and I headed to the employment office to find me a job. En route, a young man rode a bicycle-propelled popsicle cart right in front of us. I said to Jani as a joke, "That's probably the job I'm going to get."

At the employment office I learned that indeed there were no jobs left in town. On the way out, on a bulletin board, sure enough I did find a brochure about a job selling popsicles. I called the number, went to an interview, and got the job. I would earn 25 percent of the gross sales. Though I was skeptical at first, it worked perfectly. I attended school from 7:00 to 11:00 a.m., and then I put on my bikini top and cutoffs and got on the bike. I exercised all afternoon and got tan as an added bonus.

First I drove through downtown Fort Collins, ringing the little bell—*ding, ding*—to get people's attention. Then I headed north to the car dealerships, and then farther out of town to the construction sites. My bikini top, blond hair, and deep tan seemed to multiply sales. I finished in the mostly Hispanic trailer park, where I got to speak Spanish. It was especially fun with the kids, who I loved spending time with. They waited for me to arrive each day and ran along behind me through the neighborhood. Some nights I kept riding until seven. On the Fourth of July I had my biggest day, earning $250 as my cut.

One day I wanted to talk to Jani, so I rode my popsicle cart to the restaurant where she worked. I peeked over the low wall around the patio, hoping to see her. This was a sophisticated place with expensive entrees. I saw two women I knew and struck up a conversation with them. When they finished their ahi tuna salads, they looked over at my cart and asked, "Can we have a popsicle?"

"Sure," I said. I sold them two cherry ones.

Just as they started eating them, Jani stepped up to the table. She took one look at their desserts and glared at me. Already she'd been peeved about how much money I was making in my little popsicle empire, but this was the crowning betrayal. I jumped on my bike, waved goodbye, and got out of there because I could tell by the look on her face that she was pissed. She had just missed out on two dessert sales, and it was my fault.

During my last college semester that fall, I cast a metal mask of my hero Don Quixote for my final senior Spanish project. This experience affected me deeply. At the time I was reading Don Quixote's story in the ancient text *Man of La Mancha* by Miguel de Cervantes, and that inspiring character filled my consciousness.

Since I was a Spanish and art major, I combined my two passions to make something profound.

When I was taking the mask from the fire, it slipped and fell on the floor. I plucked it up quickly, but when I set it on the table, the result horrified me. Quixote's aquiline nose had a dent on its side. I spent that night squirming in my bed, fearing it was ruined and that I would fail my senior project, and thus not be able to graduate.

But the next day, my thesis advisor examined it very closely. She looked at me and smiled. "This is perfect," she said. "You even sculpted Quixote's crooked nose right."

That experience taught me to relax and know that when I put forth my best effort, everything would work out—maybe not as I anticipated, but as it was meant to be.

In December, when I graduated, my boyfriend at the time, Joel Salter, and I headed to Vail, Colorado, to work. Joel was going into the Peace Corps in Sierra Leone, Africa, so he too, needed to fund a trip. We taught skiing during the day and waited tables at night. Though we were working fifteen-hour days, we loved what we were doing. We played outdoors whenever we could, until our bank accounts were full enough to follow our dreams.

CHAPTER 11

In May of 1986, I left Vail and flew from Denver to Los Angeles and then to Hawaii to visit a friend and go windsurfing. After plying my board on the waves and relaxing on the beach for a few days, I headed to the airport to make the final leg of the journey to Sydney, Australia.

This was an important moment in my life. Years ago when I sailed with Tommy from Maine to Florida, I dreamed about sailing around Australia. Now I was going to do it. I was flying from Hawaii to Sydney by myself and I wasn't going to know anybody there. On the flight, I imagined my first encounter with the towering ship *Zebu* nestled in the magnificent Sydney Harbor. I saw myself boarding the boat and sailing away. But when I arrived at the dock, the *Zebu* was onshore perched on blocks for maintenance. It looked helpless, like a beached sea creature.

Still, its tall, straight masts and aged-wood hull astonished me. It was a 1938 Swedish trading ship that once carried timber, salt, and grain in the Baltic Sea and beyond. Like the tall ships I had loved in movies, it had graceful lines, a long bowsprit, and nearly a dozen sails.

Once all the other crew members arrived, Nick and Jane Broughton, who owned the *Zebu* and were managing the trip, had us introduce ourselves. It was a diverse group of twenty-four, and we would be together for the next three months. Five of us came from the US, and the rest were from England, Wales, Scotland, and

Singapore. The group ranged in age from eighteen to twenty-four, everyone athletic and outdoorsy.

One person caught my eye. He was a Brit named Carl who had thick black hair, a sarcastic smile, and a light air about this whole endeavor, exuding confidence that he could do this task and excel at it. Meanwhile, I doubted myself. I knew I could sail, but sailing a huge square-rigger, a boat that must have the wind behind it, across the Tasman Sea in waters notorious for their storms and high waves, made my heart shudder. While Jane Broughton briefed us on the day's duties, Carl's eyes locked with mine, and the sweetest smile expanded across his face.

Nick Broughton immediately put us to work repairing the ship. The arduous, sweaty labor reminded me of when I was growing up and we built our house in Gunnison. Here in Sydney, we filled in small holes and dings and sanded away rough spots, and we swabbed the decks and generally worked to make the ship seaworthy for our trip. Though my romantic expectation of meeting the *Zebu* on the water was dashed, something poignant grew from these efforts. I came to know the ship intimately. Meanwhile, working together hard, all day, every day, with the crew meant a lot of joking and laughing, which helped the group members bond.

When the sun set, we scrubbed ourselves in the dock's showers, gritty facilities that weren't cleaned very often. Then we headed into Sydney. Pub-crawling through the nights made it easy to get to know each other. Carl and I flirted, but most of the other women on the ship had their eye on him too, so I just enjoyed myself. Brits love to drink, and they also love to tease Americans; I was the butt of many jokes. They kidded me about the way I talked, and I kidded them about their funny British colloquialisms. When we were finally exhausted, we returned to the ship and slept in bunkbeds crammed below the bow.

Once we put *Zebu* in the water, we did some practice runs in the

Sydney Harbor. Then we set sail for Christchurch, New Zealand. This was real sailing, out on a vast sea with no land visible. I hadn't really bargained for how challenging the job would be. We worked in teams of six on two four-hour shifts every twenty-four hours. The labor was nonstop. Most of all it was dangerous, because we didn't have safety ropes while up in the rigging, climbing around the huge sails, untying them, and shaking them out so the wind could fill them.

Even with the hard work and risks, I loved feeling the breeze on my face and the strength of my arms as I scaled up and down like a monkey. Back on deck, once the sails filled, we all held on as the ship gained momentum and sped across the Tasman Sea. We were like travelers of old using nothing but the wind to propel us forward.

Our third day out, while I was at the helm, a storm blew in. The ship rocked, wind whipped hair across my face, and sea froth chilled my fingers. I turned to the first mate, Mike, who was the epitome of a salty sailor—tall and lanky, cigarette in hand, many ocean tales to tell, and, when onshore, a heavy drinker.

"This looks serious," I yelled above the wind.

"It's a waterspout tornado," he yelled back.

Where the sea had been blue, now the tornado slid along a silver pathway toward us.

He took the helm and yelled, "Get up there and unfurl more sails!"

I and another crew member climbed the rigging to open more sails so we could gain speed to run from the storm headed right for us. The boat pitched and rolled across big waves under a roiling sky, and rain slashed around us. Fortunately, I was already wearing the rain gear that I got before my last sea voyage years ago. The bib overalls and jacket were impervious to the elements, but my face and hands still ached from the cold.

One moment while up on the rigging, I wasn't sure I could hold on, the wind was so strong, my hands soaked and slippery. I worked to tie the sails tightly in place and make sure they were secure. While up there I looked across and saw Carl working as feverishly as I was. He gazed across at me and beamed a tense smile, and I nodded back. We were up there together and working as a team. Our work had to be good because in that moment we were responsible for the other crew members. If I didn't tie the knot just right and the sail didn't hold, the results could be catastrophic, and it would be my fault.

Once back on deck, I returned to Mike's side and watched him adeptly steer us clear of the storm. The waterspout passed to the south. I sat down on deck to catch my breath and felt my body relax from a tension I had underestimated.

Carl walked by with the cook, Sara, a woman who I had befriended. I knew that she had a crush on him. Carl paused before me. "Are you okay, Lana?"

His concern sent a giddy rush through my body.

"Yes," I said, my voice breathy.

With that fabulous British accent he said, "Pretty dodgy storm, right?"

"Frightening," I said.

He smiled, flashing a straight row of gleaming white teeth. He and Sara stepped closer to Mike, who stood watching the storm disappear into the darkening sky. Mike turned to us and the rest of our team who had gathered around him.

He lit a cigarette and blew out a long stream of smoke. "You did well," he said in his gravelly voice. "That's serious business." He dragged on his cigarette. "One time on the Caribbean in the Devil's Triangle, one of those came up, and I watched as a ship not far from ours got caught. It dissolved into the ocean, never to be seen again."

The group let out a low gasp and then fell silent, the only sound from the wind riffling the sails. There we were in the middle of the ocean, and he was telling us this story. I could feel how crucial this experience had been, how close we were to catastrophe. I remembered his voice when he told us to get up on the rigging. He wasn't afraid but he was stern, and in that moment I knew why.

Soon our crew's watch ended. We were so exhausted we stumbled below deck to the bunk room, where we lived nearly on top of each other. This presented its own challenge. All the crew slept on the berth deck in one room fitted with bunk beds. I had never slept in the same room with fifteen people, many of them snoring guys. Fortunately, I was usually so exhausted I would fall asleep immediately.

As well as becoming adept sailors, we learned and practiced celestial navigation. During the day or at night out on deck we would use a sextant to take measurements between a celestial body such as the sun, moon, a planet, or a star, and the horizon. We would use a nautical almanac to tabulate the coordinates and thus find out what our latitude and longitude were. Ever since I was a kid looking up at the infinite night sky in the Rocky Mountains I'd been fascinated by the stars. Now I was able to study and really understand their significance in helping people throughout history navigate around the world.

I felt fortunate to live and work with amazing people from diverse places. Each day I eagerly recorded our experiences in a journal. I wrote in Spanish so I wouldn't forget the language I loved so much, and so my mates couldn't read what I was writing. I also had an address book packed with letters that I'd picked up just before we set sail. My team members joked that if you wanted to torture Lana, just steal her address book. And it was true—losing it would have tormented me, because I loved hearing from everyone.

During one night watch, I began to visualize my lodge in Costa Rica. *The dining room and main meeting place will be like this ship*, I told myself. *It will have a towering roof, like these sails, and a wooden deck. It will have a bow pulpit that sits up high, with a view of the ocean below. It will be graceful and strong, and a center for people to commune with each other.*

Meanwhile, since Carl and I shared the same watch, we became closer and closer. We climbed the rigging together and made sure we both got down safely. We pulled up buckets of sea water to swab the deck. We practiced our nautical knots and checked each other's to be sure they were strong. And we listened to Mike's stories of peril on the high seas.

One day, the sky cleared completely, so at the end of our four to eight o'clock shift, we watched the sunset. Carl and I stood out on the bow. My hair blew in the wind and Carl was behind me. It felt like that scene from the *Titanic*, when Rose and Jack stand at the bow with their whole bright future before them. Carl touched the small of my back, and my body shivered with elation.

Sara, the cook, came up and said, "Beautiful sunset."

Carl and I had no choice but to part.

Our fourteen days at sea en route to Christchurch were full of dangerous episodes, but none so much as when we crossed the Cook Strait. It runs between the northern and southern islands of New Zealand and is one of the most unpredictable passages in the world. The varying currents, rough water, and heavy swells from strong winds make the passage treacherous. Adding to the tension, we crossed at night, the wind and currents tugging the *Zebu* in many directions. The ship creaked and groaned, unnerving us, and the wind violently tore at the few sails that were open. The strait is fourteen miles wide at its narrowest point, and I held tight to the railing as we passed the lights of the capital of New Zealand,

Wellington. Mike had us on call to climb up and reef the sails if we needed to, but we passed through without incident.

The tension could not subdue our excitement at seeing land. Mike had to talk us down, keep us calm, as the *Zebu* cleared the passage. Eventually, the sun rose, and we happily sailed down the coast to Christchurch.

CHAPTER 12

When we arrived in Christchurch, our exquisite ship and its crew were the center of attention. TV, radio, and newspaper reporters showed up to film, photograph, and interview us. The next day, the ship appeared on the front page of the local newspaper.

Some friends and I rented a car and spent three days exploring the area that stretches from turquoise waters to alpine peaks. The first day we toured the town. Our group included Carl, Sara, and two other friends. The first day we toured the town. We wandered along Regent Street with its colorful store fronts and then stopped at the city's namesake, Christchurch Cathedral, which back then was still standing. Sadly, it collapsed in an earthquake in 2011. We hit as many pubs as we could handle, enjoying the pale and amber ales, along with green-lipped mussels and veggie nachos.

We were completely happy just to be on solid ground for a few days, without the effort of staying steady on a swaying ship. While wandering around and in the pubs, I would watch Sara flirt with Carl, feeling a tinge of jealousy tighten my heart. Meanwhile, our other friend Quinn always wanted my attention, so whenever I had a chance to talk with Carl, Quinn was there by my side, engaging me with his chatter.

I was conflicted, because Sara and I had become close friends. When it was my turn to make bread, a rotating responsibility, she would tell me about her life growing up in Wales, and I told her of mine in Colorado. In Christchurch, as I sat in a cozy corner of a pub across the table from Carl, I watched Sara touch his shoulder while telling him how she learned to cook. Meanwhile, Quinn told me a story about a competition between him and his brother. I tried to concentrate, but I kept losing the thread. When we headed back to the ship to sleep, Sara gushed over Carl, and I wanted to tell her that I liked him too, but I didn't.

The next day we headed out of town in a two-car caravan. I drove one, while Carl rode in the passenger seat, and Sara, Quinn, and our other friend Aarav sat in back. In the other car, our friend Jenna accompanied a woman and two guys from the ship. I could tell that Carl was enjoying the attention from Sara and me. He smiled and joked, shooting me flirtatious glances while listening to Sara. I tried to corner Carl's attention while Quinn kept asking about my life.

We drove inland on State Highway 73 to Sheffield to stay at a sheep farm with relatives of Jenna. We spent the evening touring the paddocks and meadows where sheep grazed. The place was pastoral perfection, a broad green valley with snowy peaks rising in the distance. We feasted that night on braised lamb shank and roasted potatoes and sat around visiting with the farmers, fascinated as they discussed the gentle rhythms of their life. For breakfast we ate eggs collected just moments before from their chicken coop, and then headed out to Arthur's Pass National Park.

I was eager to explore this park featuring the highest pass over the Southern Alps and deeply gorged rivers running through dense rainforest. We entered the park via a spectacular feat of civil engineering: the road passed over towering viaducts and past waterfalls redirected into chutes along the precipitous Otira Gorge.

We planned to hike to the top of Avalanche Peak, an 1,100-meter (3,600-foot) vertical ascent that would take us to views of the surrounding peaks, particularly Mount Rolleston and the Crow Glacier on its southern face. Parking near the ranger station, we headed out on this six-hour round-trip trek. The day was cold, with an icy wind blowing down the canyon. We started out as a group, but after half an hour, I heard Sara complaining to Quinn and Aarav about her freezing hands and feet. When we paused in the middle of a beech forest, the three said they were turning back and would wait for us at the car.

Carl was as determined as I was to make it to the top, so we forged on, our cheeks and noses red from the cold. As long as we kept moving we could stay warm, even though we didn't have gloves or heavy jackets. At one point we climbed up over some rocks and Carl took the lead. When he ascended to the top, he reached out his hand and helped me up. The heat of his palm pressed into mine, and the intensity of it warmed my whole body.

We left the forest and entered into tussock and subalpine vegetation, the views opening up so we could see way down the valley to where we had started. After four hours of climbing we reached the summit, with bits of snow here and there, and views that extended to the ocean. Nearby, the white Crow Glacier nestled into Mount Rolleston.

"Wow," I said.

"Brilliant," Carl said.

We turned to look at each other, and it was as though we spoke through our eyes, a sparkling appreciation for the intensity and determination we both shared. We were not ones to turn back from any challenge. We would always push on. He took my hand, and we stood staring at the view as the mountain's powerful stillness filled our beings. After a long moment, Carl released my hand and broke the spell.

The next day, we drove back to the *Zebu*, where we prepared to head out to sea once again. Aboard the ship, I felt like I was home. We cruised north through the night to visit an Outward Bound sailing school in Nelson. At daybreak, we came into a cove where the students practiced. Each had his or her own ten-foot single-sail boat. A few of them glided over to greet us. We waved enthusiastically and cruised on by. After completing our chores, we went ashore.

We joined in the school's dinner celebration. With a group of about thirty people—students, instructors, and staff—we feasted on meat pies with lamb, sweet potatoes, and local vegetables, along with New Zealand wine. After a month of nonstop sailing, these students were ready to party, and they did. I struck up a conversation with a sandy-haired Adonis who explained that for a month they had eaten and slept on the tiny boats, without ever leaving them, so that they would get to know them intimately in all circumstances. They had endured storms and frigid nights, and they even had to go to the bathroom off the side of the boats. And I thought we had it rough.

Though there wasn't much drinking going on, we all joked and laughed late into the night. The students were beautiful and full of life and came from all over the world. I would catch myself in a deep conversation with some adorable guy, and I'd look across and see Carl doing the same with a beautiful woman. It was a bit unnerving, but I relaxed into it. The next morning we joined the students for a grueling workout. We jumped into the icy cold water of the Tasman Bay, swam a mile, climbed out, and ran six miles, all before breakfast.

That afternoon, we sailed farther north to Auckland, where we watched a leg of the Whitbread Yacht Race, a round-the-world speed marathon held every four years. Our ship was moored for a week near ten sleek racing boats. At the same time, the soccer World Cup was going on, so we would frequent the bars and watch the Brits go crazy as their team competed. Costa Rica played, too, and that was my team. Once in a while, when I had a bit of free time, I would find my mind drifting back to Costa Rica, to the warmth of the climate and the people. A little spot in my chest ached whenever I let my mind go there, as though I had left some part of me behind.

I related to the Brits' passion for the game. When I was in grade school in Gunnison we had an excellent soccer program, so I started playing and loved it. When I was in college and on the ski team, I played soccer as part of the training. We used to run six miles a day and then play a full game of soccer. Then when I lived in Santa Ana, Costa Rica, I played soccer with the boys in the village square.

Five or six of us would go to a pub in downtown Auckland. Carl and I made sure we sat next to each other, and while we watched the game, we would touch fingers under the table, always discreet, so our crewmates wouldn't know. Sara sensed our budding rapport, and she stepped back from Carl and, sadly, our friendship.

CHAPTER 13

From Auckland, we sailed north toward Vanuatu, and the climate grew warmer. Previously, we were always a bit chilly, but as we sailed closer to the equator, we started shedding our fleece and heavy rain gear. In the warmer climate I lived in a leather bikini that Tommy Martinez had gotten for me in Argentina. Fresh water was scarce on the ship, so we showered in salt water, and this made my hair blonder—even the hairs on my arms and legs shimmered on my suntanned skin. I felt strong and sexy, and my romance with Carl was growing.

As he shed his cold-weather gear, I got to see his body, his chiseled arms, flat stomach, and strong thighs. I ached to touch him all over but knew I couldn't.

We arrived in Vanuatu on a hot afternoon and were excited after eleven days of hard work at sea to anchor near a lush island. After we completed our chores on the *Zebu*, we leapt into the clear water, and I savored the feeling as it swished between my toes and across my cheeks. We spent hours snorkeling on the reef, where sea life thrived abundantly.

Carl and I swam side by side, and the beauty and sensuality of the warm water ignited my desire. Among the pink and purple coral, we saw a school of orange clown fish, a spotted eagle ray, and a giant mottled eel tucked into a cave. Carl touched my arm and pointed out to the deep where a sea turtle swam toward us, as though out of some great infinity. In that instant, Carl's touch, along with the beauty, sent such a surge of electricity through my body, I feared I might drown.

Vanuatu is a nation made of up some eighty islands that stretch 1,300 kilometers—over 800 miles—across the Coral Sea. We were swimming in the bay off Pentecost Island. It was paradisiacal, with turquoise water and white-sand beaches. The next day, we went ashore to meet the Ni-Vanuatu, the native people there.

They practiced a ritual called land-diving. On this ceremonial day, approximately ten men volunteered to leap from a crude ninety-eight-foot-tall wooden tower with vines attached to their ankles. This ritual, said to date back fifteen centuries, is the precursor to bungee jumping. The men make the sacrifice for survival and prosperity of the community, and proof of their manhood.

While the community sang and danced below, a diver stood at the top and leaped outward, flying before dropping toward the earth and swinging to a stop, when everyone cheered. As I stood watching from a grassy mound, my heart seemed to stop beating for a moment.

I related to that sense of leaping because that's what this adventure felt like, each day hurtling myself into the unknown in the Southern Hemisphere seas. The men leapt from the tower with no certainty that the vines would withstand the pressure. And yet they soared with their whole hearts, holding nothing back. That was my goal as I lived this experience.

We set sail on our last leg of the trip, headed for Cairns, Australia. During these days, as the crew members knew the trip was winding down, a sense of even deeper closeness developed among us. As we worked our shifts, cooked together, and shared a single head, or bathroom, a kind of reverence developed. We would stand on deck and silently watch the sun melt into the sea. Then someone would let out a whoop, and everyone would cheer.

A sense of playfulness also ignited within the crew. One day

I was in the galley making bread. I was kneading a ball of dough on the kitchen table when suddenly a blowfish flew through the porthole. I jumped back and watched as it flapped around on top of my dough, its bulbous eyes staring at me. Out on deck, a couple of guys laughed. They stuck their heads through the portholes, big grins on their faces. I laughed too, and then found a towel, which I used to pick up the fish and take it outside to throw back in the water, only mildly upset that I would have to start over making my dough.

Meanwhile, Carl and I grew closer. During this leg of the trip, the nights were so hot below that many of us slept on deck. That's how, one night, Carl and I found ourselves lying head-to-head talking through much of the night. At some point, he reached toward me and clasped my fingers, sending a surge of energy through my heart. With our crewmates constantly around, we still could not indulge in any public display of affection. But that night we made love with our fingers, touching lightly, clasping, and holding until I could have screamed. We did it all silently, barely moving, so no one knew.

When we landed in Cairns, we spent a few days cleaning the ship. We worked hard during the day, and at night everyone went out partying to celebrate the end of the trip. Mike, the first mate, took us to the coolest bars, where we danced deep into the night. One early morning near dawn, Carl and I snuck away from the group. Finally, we could be together. During the journey, we had confided in each other about the challenges of storms, the pounding sun, hard work, and the disparate personalities of our crew. And yet, on the ship, we could only be friends.

Not anymore.

We snuck around the boat yard in the foggy dawn, the boats like mythical sea creatures hovering above sawhorses. We picked our favorite, an antique wooden boat like the *Zebu* but smaller.

Underneath it Carl laid a blanket on the ground, and we sat devouring each other first with our eyes. After three months of fierce attraction, we paused just a moment, letting the tension build. He reached forward and cupped my face in his hand and kissed me. His lips were delicious, a combination of hops and mint and salt. Under the light of a sickle moon and with the water lapping on shore, we kissed and kissed. He reached forward and touched my breast, and I reached to touch him. He unhooked my bra, and I unzipped his shorts, and then we fell into each other's arms and made tender love.

The next day, we said goodbye to everyone, a teary-eyed departure that left me feeling dazed. Though Carl was supposed to return to England, he had extended his leave from work as an engineer by two weeks so we could be together. We climbed in a rental car and drove south to Sydney to visit his aunt and uncle. This was no short trip—2,400 kilometers (1,600 miles) that took twenty-six hours.

When we arrived, Carl's aunt and uncle greeted us with farm-grown food and a comfy bed. They lived in a home on a river that cut through a deep canyon. We lazed around with them, enjoying their chickens and sheep and most of all, appreciating each other. We were falling in love, but it was an impossible future because he had to head back to London, and I was determined to remain in Australia.

I had received an invitation to stay on with Operation Raleigh to help with a party they were throwing. With reluctance, after two weeks, Carl and I drove back to Cairns. By the time we got there, we were exhausted. We found a hotel room and fell into bed. The next morning I took him to the airport to catch an early flight. I didn't have any money, so while we waited at the gate he handed me some cash.

"Thank you," I said, kissing him. He drew me in close and

kissed me back. We stood there kissing and kissing, delighting in the feel of each other. When the flight announcement came over the speakers, Carl picked me up and held me off the ground, and I rested my cheek on the top of his head, feeling my eyes grow teary. We spoke no words about the future. With no computers and no mobile devices, we could only promise to write letters that would take weeks to reach each other. When his flight was announced again, he lowered me to the ground. I hugged him one last time and then stepped away.

Though my heart hurt unbearably, I knew I would be okay. This was what I had chosen, to live a life of adventure, always in the moment. Even with this goodbye, a part of me rejoiced in the freedom of it.

CHAPTER 14

In 1986, in Cairns, I started my job as an interpreter for the Operation Raleigh group. I met the Chileans, who I was to interpret for, and they greeted me enthusiastically. They had sailed here on the *Sir Walter Raleigh*, the sister ship to the *Zebu*. The ship had come across from Chile with a group of scuba divers who had previously been in Fiji and all over the Pacific, including Easter Island. There was to be a party for British Army Colonel John Blashford-Snell, sponsor of the program, who was coming over to celebrate the uniting of the two ships that had never shared the same port. It was also the halfway point in the four-year Operation Raleigh round-the-world tour.

I was thrilled to get the job because it sounded fun and I wanted to remain in Australia. Operation Raleigh extended the work visa I had originally obtained for the *Zebu* trip, so now I had six months that I could work here. I also wrote to my grandmother and asked her if she could help me out financially, and she sent me two hundred dollars. For a few days I felt flush with cash, but it went quickly, and since my job continued to be volunteer, no other money was coming in.

At times, it would unnerve me to be so far from home and have nothing, and to not know what I would do to survive. I've always believed in the importance of travel to soften a person's edges, to make one flexible and resilient, and to broaden one's viewpoint, so I knew all of this was worthwhile. But now I was really putting my faith to the test. Whenever I became fearful of the future, I said to myself: "If I can just stay in the moment and trust my intuition, I will be okay." This guiding power within me was just making itself known, and I was beginning to trust it. I knew it was tied to a larger power that has a greater intelligence than my own mind's. As well as this larger intelligence, I sensed that many lifetimes of past experience existed within me, and though I couldn't remember the experiences, when I was quiet I could access the wisdom of them.

I bunked in the organizer and crew camp, which was an enclave of some ten military tents set in an open meadow outside Cairns. A few days into my job, the organizers asked me if I could drive, and I said, "Yeah, I can drive." This is how I became Colonel John Blashford-Snell's chauffeur.

He is an accomplished explorer and true inspiration. In 1968, he and his team made the first descent of the Blue Nile, which traverses a series of extreme gorges cut in the Ethiopian highlands. He was the first to drive the 17,000-mile journey from Alaska to Tierra del Fuego, a trip which included crossing the notorious Darién Gap, a break in the Pan-American Highway between Panama and Columbia. He completed the first navigation of the Congo River in Africa. In his journeys he was taken prisoner, survived two gunfights with bandits, and suffered a bus crash on the Road of Death in Bolivia.

I longed to be the kind of courageous adventurer he was. Blue eyed, intelligent, and a great conversationalist, he told me of his expeditions as I drove him around. Even back then, I felt deep in my heart that everyone was equal, so his celebrity and accomplishments didn't intimidate me. I told him about my aspirations to see as much of the world as possible and to have my own lodge. One day while I took him from the camp to a meeting in town, he said to me, "Go, follow your dream, Lana. And while you do it, try to make the world a better place."

When I look back on that experience, I see how much I took his advice to heart. Years from that profound moment, I would not only follow my dream, but I would do what I could to make the world better. I would help plan and build the first bamboo sustainable school in Costa Rica. I would aid in saving the Pacific Coast along the Osa Peninsula from commercial fish farms and help save sea turtles. Projects like these became my most fulfilling endeavors.

I also befriended a British colleague of Blashford-Snell named Charles Darwin, who obviously was not the father of Evolution Theory. He was a tall, handsome explorer with olive skin and a mischievous sparkle in his eye. Women fawned over him, and he fully appreciated them. The reconnaissance man for Operation Raleigh, or the recci as the Aussies called him, he entertained me with stories of traveling to remote places around the globe to determine if they were worthy of exploring for Operation Raleigh. Awestruck by his tales, I listened intently.

In Cairns, I shared an army tent with Blashford-Snell's daughter, Victoria, who was eighteen years old. I was twenty-four, and young-hearted enough that at times we were like two teenagers at a slumber party, chatting into the night about our lives. She had a passion for cooking, which to this day she pursues with abundant success, and we both loved to travel. I put my Spanish to use with the Chilean crew from the *Sir Walter Raleigh* and enjoyed the playful nature of the rest of the staff, who were mostly from England and Wales.

My job was to keep the Chilean workers informed about the party plans and to help with the preparations. I spent my days moving between the work crew and the Operation Raleigh organizers, relaying plans, changing previous plans, and suggesting how to improve the food and decorations.

Finally, the festive day arrived.

The party took place on the *Sir Walter Raleigh* and hosted dignitaries—governors and mayors from Australia, as well

Blashford-Snell's expedition buddies, who flew in from all over the world. The *Zebu* moored right beside the *Raleigh*, the two lit up with white Christmas lights, the towering masts sparkling. I opened the Range Rover door for Blashford-Snell, who was dressed in his expedition khakis, and followed him and his daughter to the party. I only had clothes from the sailing trip, so I wore my best white shorts and a blue halter top. Once on board, I found my buddies, mostly the Chileans, and we chatted happily in Spanish.

The ship quickly filled up with some three hundred guests, all dressed in their best boating finery, the women in summer dresses, the men in uniforms and sailing wear. The sun was setting golden on the horizon, and I talked with my friends while nibbling on canapés from tables set up along the bow. I savored some fried zucchini and, since I would be driving later, drank just one whiskey on the rocks. Before my first sip, I made a toast to my father.

I felt fortunate to be on this elegant ship with all these worldly people, and to be speaking Spanish. I looked off toward the *Zebu* and appreciated its grace and the way I knew it intimately from bow to stern. I had no idea how long I was going to stay there or where I was going to go afterward, but all was perfect in that moment.

That evening, Charles Darwin strolled up, cradling a scotch on the rocks, and started telling me about a fabulous lodge up in Cape York, where he had just been on a reconnaissance mission for Operation Raleigh. Cape York is the most northerly tip of Australia, just south of New Guinea. Charles explained that Cape York is the largest unspoiled wilderness in Australia. As I listened I became more and more excited.

"Would you want to work at the lodge there, Lana?" he asked me.

"Yes!" I said.

Apparently, he had mentioned me to the lodge owner, saying he knew a young woman who was looking for a job so she could stay in Australia. He told the owner I was determined and could do anything.

The next day, I called the owner and we talked. He asked about my work experience and aspirations. I told him I loved to serve people and wanted to work in the travel industry. He hired me on the spot. Just three days later, when we'd finished cleaning up from the party, I said goodbye to my Chilean buddies and to Blashford-Snell, Victoria, and Charles. I grabbed my duffel bag, hitched a ride to the airport with a friend, and flew from Cairns to Bamaga. My new employer generously purchased the plane ticket and sent a driver to pick me up and take me the remaining two hours to the lodge.

My next adventure had begun.

CHAPTER 15

In 1986, I entered the part of my journey that would fully focus my desire to have my own lodge. En route to my new job, I flew to Bamaga, a village that sits within an Indigenous Protected Area on Cape York. Such holdings are formed by agreement with Indigenous Australians and protected by the Australian government as part of the National Reserve System. This network of parcels protects more than 17 percent of the continent's biodiversity and ecological landscapes.

As the plane circled the village I noted the red clay soil and dense jungle. A driver from the lodge picked me up, placing my bag in the back of a Range Rover. We drove through a town of some seven hundred inhabitants, past a supermarket and little shops. Some of the Aboriginals watched as we drove by. Descendants of foragers and hunter-gatherers, these people had strong features and large, russet eyes that held an ancient wisdom, their lives still connected to nature.

We traveled for two hours on a bumpy, dirty, dusty road that ended at a rustic outback camp, the Cape York Wilderness Lodge. Six modest wooden buildings, each with four guest rooms, baths, and decks, stood on stilts near the main lodge, a wooden, open-air structure surrounded by thick, dripping jungle. We parked near a flat-topped mountain crowned with a helipad.

All of this sat two hundred meters (an eighth of a mile) from the rocky northernmost extremity of Australia. A pure white-sand beach led to the stunning turquoise waters of the Torres Strait, which sits between the Gulf of Carpentaria to the west and the Coral Sea to the east. Underneath these waters flourishes the Great Barrier Reef, one of the seven wonders of the world, the largest living organism on Earth, and the only living thing visible from space. I was in heaven.

The driver motioned for me to go ahead while he carried my bags to my room. I walked through the warm sand to a little deck and the main lodge. Looking around me, I examined the open-air restaurant, an informal space with cement floors and five long tables, where guests ate cafeteria-style. I took in every detail, adding to my mind's idea book of what works in a lodge.

Adjacent to the restaurant I found the office, which was enclosed with walls but had a big open window, letting in the scent of orchids that flourished in an elaborate garden surrounding the lodge. At a large desk sat my new employer, Paul Phelan, and looking over his shoulder at some papers stood his wife, Judy. He immediately got to his feet. Tall and athletic, somewhere in his fifties, he was the quintessential Aussie adventurer, with a tan face and whiskey-colored eyes. He wore board shorts and a shirt with a tropical print. Judy had a round face, curly hair, and the wholesome look of Betty Crocker.

"Welcome, Lana. It's wonderful to have you here," Paul said, holding out his hand. I wiped my wet palm on my shorts and shook his.

"I'm happy to be here," I said, my body tingling with excitement. I was already sweating in this steamy, seeping jungle, but now, as I met my employers who I would be working with for who knew how long, I really felt the heat all around me, perspiration running down my sides. Paul explained that I would be living in a tent, which sounded totally amazing. My main job would be to look after the sailboats and to teach sailing to the guests. I couldn't wait to get started.

He led me down a path through the jungle. "The gardens are fabulous," I said.

"Yes, they are." He looked about. "Though not always."

"Why?"

"It's the peccaries. Just as soon as we get things cleaned up, the local herd—some fifty of them—comes in and tramples and roots through everything. Afterward, it's a complete disaster."

I swallowed hard, imagining the wild boars with their sharp tusks rooting around near where I slept.

We walked up steps to enter the army tent. It was tall enough for me to stand in and had a graceful wooden floor, two twin beds, a little dresser, and a desk and chair. The whole structure sat on a pedestal with stilts about two feet off the ground.

"Why is everything on stilts?" I asked Paul.

"Our rainy season is intense. Everything floods for months," he said, shaking his head. "You get settled, and I'll see you for tea at six."

Fortunately, I knew this meant dinner.

I was exhausted but so excited I couldn't rest, so I put on my bikini and headed out to the beach. I strolled on the perfect white sand and imagined myself here every day. I came to where eight fishing boats, no larger than dinghies, sat anchored offshore. Part of my job would be to take care of these, which were used often by guests. Cape York was a notable fishing destination for barramundi, a flavorful fish in the snook family that live in both salt and brackish-fresh water.

I hiked on a rugged trail farther out onto the deserted point and gazed across the water. I knew that somewhere out there stood the untamed island of New Guinea, but from there I could only see ocean. Then I looked to my left, and my heart leapt. The whole beach was covered in frangipani trees. Their shrubby branches reached upward and were topped with pink, yellow, and white blossoms. A breeze picked up and the strong scent nearly knocked me over. It smelled like gardenias, peachy and creamy. I continued walking and found that the frangipani forest stretched nearly two kilometers, or more than a mile.

I turned around and looked south toward another beach, where three sixteen-foot catamarans rested. Excited to see the boats I would be spending much of my time on, I skipped over to check them out. They were in great shape, with few dings on the fiberglass and good, resilient sails. I had never taught sailing before so my stomach fluttered with the thought of it, but I remembered all the practice I'd had on boats much larger and more complex than these, and my nerves settled.

Something like a log, brown and bumpy, floated in the water not far from shore. But then it moved, and the hair stood up on my neck. It was a crocodile. It slowly made its way through the water and then disappeared below the surface. The strait was so pure and clear, the dreamlike turquoise of paradise. And yet, this deadly creature lurked below the surface where I and my students would be sailing. A shiver in my heart made me flinch.

That evening over dinner with Paul and Judy, I learned how they came here to shed the trammels of city life. During a pause in the conversation, I asked them about the crocs. Paul explained that they are the largest of all living reptiles, with males growing up to seventeen feet long and 2,200 pounds. They prey on anything hot blooded, but humans are a delicacy for them. They tend to ambush their target and then drown it or swallow it whole. If one chases you, you aren't supposed to run in a straight line, because they are very fast and they will catch you. Instead you must zigzag, because they can't turn their thick, long bodies easily.

"They can be a problem," he said, smiling in a pinched way. "Basically, we tell the guests to keep their eyes open when in the water, and to not go out more than waist deep."

I swallowed hard. I'd hoped for something more comforting. Those little catamarans could capsize easily, I knew. "How about when I teach sailing?"

"Well, Lana, that's part of your job—to keep an eye out so your students don't get eaten." He chuckled.

I knew I would have to get my guts up in order to live, work, and take care of my students in this wild place.

At Cape York, my life perched on the edge of calamity. Each day I got up at 6:00 a.m., showered, and then slathered deet all over my body to fend off the masses of mosquitos and biting flies, and then headed to the beach. I made sure that the little dinghies, anchored in a cove, were clean and set up with fishing, snorkeling, or sightseeing gear. Some guests took the boats out to islands off the cape. I made sure their lunches were packed and that they had water, and then helped them get on their way. This process didn't always run smoothly. On mornings that the tide was too far in, I couldn't get to the boats without encountering crocodiles. This delayed everyone's plans.

Next I gathered my sailing students, usually one or two, and hiked about fifteen minutes to the southern beach where the catamarans were. First I would go out on a catamaran with the student until he or she was comfortable, and then I would board a separate catamaran and together we would sail in the most perfect conditions. The wind blew mildly and the water shimmered, crystal clear. You could look down and see the reef, with all its pinks and blues, and huge schools of fish swimming through. I'm a sun bunny and I loved living in my bathing suit, so I couldn't have been happier.

In the late afternoons, I helped the guests get their gear out of the boats and made sure they were pleased with their excursions. Then I scoured all the dinghies. After that, I headed to the outdoor sink to help clean the fish. That is where I first got to know Bruce, a fishing guide who worked at the lodge and mostly guided guests out on the Bamaga River. He was tall and blond, with puppy-dog blue eyes and the softest smile. He had a swimmer's body that was in great shape because he used it hard from dawn to dusk. His character was even-keel, always with a positive attitude.

I had met him before because all the employees lived together in a tent enclave and shared communal bathrooms. But my first day helping clean fish, I had this massive knife that was so sharp it could cut off a finger if I didn't pay attention. He came alongside me and showed where to pierce the barramundi to begin the incision to clean it. He smiled this seductive, shy smile, and my heart melted.

We got to know each other on the reef. In my time off I would head out spearfishing with him. While he fished, I snorkeled, staying fairly close to the surface so I could alert him if I saw any crocodiles drawing near. Being out in that warm water, and seeing the schools of parrotfish, clownfish, and damselfish, as well as huge seas turtles, I felt every cell in my body ignite. Adding to the thrill was the image of Bruce working the reef, his muscular body swimming with calm adeptness. When he came up with a fish that we would later eat for dinner, my heart brimmed with desire.

Sometimes, when no one was around, I would hang my leather bikini from a tree limb and head out on my catamaran to sail in the nude. I never saw anyone out there, and the feel of the sun and breeze on my skin gave me a sense of freedom beyond any I had ever felt. The briny scent of the ocean, the vast expanse of water, and that sun that I so worshiped filled me with delight.

And yet, a sense of danger always lurked. One day when my boss, Paul, and I returned from sailing, two Coast Guard officers stood with Paul's wife, Judy, in the lodge. They all wore grave faces. The officers had flown over the point in search of a crocodile, which the previous night had killed an Aboriginal man by devouring his whole lower body. The Aboriginal had been drunk and was trying to get into his boat when the croc got him. With a tool the Coast Guard usually uses to measure the size of drug boats, they estimated the croc to be twenty-one feet long. After this, we were much, much more careful while we sailed.

Still other dangers lurked in this landscape. One day, Bruce and I went out so he could spearfish. Instead he caught some crabs and lobsters and motioned for me to swim down to help him bring them up. While down there, my arm accidentally brushed against some fire coral. All night my arm felt like it was being held to a flame, and the next day I couldn't straighten it. Judy gave me some antibiotics, but they didn't help. Two days later, I ached all over, as though I had the flu. I looked at the prescription bottle and realized the expiration date had passed years before. Paul and Bruce rushed me to the clinic in Bamaga.

A doctor from Singapore immediately put me on an IV. "You were fortunate," she said. "If you had waited any longer, you could have died."

She settled me into one of two beds in their only patient accommodation. The room was a turquoise color, with late afternoon sun shining in. I fell asleep and woke many hours later in lemony dawn light. I looked over and there in the bed next to mine was a red-haired albino Aboriginal. In my hazy mind, I thought I was in heaven, because everything seemed so bright and otherworldly.

"Hi," I said to this strange presence. All over his paper-white skin, he had the most delicate freckles.

"Hello," he said in a deep voice.

I closed my eyes and opened them, realizing this wasn't the afterlife. We were the only two patients in this little clinic, so we spent the morning talking about how we got here—he had been bitten by a dog.

He left that evening, but I spent four days in the clinic, my arm continuing to burn. Finally the pain stopped, and the doctor allowed me to return to the lodge. In the coming weeks, I recovered completely.

After four months in Cape York, the off-season came. In January 1987, Jani flew to Australia to travel with me. From Bruce's father we bought a vintage, rusted Chrysler Valiant for $150 that we called the Batmobile. It was so big we could sleep in it, which was important because we had very little money. We drove south to Melbourne, flew to Tasmania, and when we returned, drove to Uluru, or Ayers Rock. It is a huge red mesa in the southern part of the Northern Territory, often shown in movies.

Our first evening there, we encountered an Aboriginal who showed us how to make fire with two sticks. He dug a hole in one and fitted the end of the other into it. Then, with his palms, he twirled the vertical stick until smoke appeared. He held brush up to the fire-maker and it caught, like a miracle—flame from nearly nothing. The simplicity of his creation touched me deep in my heart, and I appreciated the sense that focused energy could create something as intense as fire.

That night in the dusty, windblown outback, Jani and I lay awake, our tent flapping in a fifty-mile-per-hour wind. I kept thinking about those sticks. When the sky began to light we put on our boots and hiked to the top of Ayers Rock. It's no longer possible to hike it.

I stood on the top of that huge, powerful rock and thought of the flame that so easily caught the brush and grew to a blaze. My passion on this trip felt like that. Watching the gigantic orange sun come up over the horizon, I knew that when I focused my energy on what I truly wanted, it too would blaze into life.

In May, when we returned to the Cape York Wilderness Lodge, Paul offered Jani the opportunity to work there too. She helped out in the kitchen and with the cleaning. I continued to teach sailing and maintain the fishing boats, but now, short on staff, Paul gave me even more responsibilities. I did everything, including cooking and cleaning. I was happy to do it because I knew I was learning all the facets of running a lodge.

This period was not without excitement. One dark, early morning, Jani and I entered the lodge to wait tables for breakfast. The guests going fishing always ate early. As I walked between the tables, I tripped and nearly fell on my face. I regained balance and pulled out my Maglite. When I flipped it on, my skin tingled with sudden terror. Across the floor lazed a boa constrictor that was so big its girth stood four inches tall, and its length stretched to eight feet.

Jani and I watched it slither out of the room, and chills ran up my spine as I recognized the danger we had escaped. If I had fallen in its path, it could have grabbed onto me, strangled me, and consumed me whole. But I wasn't daunted. This dangerous life was my life, and I only wanted more of it.

Now that I had experience, the image of my lodge that I first imagined while sailing on the *Zebu* became vivid. My lodge started to take form in my consciousness, not just the way it might look, but the way it would be run, and what my guests might like to do. One night, at the desk in my little tent, I pulled out my journal and began writing in the candlelight.

At Cape York, there were twenty-five staff members for fifty guests. I knew I would need a similar, though smaller, staff. I would hire maintenance personnel, guides, cooks, office helpers, and guest-services people, and I wrote all of this down. I estimated that I would one day have maybe five separate bungalows and a main lodge, and the whole complex would be more refined than the Cape York Wilderness Lodge. I would build in Costa Rica because I had fond memories from there, and that lush country was nestled in my soul. I wanted to share Costa Rica with the world. I wrote COSTA RICA at the top of the page in huge capital letters.

One of the main reasons I dreamed of a lodge was because I wanted to experience people from all over the world coming to my home. When I traveled, I met fabulous people, and I just knew there was something good in everyone.

I also wanted an exotic life like I had at Cape York and on the *Zebu*. My friends from high school and college graduated and went to Europe, and came back and got married and started having kids right away. They have beautiful, interesting lives, but I wanted something unique. I wanted to go to Australia and beyond to places people rarely visited, like Vanuatu and Tasmania. I also knew that taking risks was important to me. I loved to feel my adrenaline surge because that feeling focused my attention in the present moment, and that was where I always wanted to be.

After hours of contemplating and writing, I looked through the pages and realized what I had done: I had created the first business plan for my lodge.

CHAPTER 16

Before I returned home to Colorado, I traveled from Australia to Asia. Though Jani had wanted to travel with me, my intuition told me that I should go alone. I loved the sense of freedom of traveling on my own, and I found I engaged much more with other people that way. When I told Jani this, she was deeply disappointed and likely angry. We did agree to meet up in Bangkok about halfway through my trip.

I went to Singapore on my own to see Aarav, one of my friends from the Zebu, and later, Bruce, my Cape York boyfriend. After I toured the city with them, Bruce and I headed through Malaysia and on to Thailand. From there, Bruce traveled to Nepal and I went to Bangkok to adventure with Jani for a couple of weeks before I headed to Nepal to meet up with him again.

When I arrived in Bangkok, Jani was nowhere to be found, and I received a letter from her saying that she wasn't coming because she had fallen in love. By this time, I was looking forward to her company, so it struck a real blow. It felt like a payback, and ultimately served as a huge lesson for me. It showed me how it felt to be excluded the way I had excluded Jani from this trip. Most importantly, it taught me that whatever you ask the Universe for, it will give to you. However, you have to be careful what you wish for—I had wanted to travel alone and now here I was, really alone. I flew to Nepal and tried to meet up with Bruce again but didn't find him for a while because there was no internet or cell phones back then. I sure got my wish.

When Bruce met me at the airport two weeks later we had a heartfelt rendezvous; he held me tightly among the throngs of people streaming around us, and his presence seemed to penetrate to my very core. I was so happy to have close human contact again. We traveled for a few more months in Nepal and Thailand, and then I flew to England to see some friends, and finally, after nearly two years away, I headed home. I had traveled around the world, and it had changed my life forever.

When I returned to Colorado from my travels, I have to admit I was adrift. For two years, I had spent my time sailing, swimming, surfing, and making love on the beach. I was a hippie of the Universe, a true citizen of the world, and when I arrived back in Colorado, I only felt constrained. I wanted out, to travel more, and to be away from my family, which was ruled with an iron fist by my stepfather. Just visiting my family home I felt the pressure there, to always be doing—and doing everything perfectly.

I knew I couldn't stay. And so, when a friend told me about a job leading bicycle tours in Vermont, I found out the details and applied. I raced bikes in college, so I was good at riding and fixing them, and I wanted to work in the tourism industry. This was a perfect fit. I got the job with Vermont Country Cyclers, jumped in my Honda, and drove to Stowe.

It was pure heaven spending my days riding through the New England countryside under the shade of sugar maples, beech, and yellow birch trees. We usually had about twenty riders in a group. We pedaled from one luxury lodge to the next, each providing gourmet breakfasts and dinners. At lunch, we guides set up an expansive buffet of cold cuts and cheeses, with treats such as M&Ms and the local Ben & Jerry's ice cream.

One guide would ride with the group, while the other one drove the support vehicle. Mostly, the clients were good riders and didn't require a lot of attention. Only occasionally would one struggle with the fifty to seventy miles we covered in a day. This person rode in the van so the group could continue.

Eight of us young guides shared a big house set on a meadow near the Trapp Family Lodge. On rare occasions when we were all at home, we gathered to party and play. One evening out on the broad deck, we created a whole orchestra from kitchen implements. We clanged together saucepans, tapped on glasses and bottles, and drummed on pots with wooden spoons. A woman pulled out a tambourine, a man played the guitar, and another man the djembe. We sang and played into the night, the chirping crickets supplying the harmony.

On a bright fall day, a man who I went to high school with from Gunnison, Colorado, two years younger than I was, showed up in the area to attend a Ziggy Marley concert. Cole Maguire had just traveled down from Alaska and heard I was in the area, so he came to see me. Though I'd known Cole all my life, this time I looked at his cowboy hat, dark eyes, wavy hair, sexy mustache, and a sweetness that exuded from a friendly smile, and immediately thought, *wow.*

We all went to the concert set below a grassy hillside on the shores of Lake Burlington. On that hot Vermont day, a Woodstock atmosphere blossomed. As Ziggy sang of love, taking life easy, and being free, we drank tequila straight from the bottle, the bright sun glinting off the lake. I danced with everyone, my arms in the air, my hips grooving, but mostly I danced with Cole. He was an adept honky-tonk dancer, so he felt the music deep within, and I felt it in him, and we lit the day on fire with our kissing and looping our arms around each other as we swayed together. I smiled so hard my face hurt.

My parents arrived the next day for a visit. Though I was hungover and had this gooey crush feeling, I went with them to a place called Trout Haven, a private club and resort that a friend of theirs belonged to. The lodge had three stories with a window at the top looking out at a manicured driveway. I was on the top story in a guest room with my parents when I heard a horn honk and yelling below. I went to the window, and there stood Cole wearing a cap and surf shorts looking up at me like Romeo with those fabulous dark eyes. When I opened the sash he yelled up at me, "Lana, I want to be with you."

The crush I'd been feeling all morning overtook me, weakening my knees, so I steadied myself on the window frame. I knew in that moment I wanted him too. It was perfect timing for me to find someone because, during the eight months I'd been back in the States, I'd dated but not really connected with anyone. I was ready.

I yelled out the window, "I want you too!"

I was brimming with joy, yet a reluctance nudged against my heart like a cold stone. When I paused to look at it, I recognized that serious commitment made me nervous, maybe from watching my mother and father fight, or my father's lack of commitment. Before I met Cole, I had also been entertaining a strong desire for the three months I'd been in Vermont—to return to Costa Rica.

Part of the pull to return there was Oscar, the soccer player I met while studying in Santa Ana. As much as I adored Cole, something remained unfinished between Oscar and me, and I knew I couldn't be true to Cole with Oscar still occupying part of my heart. Though Cole was fun, smart, strong, and adventurous, Oscar was Costa Rica. He had this soft, moist comfort, this luscious Spanish that rolled off his tongue, and this way of living beyond time and space that I got lost in, so far from the rigid and frantic world up north. The difference was like being on land versus inhabiting the ocean, weightless, timeless—free.

But Oscar was now married.

Cole and I talked on the phone as often as possible, growing closer every day. After I finished work in Vermont, I returned to Colorado, where he and I moved in together. For the winter, we taught skiing at Crested Butte Mountain Resort, and I also waited tables at the Powerhouse Bar & Grill. In addition, I landed a part in a local production of the musical *Jesus Christ Superstar*, so I was busy.

In our free time, Cole and I hiked and skied and partied. As the months passed, our relationship grew warmer and more intimate. He was possibly the first person in the world I fully trusted, because he was steady and unwavering in his affection for me. He was my best friend, and we also made fabulous love. With our passion for nature and lust for adventure, it was a perfect partnership.

However, when the ski season ended, Cole left to fish for salmon and halibut in Alaska. In a similar way that my heart was attached to Costa Rica, his was to Alaska. He had spent the past two summers fishing there. He liked the hard work and fast money, as well as being out on a vast and cold ocean. I was sad to see him go, but knew it was only for the season.

Two weeks after he left, Cole called with excitement in his voice. He described what was happening due to the Exxon Valdez oil spill. News of the accident was all over the media: on March 24, 1989, an Exxon tanker struck the Prince William Sound's Bligh Reef and spilled eleven million gallons of crude oil, initiating one of the most devastating human-caused environmental disasters in history. Cole told me that the area had filled with people there to do research and clean up an area encompassing 11,000 square miles of ocean and 1,300 miles of coastline.

"Lana, get your bum up here," he said. "There's all kinds of jobs to help clean this up."

Whenever I hear of the destruction of the environment, and especially harm to animals, I want to take action. The love of nature is woven deeply into my being. All the time I spent outdoors as a kid, my sailing trips, and my previous travels in Costa Rica combined to make me feel as though when nature is harmed, my very being is harmed as well, and that all our souls suffer, even if we don't know it. With Cole's news, my heart went out to the ocean and the birds and sea life. I had to do something.

And so, I launched myself northward.

CHAPTER 17

I quit my restaurant gig and drove my little Honda, which I called Acapulco Gold, to Seattle, where I took a ferry for the seven-day journey to Sitka. From there I flew to Anchorage and then went on to Seward. That place, at the head of Resurrection Bay on the Kenai Peninsula, bubbled with activity. Aid workers and researchers labored to help animals and clean up the oil, and thousands of others did whatever they could to assist the effort and make some money. I needed a job, and so while I wandered the streets of Seward waiting for Cole to come in from fishing, I put the intention out there, asked to be guided to the perfect job for me.

When evening came, I went to Ray's Bar, where Cole told me to meet him. Back before cell phones, this was how we connected. The bar was packed with a range of people, from scientists to rednecks to hippies, all talking fast and full of energy.

I ordered a beer and sat back. A woman next to me, with wavy brown hair and eyes set close together, commented on the massive crowd that swirled within the bar, and we marveled at the commotion. Suddenly, I was moved to say, "Hi. My name is Lana."

"My name is Lana, too," she said.

Smiling, I said, "I've never met another Lana."

"Do you have a job?" she asked.

That seemed like an odd question out of the blue, but I answered, "No, I just got here. I'm waiting for my boyfriend."

"I ask because I have a job interview tomorrow at ten a.m., and the only thing they know is that my name is Lana. They've never seen me." She shook her head and smiled. "I just got a better job as a vet-tech—I want to be a veterinarian someday."

"Oh, wow, a job would be amazing."

"Do you know how to cook?"

"Yeah, I've cooked at a lodge and on a sailboat. I've cooked a lot."

"Great. Do you like to be on the water?"

"I just sailed from Australia to New Zealand and back, and I love being on the water."

"Fabulous," she said. "Why don't you go to the job interview tomorrow?"

We laughed about the synchronicity. Then Cole stepped into the bar. He wore a brown felt cowboy hat, and his hair had grown longer, curling along his neck. I noted a bit of swagger that was common to many of the men in the area. They were the burly guys who endured the cold and made their way in the Alaskan wilds. And he looked burly, with a ghost of a beard and the muscles of his shoulders pressed against his shirt. When he saw me, a smile lit up his face and his eyes sparkled. He came up, lifted me off my stool, and held me tightly. That's what he always did, and I loved it; he held me and didn't let me go. Then he kissed me all over my face, down my neck, and up again, ending at my lips. All my thoughts disappeared in the pleasure of him.

I introduced him to Lana and told him about the job interview. He shook his head. "You always find your way, don't you, Lana?"

"I guess I do!"

He took my hand and we snaked through the crowd to the dance floor. Garth Brooks sang, "If tomorrow never comes, will she know how much I love her?" While Cole adeptly led me in a two-step around the floor, he sang those words in my ear with his deep baritone voice. We were both in the musical *Li'l Abner* in high school, and even back then I was impressed by his voice. I held tightly to him, swooning as he sang.

From the dance floor, we waved when his brother, Lyle, and a crew of six guys, all from Colorado, came into the bar. They'd been fishing, too. I was overjoyed to see them, and I ran to hug them all. We found a table, where we sat and drank pitchers of beer, and they told tales of their Alaskan adventures.

In the days before the internet, employers couldn't go online to vet applicants. The next day, I went to the interview. I truthfully said my name was Lana, and I got the job.

A few days later I found myself on a research ship with fourteen scientists. A day or so after the oil spill they went out and sampled the plankton along the coast. Now that the oil had hit shore, they had returned to take more samples to compare with their original ones. The ship was a tour ship that had been repurposed for this research, so I had a luxury cabin that allowed me to sit on the balcony and watch the whales, porpoises, and bald eagles. As cook, I also had full run of the ship, and I liked to spend time up on deck.

Early one morning, a killer whale raced before the ship's bow. It played, darting away and back through the clear ocean, and blew water each time it rose, so that I felt the mist on my face. It was so beautiful, and my heart ached for the jeopardy this whale and all the other ocean creatures were facing.

Mostly the intensity of my work eclipsed such concerns, though. I had full responsibility to put three meals a day on the table for the fourteen scientists and Captain Jack Scoby, who basically ran the whole ship. I woke at 5:00 a.m. and made coffee, bacon, sausage, and pancakes. The researchers came in, ate, and headed out. Then I started on lunch, usually a meal of cold cuts and cheese to make sandwiches. I cut up tomatoes, cleaned lettuce, and set it all out so the diners could eat at their leisure. Then I'd put four roasting chickens or six whole halibut in the oven, along with a dozen and a half potatoes to bake. It was nonstop for me until everyone had eaten. I washed the dishes and scrubbed down the tables. Then, finally, I headed up on deck to relax, commune with the ocean, and sometimes sit on the bridge and visit with Captain Jack.

Cole and I met up during rare times off work. The atmosphere in Seward was wild, money flowing from all the fishing and aid work. People labored long days and into the nights and then partied until dawn, hardly sleeping. Since the sun never really set, everyone stayed energized by the light and by the intensity of all that was going on. Sometimes we went to the bars late and stayed until three or four in the morning and danced until we could barely stand.

Part of our intensity may have arisen from the destruction that was happening all around us. Enjoying the company of others helped alleviate the pain of the toll the oil was taking on nature. Hundreds of thousands of sea birds such as cormorants and murres, thousands of sea otters, and hundreds of harbor seals were dying. At times the magnitude of it all was so much we just had to blow off steam. We went to the Kenai Fjords National Park, where we watched humpback and orca whales break the water's surface, and kittiwakes and puffins fly, lending us some hope.

At the end of the summer, when our work in Seward finished, we traveled west to Dillingham to fish salmon and later to Petersburg where Cole fished halibut and I waited tables in a restaurant. Then we headed back to Colorado. We left Alaska with our pockets full of cash and our hearts saddened by how little could be done for the animals. All the effort had only cleaned up about 10 percent of the oil.

Cole and I flew from Petersburg to Seattle, where we picked up my Honda. The first thing we did was go to a mall, which after months in nature felt like a sci-fi space station. Everything had hard edges lit by bright lights. It made me dizzy until I acclimated. We were dressed like lumberjacks, with our Carhartt pants, work boots, and T-shirts.

Cole pointed out a clothing store. "Go in there and drop your drawers," he said. "Buy whatever you want and leave the rest behind."

I found a flowing white dress with blue flowers that danced with every movement and some sexy, strappy sandals. I left all my clothes on the dressing room floor. When I came out, I spun, the skirt flowing out like a ballerina costume. Cole's eyes grew wide. We went to the counter where he insisted on paying. Then he grabbed my hand and we ran out of the mall into the sunshine, where he pinned me against a glass wall. He told me to close my eyes, and he rustled for something in his pocket.

"Okay, open them," he said.

When I did, I saw a necklace with a cluster of diamonds on a gold chain.

"I love you," he said.

"I love you, too," I answered, and I did, with all my heart. I felt like Cinderella. While I had been shopping for my new clothes, Cole had been shopping for another present for me, and this meant a great deal to me. Never had anyone been so kind and attentive to me.

We drove eleven hours to Reno, Nevada, at the base of the Sierra Nevada Mountains. There we got a hotel room and went to a rotating restaurant that perched high above the city. Amidst tables covered in white linen, shiny flatware, and fine china, we felt like royalty. Cole ordered champagne that we sipped, making our noses tingle. We ordered a steak for him and a stuffed baked potato for me, sat back, and smiled at each other. Suddenly, Cole stood, pulled a velvet box from his pocket, opened it, and knelt before me.

"Another gift? Cole, you spoil me."

He paused and smiled. "Lana, will you marry me?"

It was a stunning ring, a line of rubies set in gold. My head buzzed and my heart beat fast in a strange combination of elation and fear. The confusion must have shown on my face.

Cole leapt to his feet before I said anything. "Don't tell me yet."

I took a deep breath and settled into the relief, and yet I was so thrilled I could hardly eat. Someone loved me enough to want to spend his whole life with me, and it was Cole Maguire. Lit with possibility, I beamed at him. We both looked out across the city lights as they blinked and shone in a million promising colors. I did my best to take a few bites of my dinner.

When we finished, we headed out into the city. We walked down Virginia Street past the neon sign that reads "Reno, the Biggest Little City in the World" and gazed at all the neon-lit casinos. Along the side streets we found some cozy bars, where we ordered tequila shots. Bar after bar, we drank deep into the night.

The next morning we headed south again. Cole was extremely hungover, so I was at the wheel as we made our way through completely vacant desert. While I drove, I tried to clear away the tequila fog enough to make a decision about the marriage proposal. The day grew hot and my eyelids heavy, so I cranked the Rolling Stones and sang along with *Start Me Up*. "If you start me up, I will never stop . . ." I sang.

Broiling with no air conditioning, I took off my top, feeling the wind blow across my bare breasts, my hair snapping around my head. The desert spread vast and limitless before me, with a straight road stretching to the horizon. I considered our wild time in Alaska and also these past few days, living so freely with our money and so beyond schedules, with nowhere we really had to be. I looked over at Cole scrunched down in the seat snoozing and felt complete love for him and pure gratitude for our time together.

For a moment, Oscar and Costa Rica crossed my mind. I remembered the lushness of that place, the lilt of his Spanish, and the way my body felt so open and sexy under his touch.

But then I gazed at Cole and saw something less dreamlike and more real.

I met Oscar when he was single, and I'd been gone a long time. He was married now. *Married*, I reminded myself. *That interlude is over. I must face it and live in current reality.*

Cole and I were both Sagittarians. We worked hard and played hard, and we could keep up with each other. We saw life as an opportunity, and it never mattered how challenging the road ahead might look; we knew it would take us places. He accepted me for who I was. He didn't care if I drank ten tequilas and he had to take care of me. In that moment I saw us adventuring along the fabulous highway of marriage and kids. We would live in Colorado and take trips to Alaska and Costa Rica.

I pulled a Sharpie from the console, and while I drove, wrote on my bare chest in big black letters, *"¡Sí!"* I pulled over at a rest stop, nudged him awake, and pointed to my chest. He blinked his eyes as though trying to clear away the sleep. He cocked his head to one side and then the other. I looked down and realized I'd drawn the "S" backwards.

"Sí," I said. "Yes, I will marry you!"

He jumped out of the car, ran around to the driver's side, flung open the door, and drew me out. He lifted me and twirled me around and around under the blazing sun.

A trucker pulled his eighteen-wheeler out of the rest stop and honked his horn in celebration. Hoot, hoot!

CHAPTER 18

Back in Crested Butte we made wedding plans. We would get married outside at Lake Irwin, a crystalline, high-mountain lake. I chose four bridesmaids, two women I went to high school with and two I worked with at the Powerhouse Bar & Grill. My sister agreed to be the maid of honor. Cole asked four of his close friends from the area to stand with him, along with his brother as best man. We spent long dinners at his parents' house talking of the wedding, and they embraced me as part of the family.

As much as I was excited about our future, I noticed that something odd happened when my friends or acquaintances said, "Lana, you're getting married!" They reached for my hand to see the ring, and I found myself hiding it behind my back. In the night when I awakened with excess energy stirring inside me, I wondered about this. It all seemed so perfect to marry a hometown boy, to do what my friends were doing as they started families and careers. But something was holding me back. My intuition was trying to tell me something, but I was so attached to Cole that I refused to listen.

Cole got a job as the head guide at a hunting camp, and his employers hired me to cook there. I took a month-long leave of absence from the Powerhouse and promised to return to waiting tables when we finished in the high country. Six hunters, three guides, and I left Crested Butte in two four-wheel-drive vehicles pulling horse trailers ten miles in. We rode the last few miles as we led a team of eight donkeys that carried the food and hunting gear. It was fall, darkening into winter, and yet we lived in tents on a broad, grassy meadow. The kitchen tent was my domain. I got up at 3:00 a.m., made coffee, ham, and eggs, and packed lunches for the hunters who bagged deer and elk.

At dawn, Cole and the other guides left with the hunters. Meanwhile, I relaxed and enjoyed the time to myself, especially the nature, the red-tailed hawks circling, the raccoons rooting around the wood pile, and the elk bugling in the distance. Once rested, I chopped pine logs to burn so I could bake whole turkeys and hams in the wood oven. A little later, I stood under a sun shower (a solar-warmed bag of water) until I felt as clean as the air around me. I was completely grateful for Cole, for the water on my skin, the sun kissing it dry, the cool breeze, and the tall pines surrounding camp.

On our third week out, I woke up one morning feeling weak and feverish, with burning pain in my shoulder and neck. Usually, I felt healthy, which I attributed to vegetarianism. (In 1982, when I went to Spanish language school in Costa Rica, I lived with a very poor family who couldn't afford meat, so I ate beans, rice, vegetables, and fruit. I felt so robust that I became a vegetarian and have been one ever since. The diet fits me well because I love animals and never want to harm them.)

I was confounded when this pain appeared. Fortunately, the work week was over, so we headed down the mountain. The hike was difficult, since my energy was low and I had what felt like an injury, maybe from chopping wood or lifting bags of food. When we got out of the mountains, I immediately went to my childhood doctor in Gunnison.

Dr. Wolkov was tall with dark hair and a beard framing a fleshy face. He was a kind, free-spirited mountain man. In his red brick office next to the local hospital, I sat on the examination table, the paper crinkling under me. He touched my neck, which had developed a flaming rash. When he finished examining me, he looked me hard in the eye. "Lana, what's going on in your life?"

"I'm supposed to be getting married," I said, smiling a tight smile. Again I felt the impulse to hide the ring behind my back.

"Are you sure you want to do that?" he asked, zeroing in closer to me. "Lana, you have shingles, and that's not something a twenty-eight-year-old should experience. It's stress induced—your nervous system is rebelling."

My body was telling me something, and now this doctor was speaking it aloud. He wrote out a prescription and handed it to me but didn't release the paper to my grasp. It sat there pulled between us. "Lana," he said. "You need to be honest with yourself, slow down, and relax."

I nodded, not sure that I could do what he suggested. "I'll try," I said. He let go of the paper and I tucked it in my pocket. As I walked to the car, the conversation swam around in my head. *Relax? How can I do that when I'm working at the hunting camp five days a week and planning a wedding?* In the end, I didn't do what he said. It was not in my nature to stop and really look at why I was making this choice. I continued with the wedding plans: Cole and I had put together a list of about two hundred guests; we asked our community pastor to officiate; and we secured a caterer and planned the menu.

I spent my two days off a week, Thursday and Friday, in an expansive luxury home on the ski mountain, where my sister was house-sitting. It had three stories, a huge kitchen and great room, and 360-degree views. After my time in the backcountry, it was pure luxury to sleep on a king-size bed with a pillow-top mattress. On his days off, Cole went to Gunnison to stay with his family.

I took full advantage of the time off to sleep in, have a late coffee and breakfast out with my sister, Jani, and let my body rest from the grueling work. Nights I headed to the Powerhouse, where I sat at the bar and visited with friends. Jani hostessed for the restaurant and joined me whenever she could to sneak a tequila shot. With twenty different varieties of tequila, the place offered a guaranteed good time for anybody who wanted to party.

I'd known the Powerhouse cook for a year, a guy named Blake Cooper, and I'd always been attracted to him—especially his legs. Formerly a professional tennis player, he had tried out for the Olympics but didn't make the cut. He exuded a strength that I was lacking now with my inner uncertainty. So a few times a night, when he wandered through the bar, I smiled at him.

One night I came in straight from the camp dressed in my Carhartt jacket and smelling of wood-oven smoke, and he told me how sexy I looked. We laughed, knowing it was pure flirtation. He invited me to play tennis, but it was so cold we kept putting it off. But one evening, we left the restaurant together and he urged me to join him at another tavern. We headed up the street and sat on stools along a mahogany bar, where we drank so many tequila shots that we stumbled back to his place.

It was just a friendly drink, I told myself, even as my heart beat faster with one look at him. He was the opposite of Cole—blond hair, fine features, relaxed, a wealthy Denver kid. We sat on his couch next to each other in the one-room loft he rented in a charming historic house. His bed was just a few feet away. The walls held posters of skiers bursting through chest-deep powder. This, I realized, was his ideal—he was a ski bum through and through. He placed a beer in front of me on the glass coffee table and took a swig of his own. We sat quietly for a minute, and I reached for the beer, the cold bottle wet in my palm.

"You seem happy in Crested Butte," I said, since I'd noted that he was always smiling.

He nodded his head. "Yeah, I caught the mountain bug. My

parents want me to get a corporate job in Denver, but I can't. It would kill me. So, I defy them and hang out here skiing, playing tennis, biking, hiking . . ."

"I get it," I said. "We have to follow our hearts, no matter how hard it is."

"Are you following yours?" he asked, and I knew he was talking about Cole. I put my right hand over my ring, took a deep breath, and said, "I don't really know. I thought I was, but . . ."

Suddenly he leaned over and kissed me. His lips were soft, different from Cole's more dry, weathered ones. The kiss was luscious. I didn't hold back, but instead kissed him with deep intensity. He smelled of onions and garlic from his cooking at the restaurant, and of beer and cigarettes, and this added to the daring attraction. He took my hand and led me to the side of the bed where he kissed down my neck to my breasts.

We fell together onto the tousled blankets and sheets, where he ravished me, and I devoured him. I couldn't believe I was with him. All the women in town wanted Blake because he was so good-looking and good-natured. My heart leapt with the idea that I was having sex with him, the pull so strong it overtook everything. My mind shut off any thought of the future.

When we finished, Cole's face came into my consciousness, a crease between his brows and eyes so sullen they could have been looking at death.

Whenever I was in town, I met Blake at the Powerhouse, and when he finished work we headed to his place. Meanwhile, Cole stayed busy with his family and friends. I told myself the affair was just a physical thing that I needed to get out of my system before I settled down. So I kept it like that as much as I could, a sexual encounter.

But I did stay the night, and the routine and Blake's presence grew on me. He had no expectations and only wanted fun. The rest of my life felt weighty and permanent. This was the perfect antidote.

But underneath the conscious reasons dwelled something deeper. Above all, I was afraid of conflict, afraid to speak my truth. In our family, with my stepfather's silent rage constantly brewing, and also my father's anger when I was younger, I'd come to believe that telling the truth could have cruel consequences. Instead, I strove to be the "good girl," always pleasing, always content with my lot. I could no more admit to Cole that I wanted a different future than I could stand up to either of my fathers.

After Blake and I made love, we cuddled in bed and talked of our pasts. I told him that I missed the freedom I felt in Australia, with no planned future, only the ocean and a tall ship to sail every day.

Still, some days I wondered if Cole might walk in the Powerhouse and see me talking to Blake. Or maybe he'd smell Blake's expensive aftershave on my neck, or the cigarette smoke on my breath, since lately I'd come to share a few drags whenever Blake lit up. How could Cole not know that this was going on? That question came to me in the night, and as I did my morning headstand, it turned my mouth dry and made me wobble so I almost fell over.

A month into my affair with Blake, Cole and I were headed up to the hunting camp, trekking through three feet of snow. I plowed through it with every bit of energy I had, not stopping, not even pausing. My muscles ached, screaming for me to slow down, but I continued to torture myself because I felt so bad about my infidelity and how it would hurt Cole. Each week I told myself I must stop the affair, but then I didn't. My intuition was trying to tell me something, and the affair was helping me listen.

At camp, we greeted the hunters and did our usual chores. The work felt harder these days. Though my shingles had cleared up, they seemed to have taken my energy. The reality of what these men did every day, when they came back with huge beautiful elk and deer, was unbearable to me. The animals' lifeless eyes as the guides unstrapped them from the donkeys stayed with me through the nights. And while a month ago the feeling of Cole's arms around me as we slept eased this pain, it no longer did. I could hardly bear to have him hold me, I felt so confused.

When we trekked out of camp for our days off, I paced fast the whole way, eager to be on my own, free of the dead animals and especially Cole. I opened the door to the mansion, ran to my bedroom, and leapt onto the bed. I looked up at the ceiling and breathed deeply for the first time in five days.

The next afternoon, I was upbeat after yoga with my sister, Jani. When she left for work, I made chamomile tea and lounged in the living room. The phone rang. When I picked up I barely recognized the voice it was so soft and low. "Hi, Lana."

I stood there holding the receiver. *Who is this?*

"I know," he said and hung up the phone.

My mind went berserk. *Cole knows about the affair? How?*

I knew I must apologize. I still loved him, but I'd come to see that the tryst was a diversion, a way out. I drove Acapulco Gold fast through the ski-area parking lot and turned into the driveway of Cole's buddy's house, where he often stayed. I climbed out and knocked on the door. His friend answered but wouldn't even look me in the eye. He pointed to the living room and continued cooking his dinner. When I entered the room and saw Cole sitting on the blue couch, his face seemed frozen in a grimace. I stood before him in the dim twilight.

"Cole, I am so sorry. I didn't mean to hurt you."

He remained stiff and closed and just looked at me with those dark, doe-like eyes. Then he gazed down at his hands in his lap. I didn't blame him for remaining silent. All our careful plans, our future together, were dead. And as much as I wanted to make excuses, as much as I wanted to beg him to forgive me so we could return to plan our bright future, I knew I couldn't. It was a lie. I wanted something different. I wasn't even sure what it was, but something was tugging me south. With a heaving pain in my chest, I said goodbye and walked out.

I drove down into the town of Crested Butte. It was snowing hard and freezing, and my fingers were so cold they could barely hold the steering wheel. I scanned through the possibilities of how he might have learned about the affair. After about ten minutes, I arrived at the Powerhouse and burst through the double doors of the bar like some kind of outlaw, angry and confused.

My sister's boyfriend sat at the end of the bar. He worked with us at the camp, and spent time at the Powerhouse, so he likely knew what was going on. At this point I was grasping for anything to take away this pain, and I thought that knowing how Cole found out would help in some way. I stepped up to him. "Did you tell him?" I asked.

He smiled in a way I'd never seen him smile before. It wasn't friendly or kind; it was a tight-lipped, callous smile. Then he turned from me and took a swig of beer. In that instant, I knew that he had told on me.

This life is not what I want.

I walked out the double doors and headed to my car. There in the icy cold and falling snow, I knew I must get away. I felt the pull of Costa Rica. Everything would be fine if I could just get to that lush, warm place. And Oscar was there. *I could be with him*, I said to myself as I looked up at the snowy sky, the flakes falling into my eyes and mouth.

I can return to the softness.

I knew I was running from the pain of losing Cole and the guilt over the hurt I had caused him, but I couldn't think about that. I was full of sadness, but I was also full of hope. Costa Rica had caught hold of me. The heat, the swirling language, the fun—all of it had taken root deep within, and I sensed I would never be whole until I was there. My intuition was speaking, and this time, I was determined to listen.

CHAPTER 19

When I stepped off of the plane in San José, Costa Rica, the steamy air enveloped me. Oscar met me with a dozen roses. He stood holding them in his big hands, and I was startled by how handsome he was. Thick locks of black hair flowed soft and wild onto his broad shoulders, and bushy eyebrows framed his dark eyes. He had a wide stance, accentuating muscular legs. The confidence and power he exuded relaxed my heart. *All was going to be fine.* I hugged him, and for a few minutes the pain of leaving Cole and that whole life that we had envisioned together eased.

Cole and I had talked of having kids—I wanted four of them—and we dreamed of continuing the adventures—hiking, biking, skiing, and sailing—that we shared so well. One day I said, "We could live six months of the year in Alaska and make money, and six months in Costa Rica and relax on the beach."

A sour pucker had crossed his lips and a crease appeared between his brows. He'd traveled with me to Costa Rica for a vacation years ago and loved it, so I assumed he would get behind this idea that I cherished.

"No," he said. "I don't want to live in a foreign country. I had enough of that." An air force brat, he had lived in Europe and Turkey as a child. I knew I couldn't push him. But that day, our perfect union began to unravel.

A close friend's voice echoed in my mind. "Lana, what are you doing? You're so selfish. You should try to make things right with Cole."

Yes, I may be selfish. I have to be. If I'm not happy, how can I live a whole life? How can I be useful or loving to anyone, especially Cole, if I feel miserable? My intuition was telling me that this was right, and though it felt risky to follow such a quiet nudge, I knew I had to.

Now, as Oscar and I walked to his car, the moist, sexy freedom of this place awakened my senses. Even with the weight of my bags, I danced along the sidewalk. I was on a new trajectory, leaving behind the life prescribed for me by my family and culture. I had cut the leash and now sensed the heady thrill of the unknown.

When we climbed in the car, I saw a little toy dinosaur on the floor near my feet, and I awakened to the fact that Oscar was married. I still felt the thrill of being with him, but I couldn't bear the idea of hurting his wife. And now he had two little boys, as well. As we sped along the chaotic streets of Santa Ana to an apartment where I would stay with a Costa Rican friend, lights flashed and blurred in the rain, and I didn't know whether to laugh or cry.

I knew that I needed a job, so the next day I called David Kaufman, the owner of Conversa, the school where I studied Spanish on my first trip to Costa Rica. He had become a good friend. Over the phone I told him that I wanted to live in Costa Rica. In 1989, Costa Rica was receiving millions of dollars a year from the US under the USAID program designed to develop the country's economic system to keep it stable. Many gringos and a lot of Costa Ricans had benefited from the funding. David hooked me up with one of them, who had opened a travel agency. The next day I met with Don Michael Kaye.

His office sat in an old Colonial-style building next to the post office in downtown San José. I climbed an elegant stairway to the second story overlooking a courtyard with a garden. Just off it I found a messy office, its walls lined with bookshelves. Among them, a large man with thick glasses and the air of an old hippie sat at a desk.

Later I would learn that Don Michael used to be a roadie for the Rolling Stones. He surfed waves all over the world and then fell in love with a Salvadoran woman, and they moved to Costa Rica. He was especially known for riding an inner-tube down one of Costa Rica's most notorious white-water runs on the Pacuare River. He would become one of the true pioneers of tourism in Costa Rica.

He directed me to sit on the chair across from him and immediately asked about my life. I said I'd just finished traveling around the world, that I'd been to Costa Rica before, and that I spoke Spanish. As I described my adventures, a faint smile crossed his lips. I felt a nudge to add one more thing:

"My birthday is in five days."

He seemed to calculate in his head for a moment. "Your birthday is December eleventh?" he asked.

"Yes."

"That's funny. That's my birthday," he said, a smile lighting up his whole face. He was some twenty years older than I was but full of energy and had a mischievous sparkle in his eye. I sensed I'd said the right thing. Since he was a Sagittarian too, he knew I would work hard and that he could trust me.

"Lana, I don't know where I'm going to put you," he said, "but you have a job."

He invited me to come in the next day, shook my hand, and said goodbye.

I skipped down the staircase, singing, "I'm on my way to living in the land I love!"

The next day I went to work in the same building, but downstairs in a room with high ceilings and Italian tile floors. I sat at a desk in the middle of a big open lobby, with two handsome Costa Rican men at desks on either side of me. When Americans came in they strode straight to me because they rightfully assumed I spoke English.

Since I learned to work so hard as a kid, it came easily for me as I started my new job selling tours for Costa Rica Expeditions. I sold trips to Tortuguero National Park, where travelers took boat tours to see canals, lagoons, and wetlands, but most importantly, sea turtles that nested on the beaches. I also sold trips to Tortuga Island off the southern tip of the Nicoya Peninsula, where visitors experienced pristine beaches, stunning snorkeling, and all kinds of wildlife. And I sent visitors to Monteverde, which was just opening up to tourism. Located at the top of the Costa Rican Continental Divide, it sits 1,800 meters (5,900 feet) above sea level, and moisture gets caught among the peaks, creating a sumptuous cloud forest with incredible biodiversity.

I had not been to Tortuguero yet, but I eagerly read the brochures and was so in love with Costa Rica, I had no trouble selling trips. During previous times in Costa Rica, I had gone to Tortuga Island, so it was easy for me to talk of its beauty. And I once hitchhiked and rode on a cantaloupe truck into Monteverde, so I loved telling travelers about an experience I had there. One day while hiking, a friend and I encountered a golden toad, a creature that stayed branded on my brain because of its stunning orange-gold color. The only place on the planet the now-extinct amphibian lived was the six-square-mile area of Monteverde in northern Costa Rica, and I actually got to see one before the species disappeared.

The place that really caught my attention was Corcovado National Park, set on the remote Osa Peninsula in the south of Costa Rica. Near my desk hung a poster of the ocean there that I stared at longingly. The place appeared untamed, with basalt-colored sand, gnarled driftwood, and huge, crashing waves. The rainforest came right down to kiss the shore, merging two great forces that drew me. Back then, it was barely developed, with only one hotel in Drake Bay.

I was stuck at my desk selling, but I swore one day I would go there.

And then there was Oscar. What I learned only after getting to know him was that before we met, he had been involved with a Costa Rican woman, the daughter of a wealthy Santa Ana family. Her parents sent her away for a year of the educational program Up with People to separate them, and that was when Oscar and I met.

Since that time years ago, she had returned and they married and had two little boys. Now that I was back in Costa Rica, Oscar was torn between his wife and children and me. He had injured his knee so he couldn't play soccer. To make money, he drove a taxi, and when he wasn't driving, he partied hard. When I did see him, it was as though the guilt we both felt sat in the room watching us make love. It wore an ogre face that stayed in my consciousness for the many days when I didn't see him but heard of his drunken nights out at the bars.

I knew I must cut him loose but couldn't seem to find the strength. One day at work, two tall American men strode in, full of confidence. One of them was blond, with soft, almost feminine features, and the other, dark, with intense brown eyes and a shadow of a beard. They flirted with me as we planned their trip, and afterward they invited me to a soccer game that we never got to. Instead we ducked into a movie theater to see the 1988 film *The Moderns,* an erotic movie about a woman and her two lovers. We all squirmed in our seats, me sitting between these two hot men, until it was over.

We made our way out into the damp evening air and stood on the sidewalk as cars rushed by on the street and the moon shone full above us. I invited them back to the apartment I shared with my friend, Gloria, who was out for the night. The men and I drank tequila and laughed about the movie and the way it ignited our lower chakras. Meanwhile, the dark-haired man stroked his bare foot against mine under the kitchen table. Late in the night, he and I wandered into the bedroom, while his friend crashed on the couch.

A few days later, Oscar called and invited me to go dancing the following night. When I got home from work I put on a fabulous black dress that was tight and short, along with black high heels. I sat down to have a glass of wine with Gloria and waited for him to pick me up. He didn't come, though I didn't worry because he was often late. I just kept talking to my roommate, but it was getting late and I really wanted to go dancing. At ten o'clock, I felt the slow burn of anger, but I couldn't call Oscar because of his wife and kids. I always had to wait for him to call me.

After we nearly polished off the whole bottle of wine, Gloria said, "You know you're not the only one, Lana."

I set my glass down. "What do you mean?"

"He has a taxi, and he can be with anyone he wants to be with, and he probably does. You're not his only affair."

I did not want to believe her, but this idea cleaved into me. I called a taxi, said goodbye to her, and headed out to my favorite dance spot, Rancho de Macho, where I danced and drank deep into the night. It was fun, but I was sad and felt abandoned. When I asked his friends about him, they didn't know where he was. I tried to cover my sorrow but returned home heavyhearted.

Mid-morning the next day he called. "Lana, I'm so sorry," he said.

I stayed silent.

"I forgot it was my son's birthday, and I had to go with my wife."

I was still silent.

"I had to get all these chairs, and we had a party for him."

"Oscar," I said. "You can't do that to me. My feelings about you are serious."

"I'm serious about you too, Lana. *Te amo.*"

I placed my hand on my heart to calm my frustration. I didn't know if I should believe that he loved me. He promised to make it up to me, and we said goodbye. When I hung up, I wondered if his excuse was even true. At that point in his life he drank and partied so much that it was hard to believe anything he said.

I decided to back off, to not answer his calls. But this presented a new challenge. Though I had these gorgeous Americans to party with, I found that without the prop of Oscar's and Cole's love, pain crept in. Nights alone in bed, my body felt like a canyon of darkness. I hugged my pillow to stave off the anxiety, but my heart beat so fast I barely slept. During the days, I worked extra hard and rode my bike for hours up a steep mountain that led to the village of Puriscal. Nights, I hung out with the American duo and danced with my Costa Rican friends until 2:00 or 3:00 a.m.

At that point, with the loss of Oscar's adoration, I felt vulnerable and unworthy. This made me stop and examine my relationship with him. He had a wife and two kids. As I sat at the little breakfast table in my kitchen, I put my head on my arms, so sad at the thought of the way I may have hurt them. This fact suddenly seemed glaring, where before it was obscured by my need and desire. I realized I couldn't be with him. I continued to avoid his calls, and over the next few weeks, the relationship fizzled.

Even though I was selling plenty of trips, when the end of the month rolled around, I couldn't pay all my bills. Though I was careful to always pay my rent, sometimes there was nothing left for the electric bill, groceries, and of course, tequila. I could have probably continued to stumble along this way, but my dreams were much bigger than this. I never had forgotten my dream of having my own hotel.

Slowly I admitted to myself that I must go back home. There, waiting tables, I could make twice the money in half the time and save to fulfill my dream.

Fortunately, the tourist season was ending, the rainy season beginning. I promised Don Michael I would return to work for him again in December, and he was happy with my commitment. I made a flight reservation and contacted my dad, who agreed to pick me up at the Denver airport.

The night before I departed, I couldn't let go, my heart so desolate about leaving. My Costa Rican friends took me dancing at Rancho de Macho, my usual hangout on a hillside above Santa Ana. It was a big open-air place with a pit where chicken sizzled over a fire. That night, a salsa/merengue band played, and we drank tequila shots and danced until dawn, our sweat cooling in the breeze. We stopped only to catch our breath and gaze out over the expanse of lights of the city below.

My flight departed at 7:00 a.m. I had packed my bags earlier and left them in my apartment. When I arrived back there at dawn, I was so nervous and tipsy I put the key in the lock and it broke. My heart pounded for fear I would miss my flight. I had spent my last bit of cash on the ticket and I couldn't be late.

I didn't want to wake my landlord by knocking on her door, so my taxi driver-friend pushed me up through a narrow window. It was so narrow that I got stuck, and in trying to squeeze through I was like a little fish, my legs flopping back and forth. My friend started laughing and so did I, hysterically, until Marjorie, the landlord, came out.

"*Lanita, ¿qué pasa? ¿Qué estás haciendo?*" she asked. But when she saw my bum and legs hanging out the window, she chuckled and then broke into a full laugh too. This did not help because it just made me giggle more. Finally, I squeezed through and fell with a clunk onto the wooden floor. I grabbed my bags and we rushed to the airport.

I was the last one to board the plane. As I walked the aisle I felt like a wreck, with mascara smeared around my eyes and my body smelling of tequila. When I sat back and buckled my seat belt, the pain of leaving Costa Rica caught up with me, and big tears rolled down my cheeks.

I slept the whole way, and when I awoke, I felt like I had fallen out of a tree and landed on my head. When my dad met me at the baggage claim and hugged me, he asked, "What happened to you?"

I thought, but didn't say aloud, *If you only knew.*

CHAPTER 20

In May 1991, when I arrived back in Crested Butte, I started dating Blake, the tennis player with the great legs who I was with before I left. While I had been gone, we talked on the phone a lot, and he always told me how much he missed me. He lived in a house with five people at the center of town, and he invited me to move in. Crested Butte was a fabulous place to live. It was a historic coal mining town transformed into a mountain resort, with ski and bike trails. Since everyone knew everyone, it was completely safe. People didn't even lock their doors. In fact, I didn't have a key to the house where we lived.

Fortunately for me, Cole was fishing in Alaska with his brother, so I didn't see either of them. Late at night when I was tired or when I would encounter some of Cole's friends, I would feel a heaviness come over me because I had cheated on him, and my heart still stung from the loss of our relationship. But I knew it was for the best, as I was happier during this time than I had ever been.

Blake was still easygoing and fun, and that was just what I needed in my life. He was an outstanding athlete, and he partied as hard as he competed. Since my goal that summer was to have fun while I made money, and to keep the relationship casual without any ties, Blake and I were a perfect fit. We both knew I was headed back south, and so we kept our attitude light. I also knew that this trip was a mercenary one. I would work my bum off to save so I could live in Costa Rica.

I secured two jobs. In the mornings from seven to eleven I

waited tables at Paradise Café, a bustling place where I could pull in a hundred dollars in tips during a breakfast shift. Blake and I both worked dinners at the Powerhouse, he a cook and me a waitress. With a fast turnover, and a menu of enchiladas, burritos, and tacos, almost always accompanied by margaritas, the restaurant made it easy to earn more than a hundred dollars in tips per night. Between shifts, Blake and I went for four-hour mountain bike rides or played tennis. I was fit and flush with cash and dreaming about my future in Costa Rica.

I started telling anyone who would listen about my plan to drive through Central America.

One night when I was drinking tequila with my friends, one of them said, "Lana, what are you doing?" We were a tight group, all my ski and biking buddies, so they couldn't fathom that I wanted to leave.

"Guys. I know. I'm so sorry," I said. "But I have to do this. It is in my heart. I have to move to Costa Rica." It was as though my intuition was speaking through every cell of my body. Whenever I even thought of Costa Rica, my whole being lit up with joy. I knew I had to follow this quiet message.

Little by little word of the Central America trip spread. I put out an open invitation to my friends to meet Wednesday nights at a bar called the Wooden Nickel. It was an old-West-style saloon, complete with barstools and scuffed wooden floors, set on the main street in Crested Butte. Soon friends told other friends, and the group of ski racers, ski instructors, and snowboarders grew until there were sixteen people, mostly from Crested Butte, Gunnison, and Steamboat Springs.

Since I'd spent so much time in Costa Rica and was determined to go back there, I was the official group leader, and everyone was willing to listen to my suggestions. I was also brimming with enthusiasm about my dream of living in a country that felt gentle and sensual.

I had come to see the power of focusing all my energy on what I truly wanted. It had worked for me in the past. When I ski raced in college, I always kept my focus on my route down the mountain. With that much speed I couldn't afford to let my attention go anywhere else. One quick glance at a tree or a gate, and I could wipe out. I found that I could use this discipline in all areas of my life. When I wanted to travel with Operation Raleigh, I fully concentrated on it; during the elimination process in Houston, I put every ounce of my energy into succeeding, and I won my spot on the trip. This time I completely fixed my attention on my dream of moving south.

Nine men and seven women fully committed. There was Yvonne from New Zealand. She was traveling around the world, was an accomplished river rafter, and excelled at living in the moment. Sunny worked with me at the Powerhouse. She was coming on the trip with the intention of living in Costa Rica with me. A man named Klaus had a girlfriend in Costa Rica who he wanted to visit. There was also my Costa Rican friend Luz, who lived with us in our house and was headed back home. Her perfect Spanish would be a real asset. And there was my close friend Aaron, who was completely wild and loved to chat like a girlfriend. Altogether, five of us spoke Spanish fluently and four were mechanics, so at least our communication and mechanical needs would be covered.

The political part was less certain. It was dangerous to travel in Central America in the early 1990s. Civil wars and pro-communist revolutions destabilized the area in the late 1970s, and the fighting there hadn't stopped. Fearing that communists would threaten access to the Panama Canal if the countries installed pro-Soviet governments, the US poured in money to fight back. The major fighting ceased by 1990, much thanks to Costa Rican President

Oscar Arias. He negotiated an end to the Central American crisis, and for this was awarded the Nobel Peace Prize. But residual conflict continued.

Still, young and strong, we were undaunted. Three brothers, the Barney brothers, committed to the trip, but their parents didn't want them to go because a few years prior they lost one of their other sons in a motorcycle accident. The Barney boys said, "No, we're doing it," so the parents bought them a Suburban to keep them safe on the journey. We called it the Bourbon. Another friend had a Chevy van that we called *Relampago*, which means lightning. It was white lightning.

I made a quick trip to California to pick up a '71 Volkswagen Bus just for this journey. It was red and white, with polka dot curtains and a black and white checkered floor. It had a pop-up top that allowed me to stand up in the back, and inside, a little sink, table, and a foldout bed. I called it Chili Pepper.

The cars were loaded. Along with our suitcases we had five surfboards, four kayaks, two rafts, and two bicycles. We had sleeping bags and tents, propane cooking stoves, and water bottles. We carried dried beans and lentils, anti-diarrheal medications, and iodine pills in case we couldn't access bottled water. And we had a good first aid kit that we hoped we wouldn't need. Each vehicle also carried a few big army duffel bags on top that held my belongings because that year, 1991, I was moving to Costa Rica for good.

PART II

GRASSHOPPER

TAKE A CHANCE: BIG LEAP FORWARD

CHAPTER 21

As we embarked, I felt the burden of getting sixteen of us safely through Central America. My friends were capable athletes and travelers, but I had initiated and planned this trip, and so I was responsible. In order to protect us all, I told the group one night in a planning session, "No guns, no drugs." This was a non-negotiable for me, I said, because like attracts like, and we didn't want anything to do with those vibrations. Everyone agreed to comply.

This eased the weight a bit, but not fully.

In the chill of a November morning, Luz and I stood in the driveway of the house where we'd been living. She hugged Blake and Jani goodbye, and climbed in my bus. Then I stepped over and kissed Blake. It was a bittersweet kiss—maybe the end of us, maybe not. We hadn't discussed any commitments for the future. He held me tightly, wanting to linger, but I broke away and hugged Jani, who also held on too long. I pushed myself from her grasp. Neither of them understood why I was leaving, and I'd been unable to convince them of my need to be in Costa Rica. Although I was sad, as I opened the door to Chili Pepper and looked at them standing side by side, I felt relieved. I was out of there, on my way to a new life.

I climbed in, revved the engine, and pulled away. Though my heart wanted to tug me back, I shoved the feelings aside and stepped harder on the pedal. I waved goodbye to downtown Crested Butte and drove to Denver to say goodbye to my father and get a final service for Chili Pepper.

I spent a few precious days with my dad. He was excited for me, and we stayed up late into the night talking about the trip and my desire to live in Costa Rica, which he supported completely. On the designated departure day, all of my travel buddies met at my dad's apartment, and we caravanned through the city toward the highway. I didn't say goodbye to my mother, since we had experienced some tension about my leaving for good. This darkened my heart, but I ignored it and held tight to the steering wheel while I watched my entire Colorado life disappear in the rearview mirror. Behind my determined enthusiasm a jittery doubt lurked, but I focused on the highway in front of me and all the promise that stood at the end of this journey. Even though I was leaving everything familiar to me, including my family, I knew I had to follow my intuition.

I merged onto Interstate 25, headed south, and sat back relieved that all the preparation was done. Ten minutes later, my bus swayed to the left and then to the right. The steering felt like taffy, all squishy on the road. I pulled over, hopped out, and paced around the bus checking the tires. When I came to the right front, I saw the wheel was nearly off the axle. I squatted down next to it and found the bolts dangling from the threads. The Barney brothers examined it too and shook their heads. The mechanics that serviced it must have forgotten to tighten the bolts. One of the guys pulled out a wrench and secured them, and we were back on the road. This was a harbinger for the challenges my treasured bus was going to cause us on the journey.

We continued south on I-25 to El Paso, merged onto Interstate 10, cruised across western Texas to San Antonio, and then made our way south to Brownsville, where we crossed the border. Once in Mexico, we drove straight south along the Gulf, the three vehicles connected via CB radios, which we used to discuss stops for food and gas. The villages we drove through often had lofty cathedrals and town squares where locals chatted under shade trees.

Each vehicle found its special purpose. Chili Pepper was for playing cards and, of course, talking because it had a table to sit around. People rode in the Bourbon when they wanted to party, and the Chevy van, the *Relampago*, when they wanted to sleep.

During this time in Mexico the owner had to drive his or her own vehicle, so I was at the wheel all day, every day. One evening I noticed my bus getting sluggish, and the next morning it only started after many long tries. When we arrived in Puebla, a Colonial city with a gold and white cathedral, we stopped for provisions at a huge supermarket. After shopping, I tried to start the bus but the engine only whined. I tried again and again. Nothing.

The mechanics on the trip took a look at it and couldn't find the cause. I recalled seeing a big Volkswagen repair shop just a few blocks away. None of the group was in a hurry, so the guys got out their Frisbees and bought some beer to pass the time while my friend Luz and I headed up the road to find a mechanic.

Thus far everyone on the trip had gotten along well, but in the last few days Luz had been impatient, especially with me. When we were cooking or loading the bus, she would snap at me. As we walked, I brushed those incidents off, and she seemed to soften with this time together. She and I both wore cutoff shorts and tank tops, so when we stepped into the repair shop, we got plenty of attention.

I began talking to one mechanic in a uniform with the VW logo on the right shirt pocket, and another came up and listened in. My Spanish was good enough to start the conversation, but Luz, a native Spanish speaker, joined in to fully convey the problem. Before I knew it, she and I were leading the two men with their toolboxes back to the supermarket parking lot. I was overjoyed that they were coming to the broken-down bus, which meant we wouldn't have to tow it to their shop.

They conferred with each other in front of the bus's open engine compartment and reached in with their tools to make alterations. After a few minutes, they told me to start it up. I climbed in, turned the key, and the engine came to life. By now the rest of the team had been drinking beer and playing in the sun for hours. My friends offered the mechanics some beers, and with wide smiles they accepted. They ate chips and talked with us, and when we prepared to go, they waved away my offer to pay. I insisted, but they would not accept my money.

We headed out to find a campground for the night.

The next day we entered the state of Oaxaca and drove west toward the Pacific coast. We were in deep rainforest for many miles and then the road turned steep, offering vast views of the Pacific Ocean. We descended switchbacks toward a village called Puerto Escondido, where we watched a major surfing competition. The air turned hot and steamy as we entered the lively village, with white-sand beaches and rolling hills. The humid air reminded me of Costa Rica, and as much as I was enjoying the trip, I yearned to be there.

Though Mexico has a gritty beauty, Costa Rica still held my heart. Nights sleeping in my bus, I longed to hear the lilt of Costa Rican Spanish, which has its own set of phrases and idioms. I ached for the soft air, the *gallo pinto* (beans and rice) for breakfast, the friendly people, and the way everything was a little disorganized and ill-functioning, though not to the degree it was in Mexico. Costa Rica offered a slower pace, with fewer expectations, and a sense that life was richest in the present moment. Most of all, I couldn't wait to start my new adventure there and move a step closer to the lodge in my dreams.

But would my plan even happen? I had risked everything for it. Some nights, it seemed impossible with so much to do to make it real.

We found a spot right on the beach, and everyone helped set

up camp. In the past few nights we had established a routine. We never ate breakfast or lunch together, but at dinner, rotating four-person teams made food for everyone to share. We made burritos and tacos, always accompanied by corn chips. Then we sat around a campfire and ate and talked and laughed and drank cans of Carta Blanca. The team cleaned up afterward, while everyone else went out to party and check out the culture of the area.

Some of the guys were marginal surfers; they were more at home in the mountains where they skied and snowboarded. One day, four of them paddled out past the break, hoping to catch towering waves. As they sat atop their boards, looking out across the vast Pacific, the surfing competition progressed, with young men and women riding the waves as though they lived on the water. They carved turns, caught air, and surfed the tube. Meanwhile, our guys stayed off to the side, snagging a few waves and riding them on short runs.

Suddenly, the announcer yelled, "*Afuera, gringos, afuera!*"

Our guys just kept surfing, oblivious, while I got nervous. I knew that the announcer was yelling at them to get out of the surf because they were interfering with the competition.

I felt that responsibility again, not wanting us to be clueless Americans. *Damn it, wake up, guys!* I trotted down the beach, waved, and yelled at them, but they didn't even see me. *How did I ever become responsible for so many others?*

When I was a little girl, I always felt responsible for Jani and me. When things were crazy at home, Dad abusing Mom, and even later with my stepfather and his pushy aggression, I felt like I had to hold everything together, to use my own power to keep the world safe for Jani and me. It's hard for me to let go, to do the best I can, and let others experience the consequences of their actions.

That day on the beach, I turned away from the ocean, frustrated, and headed up to camp.

When I turned back around I saw my buddies had finally caught on. They rode their boards in and hung their heads, while my friends laughed at them, taunting, "*Afuera, gringos, afuera!*"

A few days later we made our way through the jungles of Chiapas into Guatemala. We drove the steep road down into Panajachel, which sat on the edge of the sapphire blue Lake Atitlán. We found an old hotel with a big deck and spacious rooms right on shore. It was run down, but the family that owned it was generous. They let my friends camp on the hotel grounds. Meanwhile, Luz and I splurged and shared the honeymoon suite.

Luz was the first Costa Rican friend I made, so she helped me get to know Costa Rica and learn Spanish. In the ten years that I'd known her she had been crazy, wild, and fun. However, on this trip she continued to be irritable. She criticized my driving and tried to pick a fight when we discussed our plans for the day. I had never experienced this side of her. I wondered if she had a family problem or maybe she was weary of me being in charge of the trip. I knew sometimes I could be pretty domineering when I got concerned for the group.

I set aside these worries and enjoyed time with my friends. One day we took a ferry across the lake to the village of San Marcos where we shopped for local crafts and wandered along the lake edge. Another day, we swam, leaping off the hotel balcony into the cool, blue water.

Luz and I shared a king-size bed in our honeymoon suite. Our third and last night at the lake, I sensed something unsaid between us. She had been surly all day, so I couldn't wait to put everything aside and go to sleep.

The next morning, she woke up, banged around the room packing, and then stepped in front of me. "Can we go to Guatemala City when we leave here?"

I shrugged. "I guess."

"I need you to take me to the airport. I'm flying home to Costa Rica." Her face was red, her eyes bloodshot and tired.

"Why?" I asked.

She shook her head. "I just have to go home."

"Luz, you have to tell me what's going on," I said. But she ignored me and continued packing her bags.

Our friends tried to talk her into staying on the trip, but she remained closed to them too. When we left Lake Atitlán we headed for the airport in Guatemala City, where we dropped her off. She wouldn't even look at me when we said goodbye. I was totally bummed that she was so desperate to get away from us, and especially, it seemed, me. My goal on this trip was for everyone to enjoy themselves, so for days after this I wondered what had happened, and then a possibility dawned on me.

When Luz and I were together we tended to ogle at guys, drink tequila shots, and laugh a lot, but I realized she never shared any experiences with men she had had. I was always the one talking about guys. Years later my suspicion was confirmed: Luz was a lesbian, and she wanted to be with me. Our honeymoon suite must have been so frustrating for her that she could no longer take the pressure.

The next day, we were on a two-lane highway headed to El Salvador, Chili Pepper leading the way. Suddenly, a VW Bus screamed toward us from the opposite direction. The driver and passenger waved their arms to stop us. "Turn around now!" the driver yelled when we pulled up. They spoke English with Dutch accents. "We just got shot at!" the man said.

We turned around, but we didn't know where to go, because this was the route south. Again, the heavy sense of responsibility gripped me. These people trusted that I knew my way in Central

America and that I would help them through safely. I missed Luz, our sole Central American resident, who would have had more ideas than I did.

I recalled a conversation I once had with my father. He had said, "The day you become responsible, you will have a better life." I practiced this truth and made sure I took good care of my own life, and it worked. But I saw how I had extended this to being too responsible for others. A palpable weariness hung over me. I felt like weeping and realized that I was ready to collapse. Every day, all day, I drove. I told others where to go, and I pored over maps at night instead of drinking and laughing and playing with my friends. I worried and worried and sometimes doubted whether we were going to make it to Costa Rica at all.

Right then, I didn't want the responsibility.

One of the guys said he had friends in Honduras, so we headed east across Guatemala in hopes of crossing the border near Copán, even though we knew there was fighting in that region too. We arrived at the border crossing in the late afternoon. As we drove up to the guardhouse, exhausted and hot, three guards stepped out. They examined our cars full of fifteen gringos, three of us blond. Luz, with her native Spanish, used to help a lot in these situations. The guard leader insisted we pay a thousand *lempiras*, money we didn't have.

He shook his head. "Well then, you will have to stay the night here. We can't let you through."

"We can't stay here," I told him in my best Spanish. "We don't have food, and it's all jungle so there's nowhere to camp." It was a desolate place in the middle of nowhere, with no stores to buy food or to get clean water. Our group huddled together, conferring. We emptied our pockets of the last of our Guatemalan cash. We did have more money, in dollars, but I knew this was just Central American *mordida*, bribery, so I hoped this fraction of what the guard wanted would suffice. I stepped back to him and put on my most flirtatious smile. His face softened, his lips turning up at the edges. I held out the crumpled *quetzals*, and he took them. He opened the gate and let us through.

Once in Honduras, we made our way along the rim of a canyon. It was sunset, and the views across the vast layers of rock, now tinted pink, were so magnificent that we stopped and climbed out of the vehicles to take it all in. We stood in a line at the very edge of the canyon. I breathed in the clear air, relieved to be in a quiet place, even just for this moment.

Sated with the beauty, we headed into Copán, a village with cobblestone streets surrounding a square adorned with a Colonial-style church. This was where visitors to the Copán ruins stayed, and just outside town we found an open spot and set up camp.

The next day, we explored the ruins. Copán is a Mayan archaeological site that sits in a green valley surrounded by foothills. A capital city in the region, Copán was occupied from the fifth to the ninth century. We strolled along the processional walkways in the central plaza and climbed the acropolis, a large complex of overlapping step-pyramids, plazas, and palaces. We examined Copán's most notable features, the stelae, tall sculpted stone shafts that glorified the rulers' heroic deeds. When we came to the grassy ball court, an ancient stadium, I stayed and let the others wander away.

By now it was late afternoon. I climbed to the top of the bleachers, sat on the stone, and looked around at the thick rainforest and the ruins. I imagined living here 1,500 years ago when this city was a thriving metropolis of some 20,000 people, encompassing 100 square miles. I could almost hear the ball players running and encouraging each other, while the crowd cheered. Today, moss covered the stairs, a living blanket, and the air was humid and full of energy from the past and the present, all connected to nature.

I considered the first two weeks of the trip and felt gratitude. We had made it through another country without being shot. We had crossed the border without giving away all our money. My bus was still running, and even though Luz had left, most of our group interactions had been harmonious.

But then I pondered my quest to live in Costa Rica and became doubtful that I could manifest all that I dreamed of achieving. Yes, I could get through these countries in one piece, but to build my own lodge someday in a foreign land just might be too big a dream.

Then I remembered a day when I stood under a waterfall and the power of its flow washed away all thoughts. Afterward, I lay on a rock and felt my skin tingle as the sun evaporated the moisture. A morpho butterfly landed on my arm, the beauty of its iridescent blue wings seeming to levitate me off the ground. That was the life I wanted, and I longed to share it with others.

We were back on the road that afternoon. As I drove, I was wary of the armed conflict in the area. We were traveling across a country that had not known peace for decades. I flinched whenever a car rushed by, and I found myself wanting to duck when we passed a Honduran army truck full of soldiers standing in the back, holding rifles. All this constricted my heart, but I kept my foot firmly on the gas pedal. Nothing could stop me from living in Central America.

At night in the middle of a thrashing rainstorm we arrived in La Ceiba, a Honduran town on the Caribbean. We were hoping to find the friends of one of our guys. They were starting a rafting business there. The area was renowned for its water adventures. Scuba divers came from all over the world to the island of Roatan just off the coast, to explore elaborate walls of coral. La Ceiba itself was just starting to grow a tourism business, so the town, set in the shadow of jagged hills, only had a few shacks and vendor stalls. We cruised the main street, feeling uneasy in its tattered darkness, and found an empty lot where we set up camp for the night.

The next morning, we started our search for the expats. At a time like this when GPS and cellular service didn't exist, we had to rely on our instincts. We asked a few locals if they knew three gringo river runners. One of them directed us to their encampment just outside town. They greeted us with kindness and invited us to camp on their land, a lush patch of open meadow surrounded by jungle, with a river running through.

For the next three days, we rafted and kayaked rivers with them, including one that had never been navigated before. We helped them map out some river runs for their new business, discussing what might provide excitement and fun for their clients. One day on the river we stopped near huge granite boulders. We peeled off our clothes, climbed up on the high, square surfaces, and jumped off. The water was warm and clean and fresh.

Everyone settled in to this adventurous life, doing sports in the mornings and lounging under palm trees by the river in the afternoons. But soon reality crept in. We had to continue south. One morning, with clear skies and parakeets screeching, we loaded up our gear and headed toward Nicaragua.

We arrived in the capital of Honduras, Tegucigalpa, by late afternoon. The people there were poor, many of them living in shanty houses set on a broad landslide. Ironically, the roads were completely modern, because outside countries had given funds to build the Pan-American Highway. It was sad that some of the money didn't go to take care of the Honduran people. We cruised through and made for the border, but we were not allowed to cross because it was too late in the evening.

We backtracked long enough to find a tobacco farm that rented rooms in its main house. Some of us stayed the night in the sprawling hacienda while others camped. Though we looked forward to sleeping indoors in beds, the place had strange energy. It was uncharacteristically opulent for this part of the world, with elaborate tile walkways and cushy furnishings.

At the restaurant that night, the owner sat like a mafia boss at a table in the corner. He wore a pressed Latin dress shirt and smoked a fat cigar. People came and went from his table, and I got the distinct feeling that he was making deals, maybe shady ones, and that the farm may have been a façade for a more lucrative business. We finished our meal and didn't linger, instead heading upstairs to enjoy a real shower and a comfy bed.

The next day, we crossed the border into Nicaragua without incident and drove to Masaya, right outside of Managua. We found a grassy spot and asked the owner if we could camp there. He was building a hotel nearby, so he appreciated travelers. "Sure," he said. This part of Nicaragua was dazzling, with a steamy volcano that glowed orange at night, a vast lake of clear blue water, and the village with Colonial-style stone buildings. Our campsite sat in a verdant meadow surrounded by trees. My friends wanted to call it home for a while.

But I couldn't wait to get to Costa Rica, just a day's drive away. We'd been traveling for a month, and we were weary and ready to settle down, wash our clothes, and sleep in beds. Unfortunately, my bus wasn't doing well. It was tired. Some days it didn't want to start, and as we drove, it sometimes overheated or had trouble shifting. One of our mechanics on the trip started riding with me full-time to help with this. Everyone was frustrated with my bus, and because of it, I felt tension from the group.

Two of my traveling friends and I walked to a bar a few blocks away from camp to call Luz from a pay phone. On a previous call to her I noted her attitude had improved, and she had cheerfully agreed to do some groundwork in Costa Rica to aid our arrival. I was relieved to still have her friendship. I told her we'd be there the next day and to get ready to party. When I hung up, an explosion erupted from somewhere beyond the bar. It was a deafening sound, like thunder hitting close, and it resonated through my whole being. It was followed by another explosion, equally loud, that shook the floor beneath our feet.

My friend said, "Lana! What's going on?"

I asked the bar owner and he explained, "It's a bomb. There's fighting *en el pueblo*."

I ran back to our patch of grass and talked to the landowner. "It's okay," he said. "Just stay here, but don't go out anymore. Don't go anywhere!"

That night, we all tucked in around the campfire, while the ground shook beneath our feet. When the noise seemed to draw closer, I grabbed some water and doused the flames to avoid calling attention to ourselves. The whole night, I squirmed in my bus, sweating and afraid. No one slept with the sound of yelling, gunfire, and bombs.

The next morning, we got up before sunrise and started loading our rigs. I climbed into Chili Pepper and turned the key, but it only made a whirring sound. I tried again and again, but it wouldn't start. I jumped out and kicked the dirt, so frustrated and feeling bad that my friends had to sit through this.

We couldn't stay here another day!

The Barney brothers pulled their Suburban in front of my bus, and with a thick chain, hooked it up to tow my vehicle south. I sat in my bus's driver's seat, tense with fear while we climbed and descended over mountains. I had no control; sometimes slack built in the chain and then released, jerking my vehicle. Other times my bus raced forward, and I pressed myself back into the seat, afraid I would rear-end the Bourbon. I lightly tapped the brakes to slow the bus down. We traveled this way for three hours, while everyone else sat packed into the other cars.

Finally we crossed the Costa Rican border. I calmed down a bit, knowing I was in my country, but we still drove another five hours. When I saw the lights of San José, like a giant bowl of gems before me, my heart relaxed and I danced in my seat.

I was in my dream country.

1975 - Training Handy Amigo.

1980 – Water skiing Blue Mesa Lake, Gunnison, Colorado.

1980 – With Jani, Gunnison High School homecoming queen.

1982 – Sailing trip from Maine to Florida on Spanish Gold.

1991 – Road trip through Central America.

1991 – The crew arrived in Costa Rica in December.

1996 - At Corcovado Lodge Tent Camp with employees.

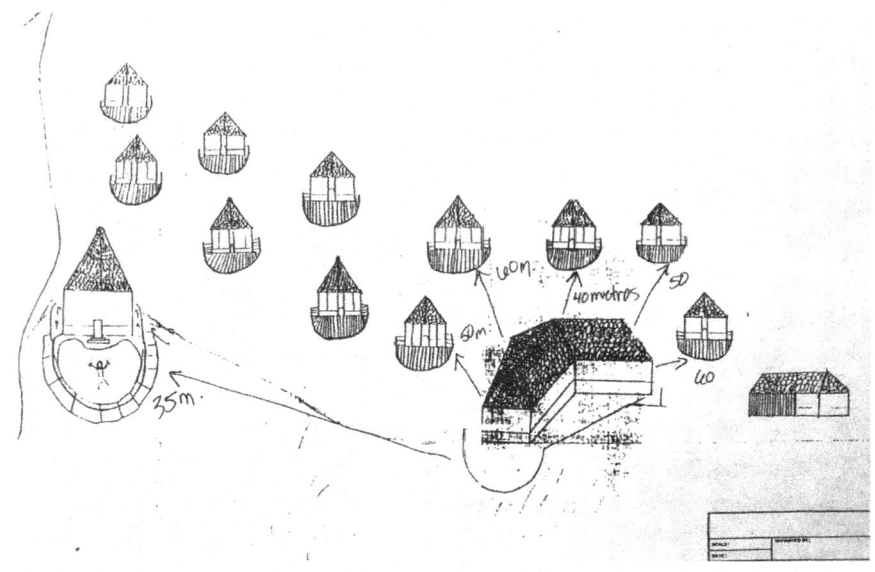

1997 - Design of bungalows, Rancho Grande, and yoga deck.

1998 - The kitchen at the author's house at Luna Lodge.

LUNA LODGE
Osa Peninsula, Carate, Costa Rica

October 1999

Dear friends, family, and future visitors to the perfect paradise;

It has been almost two years to the date since my last correspondence with many of you and perhaps the first for many more. This update finds me near the completion of a dream that I have kept in my heart for nearly twenty years. The building of what has become "Luna Lodge". It has been a long and arduous journey that many of you will have the opportunity to reap the benefits from very soon. My dream was to develop a magical and captivating rainforest resort, preserve and protect this fascinating land, and educate, entertain and open the eyes to these wonders to all who visit.

In this age, it has become a challenge to find an absence of civilization. Solace can only be found in far away places. Even here in Costa Rica, it's difficult to find areas where man hasn't made his mark. If you're interested in exploring a place that has yet to be touched by the technology of the 20th century, the Osa Peninsula is an ideal solace-seekers destination.

Luna Lodge sits on a mesa, in the midst of 60 acres, more than half of which is primary rainforest. The Carate river valley, which we overlook, is a wonderland of tropical rainforest, rivers, and wildlife. My staff and I have carefully placed the components of our lodge to naturally co-exist with the pristine environment bordering Corcovado National Park, and the outcome is nothing less than spectacular. We look forward to having you share our warmth and hospitality in a place that will truly touch your soul.

We have five secluded bungalows each with breathtaking views, private bath and deck. Priced at $125 per person with meals & tax included. Our Bar & Restaurant, "El Total Eclipse" features International Cuisine, a Sunday Brunch, spectacular views of the forest, river, ocean and excellent opportunities to observe the local wildlife.

Its ready, we've done it, mark your calendar, and make your reservations. Our official opening is on December 18th, 1999, and we are taking reservations through the millennium. Experience our location via cyberspace at http://www.lunalodge.com which provides a wonderfully vivid depiction of the grounds, activities, and all related information. Contact us by e-mail lunalodg@sol.racsa.co.cr or telephone/fax 011.506.735.5431.

Thank you.

Lana Wedmore, Owner/Operator

1999 - First marketing letter to clients.

CHAPTER 22

My Costa Rican friends knew we were coming. At 9:00 p.m. we met them at Coco's Bar, one of my favorite hangouts. It was a casual place with black and white tile floors and a bar that covered the whole side wall. The owner looked and dressed like Elvis, with a white suit and his black hair coiffed in an anvil-shaped do. He engulfed me in his big arms. We were tired from the drive, but when my friends greeted us and hugged us, we started a big party in celebration of our arrival. We danced salsa and merengue, drank tequila shots, and laughed over our adventures, not stopping until the world brightened at dawn.

Elvis agreed to rent the top floor to us, so fifteen of us slept on the tile floor in a party room, sharing one bathroom. We stayed there three days, until I rented a house in Piedades that Luz had found for me. Fortunately, rent was low in that part of the world, so I could afford to live large.

It was a big Spanish Colonial-style hacienda with a giant living room and kitchen, a yard and garage, and a fence around it, so it was safe. Most of the group stayed with me in that house with no furniture. The Barney brothers hung there for three months, surfing the ocean and kayaking rivers all over the country. Their parents even came down and stayed with us. Everyone took trips around Costa Rica, and when we were all there, we had a celebration.

In January, I would go back to work for Don Michael. Until then I used the days to get my house in order and to play. Something was always going on. My friends shared their adventures around Costa

Rica, or we made a meal that everyone pitched in to cook, or we threw a welcome celebration for some new visitor who had arrived and needed a place to stay.

All kinds of characters came through. A man named Grant McClain, who I had worked with at the Paradise Café in Crested Butte, came down. He was tall, with a soft, kind face. He looked a bit like a teddy bear. One day, I walked out in the living room and found him standing there with all sorts of clothes on. Literally he was wearing two pairs of jeans and two or three pairs of shorts. He had a long-sleeve shirt buttoned up and a T-shirt on top. And, he had socks on his fingers. I looked at him, incredulous.

"What are you doing?" I asked.

He shrugged innocently. "I hate to wash clothes, so I'm going to take a shower and just do laundry while I'm in there."

I nearly cracked a rib, I laughed so hard.

All my friends in Costa Rica knew that they could come over any time. These were people who I had met through work and through dancing and partying at local bars, and just in the neighborhood. Some of them worked in tourism, while others worked at Conversa, the language school I had attended when I first came to Costa Rica. The Americans were trying to learn Spanish and some of them wanted to find love. And my Costa Rican friends wanted to learn English and were looking for romance too. This created an intense energy in the house.

One couple that came down with us started having trouble because she was flirting with the many handsome Ticos. And then there was Klaus and Sunny. Klaus came on the trip to meet up with his girlfriend who had been teaching English in Monteverde. But he and Sunny got together on the way down, so fireworks exploded when we arrived and his girlfriend was waiting for him.

I threw my first party when the Barney brothers' parents came. The house was packed, with probably sixty people milling about. We served ceviche, snapper with mango salsa, and margaritas. Music played on a boom box, and people danced in the living room and out on the terrace. The conversation was in English and Spanish and so loud no one could hear anyone anyway, but no one seemed to care. The party went until sunrise, when I finally fell onto my mattress and slept the day away.

One day, we took a raft trip down the Pacuare River, not far outside San José. I was friends with guides at the company where I worked, Costa Rica Expeditions, so they joined us on our rafts for a day of fun on this Class III and IV river that runs through lush rainforest in the Talamanca Mountains. Twenty of us paddled two rafts and ten kayaks on the clear, aquamarine water. Klaus and I were at the front of one raft since we were both strong paddlers and good swimmers. Yvonne, our New Zealand traveler who had rafted all over the world, told us to put our arms up if we fell out of the boat, so she could pull us back up.

We romped through rapids all morning and saw monkeys, iguanas, and toucans along the shore, as well as waterfalls flowing in from tributaries, and then we stopped for lunch. While we ate, the river rose so fast that my guide friends hurried us onto the rafts, fearful that the rapids would become too large to negotiate and would trap us in the canyon.

Our first rapid after lunch, called Horrendo, had a house-size boulder in the center. We tried to skirt the edge of it, but the water raged so hard it sucked our boat in, so we had to punch straight over the top instead. We sailed over without incident, but when we headed down the other side, the boat slanted at a nearly ninety-degree angle, dumping me and Klaus in the middle of the churning hole on the downriver side.

I swam hard toward the surface but hit the bottom of the boat. I ducked down and tried again, but again hit it. By now I was completely out of air and struggling. The water swirled around me, filling my nose and ears. It seemed like some sick fate that I would finally realize my dream of living here only to die.

With no air left in my lungs, I called on that strength I came to know so well as a young girl. I kicked hard to move myself from under the boat and once again tried to surface. That time I met air. I gasped, taking it and plenty of water in. The rapids churned around me so chaotically I saw nothing but sky and waves. I remembered the safety briefing the guides gave us onshore and what Yvonne said, so I put my arms above my head.

Just as I despaired of being saved, a hand clutched my wrist and then my other one, and I left the water, slithered over the side of the raft, and plopped in the bottom. Yvonne kneeled above me, a crease between her eyes. "Lana, are you okay?"

I smiled up at her, while coughing water from my lungs. "What about Klaus?" I asked. I had seen him fall off the boat at the same time I did.

"I'm here," he yelled from behind me, and my heart settled.

My shining future would not be taken from me that day.

After three months of wild life in my Santa Ana house, things began to slow down. I was back at work now, selling trips for Don Michael like crazy, so I had less time to hang out and have adventures. Our group dispersed, most headed home. The Barney brothers put their Suburban on a banana boat and sent it to Florida. They flew there, picked it up, and drove to Mardi Gras in New Orleans, and then back to Colorado. Sunny, who hoped to live in Costa Rica, escaped the drama with Klaus and flew back to the US.

With the house empty, I had no reason to keep it. I found a smaller, less expensive place nearby in Santa Ana that in many ways inspired my future creation. In my imagination, I was already building my own lodge. This house, perched on a mountainside, blended seamlessly into nature. It was constructed around a car-size boulder. The whole house was made of dark wood and felt like the home from the television series *Swiss Family Robinson*, all the casement windows opening out onto trees and flowers. It had stairs that skirted around the boulder to the bedroom upstairs. The bathroom sat partially outdoors, with a sunken tub along one side, and an open-air garden along the other. I stepped out the side doors of the house onto a terrace, with a garden designed so that flowers bloomed year-round.

The bungalows I imagined for my guests would be like this.

During my days when I wasn't in the office selling, I rode my bike around Santa Ana.

On a previous trip to Costa Rica, I had met an old hippie from California named Jack Simms, and over the years we stayed in touch. One day he proposed an interesting business opportunity. He invited me to partner with him on the purchase of a farm in Santa Ana. To fund my portion, I used the money I made in Alaska. I didn't plan to live there because it was an investment property. We hired a man to plant coffee trees with the intention of making the land more valuable so we could sell it at a profit. That was my first experience of owning land in Costa Rica, and my first step toward funding my own lodge someday.

In the evenings at the adorable little house where I lived, I sipped tea on the terrace, surrounded by birds-of-paradise, orchids, and hibiscus, utterly grateful to be in my new home. With my job and close friends, I was confident in my decision to live there.

Little did I know that my romantic heart might put the whole plan of living in Costa Rica in jeopardy.

CHAPTER 23

I worked relentlessly selling tours, but it was hard to sit at a desk because I wanted to be out exploring my new home country. Between clients I gazed at the posters for the trips we were selling, especially the one of the ocean and rainforest in Corcovado. The coast there looked untamed, with black sand, gnarled driftwood, and huge waves that I could almost hear in my imagination. Something about that lush wildness captured my attention and wouldn't let go.

Still, dedicated worker that I was, I put my heart into the job and sold hundreds of trips.

One day my boss called me into his office and asked me if I wanted to be a guide. Joy bubbled up inside me, and I beamed a big smile at him as I told him I'd love to.

He sent me out on single- and multi-day trips. Sometimes, I took people to the dock where they caught the boat to Tortuguero. From there, they headed off on their adventure. Other times I accompanied them and took visitors up into the cloud forest at Monteverde, explaining the history of the area as we traveled. Tourism was just starting in Costa Rica, generating a great deal of excitement. Travelers experienced an unspoiled land, and I got to do it with them.

I was so full of delight I could hardly contain it. I loved meeting people and getting to know them. And as I traveled, I imagined my own lodge. At each hotel we stayed in, I evaluated the experience and picked up ideas about what to do and what not to do.

One day we were in a bus on the winding mountain road that led to Monteverde. I stood at the front and faced the passengers as I explained the history of the area. After I finished my talk, I sat next to a couple from Minnesota. I asked them about their lives, and they asked about mine. I said directly to the man, "Someday, I'm going to have my own hotel here in Costa Rica."

"Really?" he said.

"Yeah, I want to share this amazing place with others."

"Are you sure?" he asked.

"Yes, I am. I'm really sure. This is my goal."

"Okay," he said. He sat up taller, and I saw him owning some identity, his super-businessman self, with his finely clipped hair and neat fingernails. "I just want you to know, Lana, that it's going to be the first thing you think about when you wake up in the morning, and the last thing you think about when you go to bed."

I nodded. I was already doing this.

He looked me straight in the eye. "Hire the least number of employees you can have, because they're a pain in the bum."

Again I nodded, hungry for his wisdom.

"When you build, it's going to cost five times more than you ever thought."

This warning did not deter me. I didn't care. This was my dream. I thanked him for his sound advice.

We arrived in Monteverde, and I was more determined than I'd ever been.

During my time as guide, I really started thinking about Corcovado. "I want to go there," I said to my boss, Don Michael. "I've sold trips to that mysterious place. Now I've got see what's going on down there."

He took in what I was saying and nodded. Pausing, he rubbed his chin and looked over my head toward the door, considering something.

He looked me in the eye. "Lana, we're coming into the rainy season, so why don't you take a month off and head down there?"

I swallowed, shocked at how easy it had been. "Yeah! Definitely. Thank you." He was aware, of course, that this trip would make me an even better employee because I would know so much more about the adventures I was selling.

I was still in touch with Blake, the tennis player, so I invited him, my sister, and a friend named Wheels to join me on a three-week adventure. After that, my dad would come down, and he, Jani, and I would go to Corcovado. First, Blake, Jani, Wheels, and I took a ferry across to the Nicoya Peninsula to Santa Teresa, on the coast in the Puntarenas province.

At this time, Santa Teresa was barely a settlement, with only one restaurant and a few little shacks. We cruised through and found a vacant beach. It seemed to stretch for an eternity and had pale sand, clear blue water, and palm trees. We pitched our tents and made a fire pit surrounded by driftwood logs for us to sit on. Then we peeled off our clothes and dove into the cool water. It massaged my body as I swam, and then I just floated on the surface, the swells lifting me up and releasing me down. When I got out and lay on the beach, the sun warmed my skin while a pelican soared across the blue above.

This is the life I want—this watery, outdoor existence.

Everyone must feel this when they go on vacation, and maybe I was greedy, but I didn't want to go back to a dry-land, workaday life.

I want to live in this feeling all the time.

We stayed five days on that heavenly beach. We walked, played in the waves, drank tequila, talked, and laughed. My sister and I got along well, and that eased my heart, knowing that the person closest to me in the world was still my best friend. I tried not to think of my other best friend, my mother, whom I hadn't talked to in a long while.

One day, Blake and I took a walk along the shore, naked. I reveled in the feel of my palm in his, the sand between my toes, and the sun on my breasts. Blake was still gorgeous, with his muscular legs and arms, his confident smile. After all this time on my own in a new country, I savored being with him and Jani, people I knew well, and the comfort we shared in each other's presence. As Blake and I walked we encountered a Tico using a machete to cut grass that was almost as tall as he was. His head just peeked out above the top. When he saw us, he ducked down, obviously embarrassed. We continued to walk by, giggling. He didn't lift his head again.

We left Santa Teresa and drove our red four-door rental truck along the coast into the Guanacaste province to Carrillo, which has a circular bay, stunning beach, and calm, turquoise water, where we lazed, floating on the surface. Just north of there, we swam in the gentle waves at Sámara.

From Sámara, we headed farther north along the peninsula to Tamarindo, also with a fine-sand beach, but with bigger waves, which we surfed all day until we could barely stand. We splurged for the night and stayed at a little surfer's inn called Daisy's, which sat on stilts and had showers and surfboard storage on a cement slab below. After three weeks of travel, we drove back to Santa Ana, and then headed to the San José airport where we picked up my dad. We all stayed the night in my little nature house.

The next day, Blake and Wheels headed to Manuel Antonio National Park to hike and view wildlife. Jani, Dad, and I made our way south in the red pick-up to the Osa Peninsula. It was an arduous drive along winding roads through this mountainous country. I did much of the driving and found my foot heavy on the pedal. As beautiful as the terrain was, I was eager to explore the Corcovado National Park.

After eight hours of driving, we arrived in the village of Puerto Jimenez, right on the coast. It was dark and raining. This old mining town was but a clutch of shacks set along a muddy street, with one bar sporting a wooden sign that read La Indija, which the locals said meant crack in the wall.

We pulled up to a run-down hotel near a mangrove forest. When we stepped out of the truck, mosquitos attacked every inch of our bare skin, and the air was impossibly hot and humid. As we hauled our bags in, the rain pounded even harder, so hard we got completely soaked. The world seemed blurry and foreboding.

Jani screeched, "I just can't deal with this! I don't see why you even wanted to come here."

We went to our room, where Dad and Jani climbed into their beds. I could barely sit, my heart was so unsettled. This place was light-years away from what I had imagined. I grabbed a pack of cigarettes and a lighter—a habit I had picked up from Blake—and snuck outside, careful to conceal the practice from my dad. Standing on the deck, I lit up, took a long drag, and cried.

Our second day on the Osa Peninsula, I stepped outside and looked up at a clear indigo sky. The mosquitos still buzzed about, and the air still held a cloying humidity. But the shining sun gave me hope that today might reveal what I'd come here to find. We left the hotel and drove to the edge of town to pick up Juan Serreno, part owner with Don Michael of the Corcovado Lodge Tent Camp, where we would stay that night.

He insisted on driving, but I resisted giving up the steering wheel. I didn't know who he was or how he drove, and I didn't want to trust the safety of my dad, sister, and myself to him. But he stood in his driveway unmovable, so I slid over to sit in the passenger seat, where I could monitor his every move.

The truck squashed along a red mud road en route to Carate. We skirted the Golfo Dulce past little *fincas*, or farms, carved out of the forest. White Brahma cattle flapped their ears under the shade of ficus trees, and horses grazed long meadows. Meanwhile, heavy black termite nests hung from tree limbs and the vegetation thickened. Cicadas screamed a throbbing screech that grew louder and louder the farther we traveled into the rainforest.

We crossed stream after stream, bumping and squishing along, until the forest gave way to open land, where the trees had been cleared. The road simply ended. One *pulperia*, what Costa Ricans call a general store, and a grass airstrip, sat in the clearing.

"This is Carate?" Jani said. "It's nothing!" Her face held a sad grimace, her brow sweaty, blond hair sticking to her neck.

I could only agree with her. There was nothing here.

When I was a little girl and Jani was struggling, I wanted to put her inside my belly button to protect her. I had that sense now. But instead, I pulled on the door handle.

Fortunately, sometime along the drive, the dense humidity had evaporated, and when I climbed from the truck and braced for mosquitos, none landed on me.

I saw the ocean and made a beeline for it, leaving everyone behind. I was determined to find that place, that untamed feeling I sensed in the poster in my office. The hard ground turned to sand and I pulled off my sandals to feel it between my toes. A few more steps and I broke free of the coconut trees and found myself on a broad, black beach. A hermit crab darted out of a hole and ran toward the water. A bleached coconut sat next to a gnarled piece of driftwood. *Boom, boom,* the waves crashed on shore. I looked into the distance and saw how the rainforest came right down to the beach, creating a fusion of green, gray, and blue, masked in mist. This was pure art to my eyes.

Suddenly I remembered that when I first decided to live in

Costa Rica, Jani and my then boyfriend, Blake, were upset with me because they didn't want me to leave Crested Butte. The conflict came to a head one night when we were drinking. I was upset because they couldn't understand my point of view and finally I stood up and said, "I want to go to Costa Rica and dance! Everyone dances there, and it doesn't matter how old they are, or what's happening in their lives. They just dance."

Jani and Blake looked at me like I was crazy.

Shortly after that I had a dream. I was in Costa Rica on a beach backed by lush forest. I was doing easy pose, which is like sitting cross-legged on the floor. But I wasn't sitting on the beach, I was levitating above it, with my hands in a mudra, each of my thumbs and pointer fingers touching. The place felt like paradise, with a black beach and strong surf, the water clean and clear, as huge waves arced and slammed to the earth. I sang a sweet song on that clear day, a breeze blowing in my hair.

I realized now that this was where I was in the dream. This place I had never been came to me years before I arrived here.

"I'm here! I'm home," I yelled to the sky.

I wiped tears from my eyes, just in time for Jani and Dad to join me. Juan had maneuvered the truck onto the beach and, after I collected my sandals, we all piled back in and drove a mile along shore to Corcovado Lodge Tent Camp. Set next to the ocean, with a sprawling lawn, arching palms, and tents for the guests, it was my idea of heaven.

The next day Jani, Dad, and I walked along the beach to Rio Madrigal in the Corcovado National Park. The beach was just as I'd imagined, long and full of crabs, shells, and driftwood, and edged by monkey ladder vines and palm, coconut, and almond trees. In the forest, we stepped across thick trunks and leapt over streams. Spider monkeys swung above us through the canopy, while raccoon-like coatis rooted for crabs near our feet. My senses sparked to life as I practiced being a guide, spotting animals for Jani and Dad. We saw a black-headed trogon, an indigo-colored bird with a yellow breast, and sitting still in a treetop, a crested owl, the sun glinting off his golden eyes.

At the estuary where Rio Madrigal met the Pacific, we took off our shoes and waded across the clear, cool water. We sat on logs and ate a lunch of bean burritos. Hermit crabs inhabiting many sizes of shells crawled around our feet, and the tide rolled in with waves that crashed so hard the ground shook. A calm came over me like I'd never known before, a sense that this was my place—the land I'd searched from the US to the Caribbean to Australia and across Asia to find. I knew in that moment, I could stop seeking.

The next morning, when the surf was calm, we hiked away from camp. I waded into the ocean, feeling its coolness as the waves struck my calves, thighs, and belly. Even then, at low tide, they were not tame little waves, but strong ones with attitude. Jani balked at their intensity, but ultimately she and Dad followed me in. Beyond the break, I rode the swells up toward the sky and felt them settle me back. I sensed the power of the Pacific, and the peace of seeing nothing—absolutely nothing—made by humans.

When I returned to work, I told Don Michael how much I loved Corcovado National Park, and he sent me down there again for a month.

I flew from San José straight to Carate on a charter Cessna 206, the only plane that could land on the short strips in and near the park. I again stayed at Corcovado Lodge Tent Camp. The next day, I climbed on the same plane with a guide and two National Geographic photographers, there to shoot Corcovado National Park. The pilot, Alvaro Ramirez, was the only pilot in the region who could land on the short strip inside the park. No one else had the experience—or even dared to try—to land a plane on such a narrow strip of ground that ended abruptly in a wall of rain-forest.

Below us the forest was a tangle of emerald, olive, and jade green, rimmed on one side by black beach. We opened the windows so the photographers could take clear shots, and warm, soft air rushed through. After flying for a short while, the plane banked, and I saw the tiny strip below us, a carpet of grass. My mouth went dry and my heart beat fast as we lined up on final approach. Alvaro set down the wheels right where the forest paused and the airstrip began. We bumped along, the green rampart of trees at the end of the runway looming before us. But Alvaro brought the plane to a halt just where the airstrip ended and a breath away from where the forest began. We were ten minutes from where we had started but a world away in the center of the park at Sirena.

For the next six days, Tomás, the guide, and I helped the photographers set up their gear at dawn, and then we were free to explore. We walked along the trails that meandered just fifty yards from the ocean. An anteater, with his big snout, rooted along the forest floor, and a three-toed sloth, with near-invisible slowness, climbed the limb of a cecropia tree. We came to the Sirena River, where crocodiles and sharks preyed on fish. While walking back we spotted a group of peccaries, wild boars that if disturbed could be quite dangerous.

Tomás grew up in the area, so one day he stopped and said, "Lana, this was where my school was." Now, it was just vines and tangled roots. He also pointed out old stone foundations with rotting boards that once were houses. In the mid-1900s, this area deep in the jungle was ruled by a *cacique*, or chieftain, who cut down some of the primary forest to graze cattle. He made his fortune buying and, with a wide margin, reselling gold the locals mined in the Rio Claro and Sirena River. It was a good deal for everyone except one caveat: if the cacique liked your woman, you had to give her up. Thus, he had many wives and fathered some fifty children.

In 1975, when the park was formed, the families that lived there, including the cacique's and Tomás's, were forced to move outside its boundaries. Sometimes I caught Tomás looking out toward the forest with a yearning in his eyes, and I wondered if he missed those days when his village was there.

We stayed at the Sirena Ranger Station, what was once a trading post in the middle of the forest. Because it was so hot indoors, and there was no air conditioning, about ten of us slept on top of the big building's roof, our pads and blankets scattered randomly across the open space. The National Geographic photographers slept in tents. At dawn, howler monkeys roared like something out of *Jurassic Park*. I whispered to no one and everyone, "Whoa."

I have a passion for photography so I grilled the photographers whenever I could. One day, we were walking on a remote trail and I asked the two men about the best lenses for wildlife photography, and whether they used filters, and how to capture the movement of animals. They were generous with their knowledge, and as they shot, I watched them to glean yet more.

We left them behind so they could do their work. Tomás and I hiked down into a creek bed and, suddenly, he whispered, "Lana, we'd better turn around. We'd better go get those guys."

"Okay," I said. It was dusk, and it gets dark almost instantly in the rainforest because the vegetation is so thick. When the sun stops shining, all seems to go black. We turned around. I looked down and my breath caught with what I saw: a puma track indented the footprint I had left just moments before. My heart nearly pounded out of my chest.

"There is a puma watching us," Tomás whispered. His hand pressed into the small of my back, hurrying me along.

In the fading light, we found the photographers and hiked double-speed back to the ranger station.

I should have been scared, but I was falling in love with Corcovado. The wilderness was strong and free and beautiful, and it would never be completely tamed, but it felt like home.

On one of our last days at Sirena, Tomás wanted to show me the Rio Pavo, a remote river about ten kilometers, or six miles, from where we were staying. We had hiked for a few hours when the dense forest opened up to a glistening waterway. It was knee-deep, surrounded by thriving tropical vegetation. In the center, a blue heron sitting on a sandbar took flight, its broad wings flapping in long arcs. We waded through, mud shifting beneath our feet. As usual, I was just wearing my bikini. I admit I was pretty naive about what could happen to me.

Tomás was a short, muscular block of a man. Mostly, he hiked in front of me. But on this day, when I was trying to hold my footing in the water, he turned around, reached out his meaty arms, and grabbed me around the chest, pulling me into him. I smelled his salty sweat and the burrito he had eaten at lunch on his breath. I pushed my arms into his chest.

He resisted, grasping me tighter.

I slammed my fists against him and broke away, nearly falling in the water.

I struggled through the current to the bank. With my distress, the Spanish got stuck in my mouth, but I managed to say, *"No puedes hacer esto, Tomás!* We . . . work together. You're supposed to be my . . . *profesor!"* I tried to be strong, but I was afraid. Sex had always been a beautiful consensual act for me. Never had I felt pressure or violence around it.

Tomás stood there, looking at me with his dark eyes framed by thick brows. His expression revealed no remorse, and I realized if he wanted to, he could really hurt me, and no one would know. I didn't yet grasp the lay of the forest, and we were in a remote place. I was not even sure how we got there because I had trusted and followed him.

Still I stumbled across the Spanish words. "You're . . . married and you have kids," I said. "Don't do this!" I had met his family, who worked at Corcovado Lodge Tent Camp. Finally, my Spanish cleared. "I will tell, and you will be in so much trouble."

He turned from me and practically ran away down the trail. There I was in the middle of Corcovado by myself, not fully knowing how to get back. It was growing dark within the dense foliage surrounding me. In any moment a jaguar or peccary might dart out and come at me. I took a step in the direction we came from and then continued along the barely discernible trail with no markings, following my intuition through the forest. It seemed to take forever to find my way back to the station, where I collapsed on a hammock.

A week later, I was strolling along the beach when I saw Tomás and his little girl, Cindy, walking toward me. She wore a white dress with red polka dots that I had bought for her. As soon as she recognized me, she came running. I kneeled down to her height.

"Lanita, Lanita," she yelled, flinging herself into my arms. We hugged, and then she stepped back and began telling me about the starfish she saw alongshore. I listened as she demonstrated with her little hands how big they were. Meanwhile, Tomás arrived. He stopped near us and watched.

When I stood, I looked him in the eye, and we paused for a moment that way, staring at each other, little Cindy between us.

He nodded subtly, and I sensed that he got it. He knew that he had to respect me.

But even still, the incident stayed between us like a quiet drumbeat.

CHAPTER 24

When I returned to San José, I told Don Michael about my adventures. We sat in his office and I could barely stay in the chair I was so excited about Corcovado. Over the years, we had become close, so he wanted me to be happy; he knew if I was happy I'd do a good job. He smiled his broad, ageing-hippie smile and nodded.

He sent me to a training course to learn more about the Osa Peninsula and Corcovado National Park. I learned the geography, the natural history, and the habits of the animals there so that I could be a well-educated guide. I was continually astonished by the place. It is the second largest national park in Costa Rica, encompassing 164 square miles. It protects more than 700 species of trees, 140 species of mammals, 463 different birds, 117 amphibians and reptiles, 40 types of freshwater fish, and 10,000 unique insects.

Corcovado is home to 220 different species of butterfly and to the largest population of scarlet macaws in Costa Rica. At the Llorona, Sirena, and Carate beaches, various turtles—the olive ridley, leatherback, green, and hawksbill—frequently nest. The park is also a sanctuary for several endangered species, including the jaguar, cougar, tapir, ocelot, giant anteater, and American crocodile.

Once I was familiar with the area, Don Michael sent me down to work at his Corcovado Lodge Tent Camp and to guide travelers through the park.

This was pure heaven to me, and I strived to be what I thought of as the "Guide with the Mostest." I got to be in nature and wear my bathing suit top and shorts. My whole life, I had always been in my bikini whenever I could. I took people through the park and got to know them. I hiked every day and saw fabulous animals and got to know them too.

Soon, Don Michael bought an expedition raft, the kind used to float down the Colorado River through the Grand Canyon. With it we took people into Corcovado by sea. Once we landed on shore, Tomás and I guided the clients into the park in two groups. If there were twenty people, I took ten and he took ten. We headed out on different trails, one along the beach and the other through the forest. At an endpoint, the trails met, so we all had lunch together. Then Tomás and I switched, so the travelers experienced each of us. I was meeting many people while getting tan and fit, all of which I loved.

One day, my group had just met up with Tomás and his clients when I heard white-lipped peccaries gnashing their teeth, an eerie sound like hail hitting a tin roof. These boar-like animals with thick gray hair, little ears, and long snouts can be dangerous if they feel threatened. Their upper canine teeth grow outward and upward forming clearly visible tusks that they use to crush hard seeds and slice into plant roots. They also use their tusks to ward off predators, which unfortunately may have been the way they viewed us.

I stopped and listened, hearing the boars' chomping grow louder, and I could smell their distinct skunk-like scent. They tended to run in large packs, so I knew we were in trouble. Tomás and I exchanged a serious look. "Okay, everyone," I yelled to the approximately twenty travelers. "We've got to get up high, on a log or something. Now!"

Tomás and I looked around and found a huge fallen tree.

"Over here," I yelled to the group. They ran to us, and we helped them onto the log. Tomás and I climbed up after them. The peccaries filtered out of the dense brush, more and more of them until I counted about fifty. I breathed fast, and my palms sweated as the peccaries arrived at the bottom of the log. Their snouts pointed up at us, sniffing. Their bristly hair crested on their backs, which meant they were excited. The log had a broad girth that set us a few feet above them, but they were relentless. With their snouts, they butted at our perch—they were trying to tip us off. The peccaries were not tall, but if they had stood on their hind legs they could have nibbled our feet. The log rocked beneath our feet. If one of us fell to the ground, they might attack the person, using their teeth and hooves as weapons. With so many peccaries, it could have been deadly.

Finally, unable to move the log, they gave up and wandered away, their wiry tails swaying.

Joy and relief filled me. I climbed off the log and helped our clients down, who were stunned into silence. I scanned the group to make sure everyone was okay, that there were no signs of shock or over-heating.

One person said, "Wow," and another said, "Incredible," and then they all talked and laughed at the same time, thrilled with the experience.

As we hiked back to camp my body vibrated with the excitement of having succeeded in keeping my clients safe.

At Corcovado Lodge, I lived in a tent set on a grassy oasis right next to the beach, where palm trees arched and waves crashed on shore. The manager of the camp, William, was having problems at home, so he was distracted. This had been going on for a while, and I feared that the lodge's business might suffer because of it, so I worked extra hard.

One evening my boss, Don Michael, called me on the radio and said, "Lana, will you be the assistant manager?"

"Yeah. I'd love to." I leapt in the air, excited to be taking another step closer to running my own lodge. I was eager to learn.

One day the manager was gone, so I was in charge of the workers. Costa Ricans love to talk, and during a coffee break all the workers were chatting. They sat down by the shore sipping coffee, and Tomás hung out with them.

Though very close—Tomás had taught me so much—we still had some residual tension from the incident at Rio Pavo.

As the morning progressed, the workers continued to hang out drinking coffee. Plenty of tasks needed to be completed: We needed to cut the grass and trim along the edges with the weed whacker. We needed to collect the fallen brush and coconuts from a recent storm and fix a spot on the restaurant roof that was leaking. I walked over to them and said, *"Ya vamos a trabajar. Ya, es tiempo!"* But Tomás and the others just sat and smoked cigarettes and sipped their coffee.

I walked away, not yet upset because I understood that they didn't have that much spare time. I waited another fifteen minutes, getting irritated, but they continued to sit. I walked back over and said to Tomás, "Okay, come on, get up. I need you to go down there and chop the weeds with the weed whacker."

Nothing happened. At this point I was angry. I went down to the grassy area to do the work myself. The weed whacker was a big machine. It came with a vest that held the machine in place on your chest. I pulled the vest on, but it was so big I couldn't fasten the snaps.

The workers saw that I was struggling, but they still didn't move.

When they ignored my request again, I felt like I had failed my first real test as assistant manager. Part of the challenge was that in this Latin country, men dominated, and I didn't know how to supervise people who viewed me as a person without power. To overcome this, I knew I needed some new skills.

Finally, a man named Don, who was the captain of the raft, a big African American guy with the most beautiful smile, came up to me and spoke in English. "Lana, it's okay. Don't worry. I'll do it later."

I turned to him, and it was as though he could read my feelings. "Just let it go," he said.

"I've got to do it. They're not going to do it."

"No. No. Just let it go. I'll do it for you."

I thanked him, handed him the vest and machine, and strode into the office. I was fuming at those men, and while my fury ate me up inside, they calmly sipped coffee. I took deep breaths to settle down and realized, for possibly the first time, how challenging my goal of building a lodge in this country might be. The thought saddened me to a point where I sat and put my head on the desk.

But then a monkey squealed in the forest, a funny sound almost like a giggle, and it brought me back to why I was there. *I must do what I can to fit in this male-dominated, wild world.* I recognized how tongue-tied my Spanish was and saw that I was not good at expressing myself in Spanish when I was angry. I had not really been angry in Costa Rica before this, so I had rarely needed those kinds of words. I committed to expanding my vocabulary. It was a wake-up call for me.

Meanwhile, Don became one of my best friends, and he modeled for me a steady strength. One day soon after this, seven guests en route to the lodge couldn't cross one of the rivers because of a downpour. Don waded across the water, and as dusk fell, organized the group into a chain. Everyone held hands, and they waded together, Don in the middle. When they wobbled and lost their footing, it was thanks to him that they regained their balance and made it across.

This was what Don did for me each day. He held that steady

balance, so I could move across the river of this challenging country to the shore of my dream.

I worked at Corcovado for a month at a time and then got three to four days off, when I returned to San José and played with my friends. Whenever I went, I had a blast, dancing with them and riding my bike around Santa Ana, but I always missed the quiet mystique of the Osa Peninsula.

The lodge manager, William, was gone a lot, so I continued to learn how to run the lodge by simply diving in and doing it. He returned periodically, but he was having so many problems with his family that he was exhausted. I was extremely responsible, and he knew that. I don't think he did it on purpose, but he took advantage of me.

One day, I looked all over for him in the office and on the veranda. I went to his tent. Finally, I peeked in a vacant tent, and there he was, lying on the cot snoring. He had a big belly, so I called him Baloo after the bear in *Jungle Book*.

"Baloo," I said, "get up. I need your help."

He did.

But then he realized his hiding place was no longer a secret so he began to rotate his sleeping spots. He knew which tents were empty and he went there. I still found him when it was really necessary, but most of the time I just winged it and through this learned how to manage a lodge. Because he knew how much I was helping him, Baloo ended up being one of my closest friends in Corcovado.

During the high season, the lodge was full, and the employees scrambled. This was when the real shift came in my relationship with them because I worked right alongside them. When the restaurant was busy, I bussed tables. When the bar was overflowing, I took drink orders. When we needed a clean tent in a hurry, I helped the housekeeper tidy up, and when the grounds were covered with driftwood from a storm, I picked it up. The employees saw this.

They seemed to realize that I had a big heart, but I worked hard, and I expected them to work hard. And they did.

I came to love being assistant manager. I felt I had found my home on the Osa Peninsula. That was, until one day my former fiancé, Cole, showed up.

CHAPTER 25

One evening as I totaled the bills for the next day's checkouts, the radio-phone rang. I picked up and smiled when I heard my friend Elena's voice. With no other phone there at all, I was always pleased to hear from her. We sometimes chatted in the evenings, when the radio line was used the least. The rest of the time it was an open channel, so even the bus drivers for Costa Rica Expeditions could tune into our conversations. This had led to a lot of gossip and interest in "what was going on with Lana in Corcovado." Tonight, though, Elena was calling for a real reason.

"Hey, Lanita," she said. "I have an interesting message for you."

"I'm listening." I sat in my chair and wondered what this surprise could be.

"We got a call here from a guy named Roy Sanders from Gunnison. He and his friend Cole Maguire are coming to Costa Rica, and they want to see you."

My mouth went dry and my heart fluttered at the mention of Cole's name. With all the work I'd been doing, I had forgotten him, my adorable, rugged ex-fiancé. His passion, his laugh that shook his whole body, his generosity and sincerity—it all came rushing back.

Immediately, I shoved the images away. *Cole hates me. Why would he come here?*

I took a deep breath. "Okay. Tell them to come down."

"Good," she said. "They fly into San José on Friday, so you can expect them on Saturday morning."

"Great," I said, trying to blanket my apprehension with an enthusiastic tone.

A few days later, I stood with the tent camp's horse wrangler, Urbano, at the dirt airstrip in Carate as a Cessna 206 landed. Roy climbed out first. He was like an elf, small, with a head and beard of bushy red hair, and he was full of love. He gave me a big hug. A few other guests climbed out of the plane after him, including Cole, but I didn't have time to greet them or him because another Cessna full of guests had landed, and they rushed over to say hello.

When I turned back, Cole was standing right in front of me. He was handsome as ever, with his curly hair and dark eyes. We looked at each other, pausing as the breeze blew off the ocean and a pair of scarlet macaws squawked from a treetop. His face registered a confused combination of joy and what seemed to be fear, or maybe even anger, a crease between his brows. He moved in to hug me, fast and stiff.

I excused myself to gather the group, while Urbano loaded all the luggage onto a horse-pulled cart. I led the eight guests on the forty-five-minute walk along the beach back to the tent camp. They raved about the flight in. Roy and Cole talked of the forest's impenetrable green and the stunning way it met the Pacific, but I didn't really have time to visit as I fielded the other guests' questions. When we arrived at the lodge, I checked everyone into their tents and returned to my daily duties.

That evening under a full moon, Cole and I walked the beach. As our feet swished through the sand heading away from camp, we remained silent. Waves pounded the shore. The full moon lit up everything, including Cole's closed expression that reminded me of the last time I saw him, when I apologized for cheating on him.

But then we turned back toward camp and everything felt lighter.

"You like your work here?" he asked.

"I love it. It's challenging every day." I thought of all the trials I'd had here, and as a woman in a Latin American country, I had to learn to be assertive. "I love speaking Spanish every day," I said, "and meeting people from all over the world. I thrive on the constant change. Nothing is ever the same in the rainforest." I gazed at a silver cloud racing across the sky.

"What do you mean?" he asked.

I thought of life there and realized how unique it was, living in a tent, completely off the grid. "Once we turn off the generator at night, all you hear is nature, and the air is so still and . . . sacred. Everything is lit with candles." I looked over and saw that he was interested in what I was saying. "But when something goes wrong, it's sink or swim. We have to deal with it in the moment. We have to fix the generator, or the water pump. There's no calling the repairman."

He nodded, taking it all in. "Sounds amazing."

"Yeah, it is." I smiled, savoring this world I'd found myself in. We walked more, and I sensed he now had a deeper appreciation for this place, and I wanted him to appreciate me. I was tanner and more fit than I'd ever been, and for some reason I wanted him to notice that, to be impressed by it, and to be mesmerized by my life here. It suddenly felt so important that he see it all. But I shook away that need. "And you? What's happening in your life?"

"Things have been good in Crested Butte, but I'm headed to Alaska again right after this trip."

Alaska. I remembered our times there, working and playing hard, those days that literally never ended, the sun barely setting, leaving time to be young, to hike and party and make love. The memory ignited my whole body, and I sensed the same was happening with Cole. Our attraction was so strong, the sex so good.

I heard a faint sound above the waves. It was someone breathing—a woman sighing. Cole must have heard it too; he glanced at me and raised a brow.

We were back at the tents, and there, in the glow of one of them, a woman's silhouette cast against the candle-lit fabric as she sat atop her lover. The canvas tents were rectangular, with pitched roofs. Each had two beds hugging opposite walls, a side table in between. The woman rocked atop her lover on one bed, a window alongside them. Sheer curtains blew in the wind, adding yet more romance to the moment. The woman arched her back, sighing and moaning with pleasure, while the waves broke and the moon shone. Cole's fingers brushed mine and didn't retreat, his palm hot as he grasped my hand. He squeezed and then let go.

I felt fire coming off his body and my own. We continued to walk past, and I realized I was holding my breath as desire filled me. It glowed in my nipples, and I swore I could see a bulge in Cole's shorts. He caught me looking there and laughed, and I started laughing, and then we realized the couple might hear us, so we ran away, down toward the ocean.

We kept laughing as the surf cooled our feet and our passion. Even though the incident had ignited us both, we couldn't go there. I didn't know how he felt about me, and he didn't know how I felt about him. *I* didn't even know how I felt about him. We really cared about each other but when we walked back up to the tent camp, I hugged him and left to sleep in my tent alone.

As I undressed, my intuition was telling me that renewing this relationship could jeopardize my whole plan of living in Costa Rica, since I knew he would never move here. He wanted to live in Alaska and was adamant about that fact. I would live in Alaska and Costa Rica, but Cole wouldn't. He only wanted Alaska. Realizing this helped calm my excitement so I could fall asleep.

In the morning, however, thoughts of our electrifying beach experience zapped around in my mind. My heart once again accelerated, but I shook away the feelings. *No, no, no, no, no.*

That day, I guided Cole and Roy through the park. Both of them loved nature and animals, so they were riveted to the beauty surrounding us, vines draping above our heads and roots swirling beneath our feet. Cole especially appreciated the strangler fig trees. These germinate on the bark of other trees and then root down and climb up, engulfing the host as they compete for sunlight in the crowded forest. Ultimately, the host tree dies, leaving the strangler with a hollow core, its trunk tall and eerie, gray bark studded with stark, chaotic branches.

We also saw a sloth, woodpeckers, and peccaries. By the end of the day, Cole and Roy were drunk with the beauty and stumbled into the restaurant for dinner.

The next two days while I worked, they played in the ocean, snoozed in hammocks, and got to know the other guests. Their last night, we did tequila shots in the tent camp's bar. Somehow we hatched a plan over dinner to return to San José, stay at my house in Santa Ana, and then travel together to Nicaragua.

Really? I said to myself once I was alone in my tent. *How in the world did this happen?*

Rainy season was about to start in Corcovado. While it's spring and summer in the US, here a dozen inches of rain can fall within a few hours. Tourists barely come, and the heat and mosquitos bear down on any living creature near the beach. The tent camp activity slows down, so it was a perfect time for me to leave . . . with Cole.

I was apprehensive when they invited me because there was a part of me that felt the flame picking up again, and my intuition was telling me not to follow that spark. But before I knew it, we were at my house in Santa Ana. Roy was asleep on the couch downstairs and Cole and I stood looking out my bedroom window at the view of the city.

The electricity between us had continued to build. In Corcovado, we could not act on it because I was not allowed to fraternize with guests, and there really was no privacy. But now we were alone and drunk from dancing and drinking tequila at Rancho de Macho. Cole pulled me into a hug, and it felt like I'd arrived home after a long absence, so safe and encompassing, his scent as familiar as my own. We fell onto the bed and couldn't get our clothes off fast enough. I melted into his adept touch, and we got lost in our lovemaking.

The next day we took a boat down the San Juan River in Nicaragua. The first thing I noticed as we headed deeper into the country was how quiet it was. In Costa Rica there are so many birds and bugs, so much life, that the air throbs. It's like listening to nature's symphony. But in Nicaragua, as we made our way down the muddy river in a two-level ferry, the animal music disappeared. I was so confounded by this that I headed to the top deck and stood listening. Yes, it was like Costa Rica, with its moist air and heat, but I only heard the churning of the ferryboat engine and the passengers talking.

Along the journey, the boatman stopped occasionally to drop off food supplies to villages. When we arrived at our destination, El Castillo, we were hungry, not having eaten all day. We asked the boatman for food, but he just shrugged and shook his head.

We climbed off the ferry onto a dock at the best hotel in town. At check-in, we asked the man at the front desk where we could buy food. He paused as though thinking and then told us it was hard to find food in town right now. Cole and I made our way to our room, and Roy headed to his. Tired from the journey, we went to bed hungry that night and fell asleep immediately.

The next morning I got up early, my stomach growling. I walked the main street, where I found no shops or restaurants selling food. A little boy with huge dark eyes and flamboyant confidence tagged along with me. I asked him in Spanish if he knew anywhere to get fruit or beans or rice. He motioned for me to follow him. We wound through back dirt streets to the very edge of town. I smelled the bread even before we arrived.

The boy led me to a yard in front of a little house made of concrete blocks, where a woman was just pulling loaves out of her outdoor wood-burning oven. They were puffy little treasures that smelled a little smoky, making my mouth water. She invited me inside to a kitchen pantry full of canned food, which served as a little neighborhood store. I picked out a few tins of tuna and gave her some *córdobas*. She took them with a smile.

Thanking them both, I returned to the hotel. Cole and Roy clapped when they saw the food. On a veranda overlooking the river, we ate tuna sandwiches, which, even though completely plain, tasted delicious.

The absence of animals became especially haunting when we visited the Reserva Biológica Indio Maíz, a national biological reserve. We spent an entire day hiking through the forest and saw no wildlife. When we left the park, I asked the ranger about this, and he said it was because of the war that had ended recently. The people were poor and had nothing to eat, so they killed all the animals and birds. My heart ached with this news.

In Nicaragua, life felt desolate without the animals. I tried to make the best of it, but everyone seemed sad without them. At the hotel in El Castillo we met expatriates—Europeans and Americans—who sat around and drank all day in a quiet desperation. They seemed stunned by the lack of lyrical bird calls to adorn the air and fish from the river to eat.

I did find that the village, El Castillo, was beautiful. We visited the Fortress of the Immaculate Conception, built in 1673 for protection against pirate attacks. As we stood atop the fortress, a dark, moss-covered ruin, and gazed down at the river and the village, I felt gratitude return. This was an amazing town accessible only by boat, so it had no paved roads or cars. The quiet just for that moment seemed a blessing.

After five days, we left Nicaragua on the same boat that brought us. When we crossed the border into Costa Rica, I immediately saw the difference. Birds zoomed across the sky, monkeys swung on tree branches, and butterflies flitted in and out of the boat. Families picnicked along the river. They waved, and the kids ran and played. The brightness and joy in my home country calmed my body and mind. Cole sat next to me on the ferry, and he took my hand and smiled. We were all relieved to be back where life thrived. He looked at me with his dark eyes, and I again felt that flame that had dampened during the time in Nicaragua light up.

"You want to go back to Alaska with me?" he asked.

Before I even knew what I was doing, I nodded and said, "Yes."

My mind raced as we took the bus back to my place in Santa Ana. *What am I doing?* I asked myself. I knew I was going against what my intuition was saying. But there were reasons. It was the rainy season in Costa Rica, and I couldn't make money. In Alaska I knew I could, a lot of it. But even more than that, I had some hope, some dream of a life with this man. Yes, we had differences in where we wanted to live and what we wanted to do with our lives, but to be able to spend our days together won over that. Still, I wondered, could I leave Costa Rica?

I asked the Universe what to do.

Even though I had my doubts about the decision to go, in that moment I refused to follow my intuition. Another part of me believed in this journey. My attachment to Cole and the life we could have together had returned, and even if it came to nothing, at least I would know for sure.

The next morning Cole and I were sitting on the patio holding hands, when two doves, what I call love birds because they mate for life, flew over. They were pristine white and they flew in tandem, their wings nearly touching as they soared across the flawless blue sky. I smiled and squeezed Cole's hand. For me, this was a sign, that yes, I could go, I would go, with him to Alaska.

CHAPTER 26

Two weeks after Cole and Roy departed, I was on my way to Alaska. I flew from San José to LA, LA to Seattle, and Seattle to Anchorage, all in the same day. Cole picked me up at 1:00 a.m. He was waiting at the airport gate, and when we embraced, he lifted me off the ground and twirled me around. We made our way out into the cool, dry air to his truck, and even though it was the middle of the night, an eerie pink-yellow light filled the sky. Alaska was so different from Costa Rica, the opposite really. In Costa Rica, the landscape had curves and supple outlines, the air warm and moist, while the land in Alaska had hard edges and the air was crisp, as though it might break.

"What do you want to eat?" he asked as we cruised through the outskirts of the city. We stopped at a massive supermarket. It was the first store I'd ever been to that was open twenty-four hours. We stepped in and Cole said, "Lana, buy anything you want."

I went straight to the ice-cream counter and ordered a double scoop of chocolate-chip cookie dough. When I ate it, I relished the feel of the coolness on my tongue and the sweetness of the chocolate chips, but most of all, I was thrilled to be up late with the man who for many years was my closest friend and lover, and now was again.

We drove through the night and arrived at dawn in Wasilla, where Cole lived in a rental house near Wasilla Lake. The lake was a wonder: surrounded by grass, steely blue, and still covered with ice. Craggy peaks topped with snow towered in the distance.

We stood on the porch of his house, and he grasped my arm and pulled me into him. We stayed like that for a long time, while birds chirped around us and a cold breeze blew off the lake. He tilted his head down toward me and kissed me, and it felt like something I'd lost for years but found again, his lips on mine, his mouth with a sweet taste that could only be him. In that moment, I was ready to leave the whole life I'd built in Costa Rica for this dream of love. I would have a husband, and we would face the world together, rather than my current life that was magnificent but run on my strength alone.

A few days later, we drove south through the Chugach National Forest to Seward, where Cole already had a job on a halibut boat. I asked around for work and fairly quickly found it on a longline halibut fishing boat. It was owned by my old friend Captain Jack Scoby, who I had worked for on the research ship after the Exxon Valdez spill. Cole and I said goodbye and headed out in the early dawn.

Our crew consisted of four men and me on a forty-foot longliner. We cruised to open water and started work. First, we unreeled about five miles of ground lines with bait. Later in the day, we pulled the lines in. We removed the fish and cleaned, iced, and stored them. We rebaited the lines and repeated the process. It was messy and smelly work that took all my strength.

We were on a forty-eight-hour run, during which we worked nonstop to catch all we could. I soon learned that the captain was counting the ratio of halibut to other kinds of fish. By law, we were allowed 80 percent halibut and 20 percent other fish, such as rockfish, sablefish, and tuna. If we took in more than that amount of other fish, we had to throw them back.

We toiled at this dangerous work for hours and hours, with hooks and huge fish flying. I was exhausted after almost two days of labor. Suddenly, a rockfish as big as a person came up out of the water with his eyes bulging, because of the air pressure from being pulled up from the bottom so quickly. He was dead, but his freaked-out expression stopped me cold. I knew at this point we were over our limit of other fish, and I would have to throw this gorgeous creature off the boat.

I grabbed him and unhooked him. I was cold, wet, tired, and hungry. I thought, *What am I doing?* I realized I didn't want to be there, because I was into *caring* for animals. I was a guide, a person who saved these creatures, not one who killed them. I took the fish to the edge of the boat, threw it off, and solemnly watched it float away behind the slow churning of the water behind us.

Next came an even more brutal task. As we headed back to shore we checked the catch, and sure enough, as I already knew, we had too many other fish besides halibut. The boss said, "Flip them over the side." We poured out whole containers of incredible, edible fish that we had killed, and they floated on the surface behind our boat like victims of a massacre. I was sure some other fish would eat them, but to me it was still a horror. I kept asking myself, *What am I doing?* My intuition was calling to me once again.

Despite these doubts, Cole and I grew closer. Nights when we were off work at the Wasilla house by the still-frozen lake, we snuggled together on the porch and watched the sun set over the mountains. It was always different. Some evenings a torrent of pink and purple swirled; others, a calm persimmon melted to black; and once in a while, the water, mountains, and sky shone in varying shades of gold.

Now in the spring, the air was cold, and the wild storms that blew through drew us together in a kind of desperate clench. Neither of us wanted to be pulled away, but who we truly were seemed to do just that, and so we clung even harder. When we hugged, it was with all our strength. When we talked, it was with an intensity of the present moment, which seemed to be all we had. And when we made love, it was with our whole bodies, arousing all of our senses with touch.

One night in front of a sparking fire, he moved his eyes across my face and smiled in a shy way. "Lana, you want to get married?"

During this time in Alaska, I sensed that I was losing some part of me that I had built over many years, that was especially developed through the high school leadership conferences and leading the student body of Gunnison High. It was the part of me that was a leader, that wanted to build something amazing. I was like the train going up the challenging hill, saying, "I think I can, I think I can." I was still exercising those skills in the back-breaking work in Alaska, and in my relationship with Cole, but somehow none of it felt like my own life.

When I was a cheerleader, I was strong but I was also light. The other girls would throw me up in the air and catch me, and I was usually the one at the very top of the human pyramid, standing high above the ground, my arms reaching for the sky. I learned to be confident and strong.

Later, when I ski raced at Fort Lewis College in Durango, Colorado, I ran slalom and giant slalom. In those events, you go really fast, screaming around gates where the snow has turned to ice. I could do those things because I fully believed in them—and in myself. I was the leader of my own destiny. But back in Alaska again, I felt more like a follower.

Even with those feelings, when Cole asked me to marry him, I looked into those gorgeous onyx eyes and felt like I couldn't refuse, like I had to agree to this life with him. I knew that this was the second time he'd asked me, and the first had been a disaster, but I pushed away that truth.

"Yes," I said. I heard a faint voice of my intuition within me protest, but I shook it away.

My true self only wanted the life I loved in Costa Rica. But while my days there were lush and fun, surviving could be challenging. Half of every year on the Osa was a wash financially for me because of the rainy season. And I wanted this companionship, this love in my life. I wanted to be a woman with a man by my side.

Though Cole seemed assured about our new life together, he didn't fully trust me. Sometimes I caught him looking at me with a scared and angry crease between his brows, and other times in the middle of a big hug, he'd pull away fast. This distrust seemed to intensify when we were with his brother, Lyle, who lived with his wife in a town a half hour away.

Lyle and I had always been close, even before I got together with his younger brother. I loved him, and he loved me too, but he was not happy with me. Their whole family was wary of me. Sometimes Cole, Lyle and his wife, and I went country dancing at a bar in Wasilla. Lyle and I jitterbugged together—he was an accomplished dancer—and it was fun, but he never really looked me in the eye. He didn't want Cole to get hurt again. This weighed on me. I didn't want to hurt Cole either, but each day my heart became more uncertain.

One day Cole and I drove to a lush valley that swept up toward jagged peaks. At a little airstrip he climbed into an ultralight, a small, single-prop plane with one long wing stretching across the top and a small cabin beneath. His pilot friend, Joe, took him up. I stood on the tarmac and watched as they climbed above the peaks and swooped close to them, the little plane's engine barely audible above the sound of the breeze.

When they came back down, it was my turn. I climbed in and buckled the seat belt. The engine roared, and then the ultralight, which felt like it was made of sticks and thread, rumbled along the runway and took flight. It was exhilarating to be so unprotected from the elements. We climbed in broad circles until we rose above a towering ledge. Below us, mountain goats hung by the tips of their hooves to the edge. They were stunning creatures with curled horns and haunting, dark eyes. One of them was so close to the edge, it seemed he could fall with a puff of wind. The pilot flew near it. He circled around and around getting closer and closer, so I could almost touch the creature.

I wanted to stop the pilot from going so close to the goat, but he wouldn't. He wanted me to really see it. I yelled up to him, "Let's get out of here," but he must have thought I was saying how cool it was, because he only smiled. The mountain goat, with his little gray goatee, looked up at us with a forlorn expression as he balanced on the edge.

That was how I felt in Alaska, like the goat, clinging to the very edge of life. I closed my eyes. *What am I doing to myself?* My intuition whispered to me once again.

Back on the ground, I told Cole about seeing the goat, but I didn't share with him my reservations about our life there. We continued enjoying each other, but my heart was completely uncertain.

A few nights later, Cole took me to a new friend's house. We walked into a regal log cabin, and in the entry hall I saw a four-foot-long salmon attached to the wall. I stopped, stunned by its shimmery skin, its dead eyes, and mouth frozen open. In the corner of the living room, a polar bear stood, its legs staggered as though it were walking, its nose turned up, sniffing the air. In the billiard room a grizzly bear pelt lay flattened out on the floor, its head still attached, mouth open, so as you were playing pool you could pause and put your foot between its jaws. The place was full of animal trophies—actual stuffed animals.

Cole's friend guided us through, proud of his hunting and

fishing conquests. He was tall and chubby, with a red face and alcohol-swollen nose. Finally, we arrived at the kitchen, where we encountered a mountain goat trophy, similar to the one I saw while in the ultralight. My heart ached for the difference between this dead creature and the living one.

There were so many stuffed animals I couldn't count. The house was filled with trophy after trophy after trophy. I turned to Cole and said, "I've got to go for a walk."

"What's going on, Lana?" he asked. He knew in the past weeks a part of me had shut down, and now I was like an iron bank safe, with its locks completely barred.

"Sorry, but I've just got to go. I've got to go for a walk." I didn't want to tell him why at that moment. I strode out the back door and stood among the trees, breathing the piney scent. We hadn't eaten dinner yet, so I didn't know what to do. Besides all the dead animals in the house, the dinner was going to be almost all meat, and I was a vegetarian. I could hardly breathe, my chest was so constricted. Costa Rica was calling me again. But this time, it wasn't some soccer player that was drawing me, it was not the partying and fun, and I wasn't running from my family. It was a deeper calling, as though the Osa was my very soul, and it was summoning me back—to me. I could no longer ignore my intuition.

Cole came looking for me, and when he saw my face, he knew. He went back in, apologized to his friend, and we drove back to his house by the lake. We stood on the deck with an infinity of stars above us and looked at each other.

"Cole," I said.

"I know, Lana. This isn't going to work."

I was relieved that he said it. We didn't fight or argue, we both simply knew.

Two days later, I packed up and flew to Colorado. I lived with my sister and worked at the Powerhouse for four months until the rainy season in Costa Rica ended. Then I headed south again, more certain than ever that I wanted to be on the Osa.

PART III

WHALE

DIVING DEEP: CREATING FROM THE
INNER SOURCE

CHAPTER 27

When I arrived back in Costa Rica in January of 1993, I met with Don Michael in his new office, still on the second floor of the Colonial-style building in downtown San José, but now down the hall. It was a larger room with more wood accents, and was organized, papers neatly stacked and pens in a cup on the corner of his desk. He still wore thick glasses and an amused expression. We smiled broadly, happy to see each other.

He said there was an interim manager at the Corcovado Lodge Tent Camp who wasn't working out well. "Do you want to be manager?" he asked.

"Yes!" I said, elation brimming in my heart. I couldn't contain myself, so I got up from my chair and hugged him. I could hardly believe it. I had trusted my intuition to return to Costa Rica, and had my first job as a hotel manager.

I flew down to the tent camp two days later, so excited I could hardly sit still in the Cessna. After my time in Alaska, my sense of purpose was more focused than ever. I remembered what Dr. Reum said about everything I did pointing to my goal, and I could see that managing this lodge would teach me how to one day manage my own. I also wanted to do an impeccable job for Don Michael.

When I was a child living in faculty housing at Western State College where my mom and stepfather taught, I shared a bedroom with Jani and my stepsister, Devi. I slept on the top of a bunk bed, and against the adjacent wall hung a framed poster with an aphorism in bold print: "Anything worth doing is worth doing right." It was the first thing I saw when I got out of bed each morning, and I took its message to heart. This became my mantra as I arrived back at work and threw myself into the job.

I got up early every morning and did yoga on the deck of the tent camp's Hammock House bar, with a full view of the Pacific. Then I headed to my office where I was ready and organized for whatever the guests needed. I walked the departing guests to the airstrip, discussed with them what they liked and didn't like. I also picked up new guests; as we walked back to the lodge, I told them how things ran at the tent camp and briefed them on what they'd see in Corcovado National Park.

I kept the restaurant and cantina moving well, sometimes pitching in when the waiters were swamped. I organized my crew to keep the grass trimmed neatly and the beach clean of debris. I intervened when workers argued, calming them down and coming up with solutions. Late in the evening, I did the paperwork, running the guest tabs, tallying the profits, and gathering the cash, checks, and credit card receipts to put in the safe. When I finished, I was exhausted.

Some nights Carmen, the tent camp's cook and caretaker, came into the office.

"Lanita," she said, *"Venga—tienes que comer."*

I would suddenly feel how empty my stomach was and put aside my papers to follow her to the kitchen, where she served me a plate of food on the rough wooden table.

I wanted to do a good job for Don Michael and my employees. This was a practical school, where I was getting paid to learn. My dad always said, "Responsibility is freedom and freedom is responsibility," and I held this truth dear. I claimed all the responsibility for running the lodge. Don Michael barely ever came down to check on the business because he trusted me. Since we had the same birthday, and we were both Sagittarians, he understood that we were alike. We were blunt, honest, transparent, and workaholics. He relied on those qualities in me and knew that I was going to do a good job.

I was without a mate in the rainforest, and I knew that nature was my healer. So whenever I was not working, I spent time with my animal friends, and of course, the ocean. I walked on the beach in the moonlight, and that was when I remembered how much I loved Corcovado and its wildness. Crabs scurried near my feet and frogs croaked their sweet song. With the moon shining, the clouds took on a silvery glow and reflected off the ocean, turning it pewter. The waves slammed onto the beach with such force I could feel their power throughout my whole body.

As I worked toward my dream, a young Costa Rican named Fabio, who looked like a Greek god, stole my attention. He moved about my life, helping me when I didn't even know I needed it. He closed up the shop, swept the porch, and soon even walked me to my tent at the end of the night. He was as hard a worker as I was, and always considerate. Besides, he was adorable, with a lean, muscular body and a chiseled face, framed with long, wavy hair he wore in a ponytail. He was always ready to take care of me.

Fabio and I became good friends.

I was usually up late, organizing the office for the next day, and especially preparing the bills for the guests leaving in the morning. Fabio waited for me to finish before he turned off the generator. This was always a special moment, when the engine's rumbling stopped and the whole camp went dark and quiet, and we lit candles to read and finish out our evenings. I watched him move as he secured the doors and shutters against the weather and the animals of the park, where even pumas roamed.

We watched each other for months but knew we couldn't

touch because the company had a strict policy against employee fraternization. One full-moon night, instead of walking me to my tent, we detoured along the beach to the water's edge. Waves crashed and sand slipped between our toes. Soon this became a nightly ritual. We talked of our families and childhoods, of our disappointments and dreams.

I told him about growing up in a small town in Colorado, and he told me about growing up as the son of local gold miners. For many years his family lived in a tiny hut alongside the beach. When he was ten, a candle fell over and burned down their home. His father built a new house out of rich cristobal wood near a waterfall uphill from the tent camp. Many years later, that house also burned. Now Fabio lived in a tent at the lodge.

On an especially stunning night while we walked the beach, with a full view of the Milky Way lighting the sky, his fingertips brushed mine, sending tingles through my whole body. We held hands on our walks after that.

A few weeks later, on another full-moon night, the sky was so bright it could have been daytime. I loved those nights, especially on the beach, when the palms swayed and their shadows danced on the sand. I was absorbed in the beauty.

Fabio broke the silence. "My father tried to kill me."

"What? *¿Que pasó?*"

He paused. "*Es que* . . . when I was thirteen, I wanted freedom. I was the oldest kid, so I had to work hard for my dad with his gold mining. And I took care of my brothers and sisters. But, I would sneak away in the night to mess around with friends."

He paused again.

"*Sigue, sigue,*" I said, encouraging him to continue.

"One day we were working on a hillside, and my dad was angry because I was gone during the night. He had cussed me out twice already. Suddenly I looked up and saw a huge boulder rolling toward me. I ducked my head out of the way just in time. It scraped my back. 'Next time you think hard before you run away in the night,' my dad yelled."

Again Fabio paused. I stopped walking, turned, and hugged him. He held onto me so hard I could barely breathe, but I didn't let go. I sent all the love I had to his heart. He shook in my arms, crying, and then he relaxed.

We walked farther, hand in hand. Suddenly he started running toward the forest, tugging me along.

When we came under the darkness of a banana tree, he kissed me. Our tongues interlaced and our bodies pressed together so closely we could have been one person. There, hiding from the moon's bright light, I touched his cheek, still moist from tears. He ran his hand over my breast and pinched my nipple, sending a stream of golden light through me. At the very edge of the rainforest we made love, the most passionate I'd ever had. As we finished, the tide drew in, drenching us in cool water.

Suddenly, I pulled back from our kiss, realizing what we'd done. I was his supervisor, and he was only eighteen years old. I was thirty-three. We could both lose our jobs. I pushed away from his grasp, stood, and strode back to my tent.

In the coming weeks, I tried to fight my feelings for him. But one night we walked on the beach and talked, and it was completely romantic to be out there with the waves and trillions of stars. We kissed, and it was too fabulous to stop, so we surrendered to our passion once again.

Most nights at work, as evening came on, one of us would whisper, "I'll meet you there." He would turn off the generator and instead of going to my tent, I would climb a steep trail up through the forest. High above the lodge sat a charming vacant house with a thatched roof and a big balcony. The caretakers lived in a hut below, but Fabio knew a secret way inside the empty dwelling through a back door with broken hinges. Our whispers at the end of the day to meet referred to that place. It was a ten-minute hike, so we rushed up the hill separately and arrived panting. The house had a full view of the ocean, and we often stood staring out at the silver of the endless Pacific before we ravished each other.

We worked hard during the day, and in the evenings, we did what we must to be together. We went to the empty house or we made love on the beach. One afternoon, we were headed up to the house, but we stopped for a kiss. The passion overtook us, and we became like Tarzan and Jane in the forest. Fabio pressed me against the buttress roots of a ceiba tree, while we made hot, sweaty, slippery love.

On another day I had a meeting in Carate. Fabio and I set out in the late afternoon to ride horses to the little shop there. The owner wanted to talk with me. When night fell we rode back, galloping through the shallow water in the moonlight. We stopped at a secluded spot and made love on the beach, the sand covering our bodies so that we had to dunk in the waves to clean ourselves before completing the trip back.

The employees started to suspect what was happening. One night around 4:00 a.m., a guide for the lodge who was sleeping with one of the housekeepers snuck away from her tent. He bumped right into Fabio as he stole away from mine. They both stopped for a moment and their eyes met, but in the end they nodded in silent conspiracy and returned to their own tents.

Little by little word got around, but we still tried to keep the affair hush-hush. The employees were loyal to me so they didn't gossip about the relationship beyond the lodge. They knew how much Fabio and I cared for each other, and they seemed to respect that. This freed us up a bit, so that Fabio came to my tent late most nights and left early in the mornings.

We worked every day straight for a month and then took five

days off to go traveling. We couldn't go to my house in Santa Ana because I had a roommate, and we couldn't go to any public places because we needed to keep our relationship secret. Instead we went to Manuel Antonio National Park and to a mountain inn near Palmares, where we could relax and be together. We got to know these places deeply, mostly because Fabio was a native, and that opened locals' doors to us.

I was still planning for my own lodge as I worked as the interim manager at Corcovado Lodge Tent Camp. I wanted land on the beach, since that was what tourists seem to like. One day I found a parcel near the tent camp, with the same stunning, black beach. To research purchasing it, I flew across the Golfo Dulce to the municipality in Golfito, where government records sat in an archive.

Unfortunately, I learned that though the land was for sale, its borders were not well-defined, creating confusion over where the government-owned beach stopped and the private land began. The next day I heard that my boss Don Michael thought he owned it. I didn't want any conflict with him, and I didn't want to spend years trying to sort out boundary issues, so I let it go. A few days later I learned that Don Michael ultimately was not the owner, but that didn't alter my decision.

It was hard for me to let that one go. For days after as I walked to work, I dragged my feet in the sand. At my desk, I listlessly completed my chores. My employees knew I was struggling, so they were extra patient and kind. One day, one of the lodge workers, Pedro, came to me and said he had land he was looking to sell.

"Really?" I said, growing excited. The next day, Pedro and I walked along the beach to Carate and then climbed an old gold-mining road that traversed through a rocky river valley. As I hiked, I grew more and more doubtful. I really wanted beachfront property.

This place was completely forested and nearly inaccessible, but I continued anyway.

Finally, after hiking for an hour, we stopped on a mesa surrounded by rainforest. The grass stood so tall I couldn't even see the Pacific down below, and I heard many bird calls. When I looked around, I realized we were in an orchard. Avocado trees rambled across one area, mango and cacao trees in another, while lemon and mandarin trees stretched to the sky next to us. I climbed farther along the trail and even found a cashew tree. There were a hundred fruit and nut trees in all, Pedro said. Two small abandoned structures, one a house, the other a shed, sat at the orchard's edges.

Pedro explained that an earlier owner of the land got it from a gold mining company. That owner had to make the land produce, so he burned the forest, planted the trees, and lived here with his family. Years later, Pedro and his friend Chon wanted to buy the land, so they mined gold from the same hole that had been closed down. They offered the owner gold from his own land, and he took it. For many years Pedro and his friend lived on the land, but when they started working at the tent camp, they moved over there. They were no longer using the land.

We climbed higher into primary or old-growth rainforest, which had never been cut or burned. The area had subtle but important differences from the rest. Most of the trees were huge, with thick trunks like gothic pillars. It took trees like that some sixty years to form a canopy, and most of them were hundreds of years old. High above us, their tops billowed outward in large umbrella-shaped crowns. A secondary forest will have many younger trees with narrower crowns, and various pioneer plants such as bamboo and smothering vines.

Pedro explained that the property was seventy-five percent primary forest. The number hit me in the chest. *Wow*, I thought, *that is poignant.* I looked up and saw the life of the canopy, rich and sprawling. I could also hear the creek that ran through the land, a sweet sound as it frolicked over rocks. Below lay the orchard and the azure ocean, which I could see from up there, and even hear faintly as the waves broke on the shore.

I have to protect this, I said to myself. And then I thought, *I need to have this. It's just so beautiful. I want to live here, and I have to build something to share, and that is my dream, to build my lodge.*

I realized this was the place.

In the coming years, this land would be my nemesis and my savior, but that day it was the budding manifestation of my dream.

CHAPTER 28

Four months later, I embarked on the task of purchasing the property. I flew to San José and headed to the Banco America Central, where I had a savings account. Much of my money was from the farm investment I made in 1991. After three years my partner agreed to buy me out of that deal. My father and sister had invested in my new business, and that money was also in the account.

I was a bit uneasy about purchasing rainforest in the Osa. Everything there was so unstructured. Even my offer to Pedro seemed like some kind of dream. The day after I saw the land, I was working in my office. When Pedro passed through, I asked, "How much do you want for the land?"

He paused and moved closer to my desk. A subtle smile played across his lips, as though he were trying to contain his enthusiasm. "Thirty thousand dollars," he said with conviction.

"Hmmm." I pretended to consider spending that much. "Will you take twenty thousand?" I asked. That was all I had. I gripped my hands together under the table, hoping he would say yes.

He tipped his head to the side and narrowed his eyes, as though calculating. I knew this was just a ruse as well because no one could really know what that land was worth.

I squirmed in my chair and my heart beat fast.

He bit his bottom lip and nodded his head. *"Sí, por supuesto."*

I leapt up and ran around the desk to hug him. He remained a bit stiff, but I could tell he was overjoyed.

Even as I pulled my money from the bank, I was certain of this step in my life. My excitement blew away any other concerns. My intuition was telling me this was the right choice, and I would move forward undaunted.

The attorney I had used on the other real estate transaction, Ingrid Reischfledger, was helping me with this one. She told me to get my money so I did, all of it in cash. It was intense to withdraw so much in dollars from a Costa Rican bank. I carried the three small paper bags of bills, amounting to $20,000, in a backpack hanging over my shoulder. I knew that I needed to keep it safe for this transaction, so I called my old flame, Oscar, who was still driving a taxi. He took me to Ingrid's office, where Pedro and I were to sign the papers. He was kind and businesslike as we cruised through the busy streets to San Pedro, one of the many suburban towns surrounding San José. He said he'd wait for me, and I thanked him.

When I entered Ingrid's office, she greeted me and led me to her desk. "Lana, I have to talk to you before we sign the papers," she said.

Her office sat on the first floor of a historic home and was tidy and full of Old-World charm, though it smelled of cigarettes from her chain smoking. She looked seriously at me. Ingrid was about my age, so we had an open rapport. As well as helping me with the last real estate transaction, she had represented me on other matters, so I trusted her. Like me, as a businesswoman in this male-dominated country, she had to work hard and believe in herself, which she did. She also believed in me.

I listened closely.

"Lana, we're not going to give them all the money, because the land isn't titled yet."

I nodded, feeling my heart shrivel. I wanted the whole transaction to be complete today so I could own the land.

"We're only going to give them a third of the twenty-thousand," she said. "It's going to be in cash, and they've never had this much money in their lives." She raised her brows at me.

"Okay. Fine." I grasped what she meant. Pedro and his friend Chon were small-town Ticos who lived from paycheck to paycheck, probably without any savings or investments. In fact, Chon didn't even have a bank account. The scale of this transaction was larger than anything they'd ever experienced financially.

I took the money out of my pack and counted out the $6,666.67, using some smaller bills and change from my purse. I wound a rubber band around the bills and placed them and the change in one bag. I put the remaining money in another bag.

We headed into the conference room, an elegant space with crystal chandeliers and Italian tile floors. Pedro and Chon and their wives sat on the far side of an oval mahogany table. I greeted them happily and sat across from them.

"Lana is only going to pay a third of the money today," Ingrid told them. "She will give you the rest in cash when the land becomes titled, because we're not really sure how long that's going to take."

Pedro nodded but looked skeptical. His usually joyous face seemed to close a bit; his lips formed a thin, straight line. I pulled out the paper bag with the cash, and took the bundle of money from it, one-third of the total price. His expression softened.

Ingrid put the papers in front of them, and they took some time to read through them. I tapped my foot on the tile and fidgeted in my seat. Some part of me feared that the deal would crumble before it ever began. Finally, Pedro and Chon signed.

Ingrid passed the papers across to me. I looked over them and down at the line with my name printed beneath and could hardly believe that this was happening. It was truly the beginning of a whole new part of my life, a target that I had been aiming for since before I even set foot in Costa Rica. To honor the moment, I took my time signing my name. Then, with a big smile, I slid the money across the table to Pedro and Chon. I was happy that it went to them, who I respected and appreciated.

Gingerly, Pedro lifted the bundle and change from the table and stuffed it all in an old leather saddlebag.

We all sat there for a few moments as Ingrid gathered up the papers.

"*Vamos a almorzar!*" I said, figuring we should celebrate over lunch.

"*Sí, de fijo qué sí,*" Pedro agreed.

Ingrid said she had work to do, so the rest of us crammed into Oscar's taxi and headed to downtown San José, which had an interesting mix of Colonial-style buildings and modern high-rises. I took them to lunch at an Italian restaurant in a historic home, where we feasted on pasta and pizza. Pedro and Chon and their wives had likely never been to a big city. They gazed with awe out the windows at the tall buildings and all the people and cars bustling by. Meanwhile, I was so excited I mostly picked at my pasta primavera. I looked out at the street where people dressed in bright clothing strolled along, and I couldn't get over the fact that I owned land in this country. I was truly a local in Costa Rica now.

Pedro was more jovial than I'd ever seen him. I asked what he would do with the money. He looked at his wife, then back at me and said he didn't know. Chon said he was going to buy property in La Palma, just north of Puerto Jimenez, and build a house.

"*Qué bueno!*" I exclaimed.

After lunch we dropped them at the bus station and Oscar took me to the bank where I intended to re-deposit the cash. I put my piles of money on the counter between a clerk and myself. She looked at them, paused, and then excused herself. She returned accompanied by a rotund man with a thick mustache. He introduced himself as the bank president and invited me to his office.

We sat across from each other on either side of his broad,

immaculate desk. He explained that he knew I had made a sizable withdrawal that morning, and that he had a proposition for me. In Spanish, he asked, "Would you like to put your money in Costa Rican *colónes,* instead of dollars?" He paused, rubbing his fingers over his mustache.

All this attention was making me a bit nervous, but I looked out the window at the blue sky, and my heart settled.

"If you put your money in *colónes* now, I will give you a thirty-two percent interest rate," he said. When I looked at him skeptically, he explained that the bank prospered by loaning dollars to American corporations.

My head reeled. Just by putting my dollars in *colónes* I would earn fifteen times the interest I was previously earning?

I barely hesitated before pushing the money across to him. "You're on."

During the next year as I waited for the land to be titled, I continued to work for Don Michael, and to learn. Fabio and I snuck away from the tent camp whenever we could to spend time together and bask in the land's beauty. As I walked guests along the beach to catch the plane to return to San José, I would look up at the mesa and say, "That's my land and someday I'm going to have a lodge up there, and I'd love for you to come visit."

One day I took a young couple from the US up to my property. We explored the land and found three towering waterfalls. We swam and floated in the pools while the mist caressed our skin. Hummingbirds dipped and zoomed, and monkeys swung from branch to branch above us. I became elated as I realized I was already living my dream.

Another time Fabio and I brought up a guest named Jan Murdoch, a friend of mine from Crested Butte. As we hiked along the river, a *fer-de-lance,* Costa Rica's most venomous snake, slithered out from the base of a baco tree. Before I knew what was happening, Fabio had ducked down and grabbed it, and held it by the head out in front of him, its four-foot-long body writhing. Fabio smiled courageously, as he stood there in his rubber boots, a machete hanging from his hip. He looked like Tarzan, with his muscular arms and legs and tan skin. I knew that he had done this hundreds of times, ever since he was a kid, and that he loved the adrenaline rush, but I didn't like it one bit.

"Fabio," I yelled, "*¿Qué está haciendo? ¡Es tan peligroso!* You can't endanger Jan and me—and yourself—this way."

His smile dwindled. He stepped into the forest and released the snake.

We came to the land, where I showed Jan the house, which was small but crafted from exquisite cristobal wood, a hardwood streaked with red and yellow grains. Even the toilet seat in the outdoor bathroom was made of this wood. The kitchen/dining area was open air, like a covered porch, with views down the valley. A wood-burning cookstove and a small table sat on one side. Through a doorway were two bedrooms, one with a few boards on the dirt floor to serve as a bed but no mattress. In those rooms, casement windows opened out to the forest. The outdoor shower was surrounded by plastic with no roof, so during storms, we showered luxuriously in the warm Costa Rican rain. Though I wasn't living on the land yet, I would play in the waterfalls, shower off in the open air, and then head back to the lodge.

A low wall stood next to the house that was so covered with cherry tomatoes it looked like a Christmas tree. We all ate the fruit, laughing as the juice ran down our chins. As we hiked along the mesa, I pointed out at least forty pineapple plants, along with many avocado and mango trees. Jan was in awe. When we got to the top of the hill where the primary forest began, I couldn't get over the feeling of being in a fairytale, and I was a princess. Just to make sure it was all real, I touched my hand to the trunk of a kapok tree. The feeling of rough bark assured me I was not dreaming.

I returned to the US for a three-week visit to see my sister and dad. Occasionally I made this trip, just to remain in touch with them. I stayed in Denver with my dad and didn't even go to Gunnison. I didn't want to take the time. On the flight from Denver back to Costa Rica, I noticed that my heart was heavy because I hadn't spoken with my mother for so long.

Fortunately, I got distracted from the sadness by an adorable man sitting next to me on the flight. He was short, with blond hair, blue eyes, a fit body, and the air of an adventurer. He introduced himself as George Schmidt and told me that he was headed to Costa Rica to bum around with his surfboard. "I'll be camping on the beach," he said with childlike enthusiasm.

I told him I had some land in the Osa. Then I had a brilliant idea. "There's nothing on the land but a little house, a shed, and lots of fruit trees," I said. "But if you want to stay there, you can." When the plane landed, I told him where he could find me if he decided to take me up on the offer. I hoped he would because it would be helpful to have someone there to look after the place.

He showed up in the tent camp lobby a month later. I was so happy to see him, I rushed around my desk and hugged him. He hugged back, a bit tentatively. That evening, Fabio and I hiked with him up to the land, where we helped him get settled in the little house.

George didn't just live there, he inhabited the place, made it his own, and did improvements. Near the house, he built a shrubbery arch of hibiscus, which blazed with red flowers. He pulled weeds in the vegetable garden and cleared away vines and plants to expand it. When Fabio and I went up every five days or so, he played guitar for us and sang songs about love. All he really wanted from life was to surf, play guitar, and sing, so the land was perfect for him. Occasionally, I sent him some rice and beans, a gift of appreciation.

One day I received a note that he wrote and gave to a gold miner who was coming down to Carate. It said, "Lana, I saw five toucans in one tree and six scarlet macaws in another." I turned it over to look at the back, but that was all the note said. I chuckled at his uncomplicated appreciation for the rainforest.

He lived up there for four months by himself.

Shortly after George bade us farewell, Ingrid, my attorney, sent word that the land was now titled. With the news that I was an official owner of land in the rainforest, I danced around my office.

My next day off, I drove to San José to withdraw money to make the final payment to Pedro and Chon. My money had sat in the bank for a year earning 32 percent interest. I now had a bit of a cushion so I was pleased that I didn't have to withdraw all my savings. The money sat next to me on the seat on my way back to Puerto Jimenez, and I couldn't wait to trade it for that spectacular land. I deposited it in the bank there.

The next day, Pedro, Chon, and Chon's wife, Candida, met me at the bank. We sat at the president's desk with the manager, who handed me two cashier's checks. I signed them with a flourish and pushed them across the desk to Pedro and Chon. They each picked up the checks and quietly stared at them. It was so much money for them, so I just let them take it in while I smiled at Candida.

I was buzzing with the excitement of finally having titled land on the Osa Peninsula, so I jumped up and slid my chair in. "¡Gracias!" I said to the bank manager, Pedro, Chon, and Candida.

They got up, their eyes glassy with excitement. Pedro and Chon fumbled to put the checks in their wallets. Once they did, we all walked out into the sunshine. I wanted to skip along the road, but I restrained myself, and we all headed on our way.

I used the interest money I had made to hire a young couple, Joselito and Soila, who had a five-year-old son, Hereld, to stay up on the land and start preparing for the construction. Hereld was adorable, always wanting to help.

Fabio and I made a map of where the buildings would go, so the couple had an idea of what to do when we were not there. They cleaned around the fruit trees and cut away the weeds where I envisioned the *rancho grande* and the bungalows would go. They planted more fruit trees and some flowers that would enhance the grounds. They chopped down the grass that was taller than I was, and I glimpsed my first view of the ocean from the *rancho grande* site. But the most important thing for me was that they were on the land to protect it from hunters and gold miners.

For the next year, I worked hard at the tent camp, but each week it seemed to need more maintenance. One day an older gentleman guest came to me while I was fixing a door hinge in one of the bathrooms. He had a head of brilliant silver hair and deep blue eyes.

"Lana, I want to tell you something," he said.

I stopped working and faced him.

"My daughter was here last year, and she told me I had to come here to see this place, because of you."

I smiled.

"You run a really tight ship," he said. "My daughter also told me it was the most beautiful place she had ever been, and my son came here three months ago, and he told me the same thing." He looked me in the eye. "Now I'm here, and I see that they were right. You do run a tight ship."

I nodded and said thank you.

"But," he continued, "to be blunt, your ship is falling apart."

My knees grew weak. I'd tried to hide this. The doors were

falling off the hinges, the main lodge roof leaked, and the canvas of some of the tents had worn thin. "I know, and I have told the owner this, but he never wants to put money back into the place."

He nodded. "That's what I figured."

"Thank you for your honesty," I said.

He smiled a bit bleakly and strolled toward his tent.

I resumed screwing in the hinge, frustrated because I really did work hard and I was proud of the place. I hated to see it deteriorating.

I slept restlessly that night, the man's words swimming circles in my head. At dawn, I realized his critical view of the lodge was meant to be. He was respectful, but he had delivered an important truth.

What am I doing? I asked as I pulled on my sundress. I was putting so much hard work into the place, and without real upgrades, my energy was wasted. I was extremely thankful for Costa Rica Expeditions because it had supported me for nine years, first as a sales agent, then as a guide, later as assistant manager of the lodge, and now as manager. I was especially grateful for the seven years I'd spent here on the beach.

But that morning my intuition was speaking to me again. I got a strong sense that it was time to focus on my own project. I strode to the office, and there on the shelf in a frame sat a quote from Goethe. Whenever someone called me on the radio I picked up the receiver and saw the quote, but this day, it seemed to say, "Lana, it's time."

"Whatever you can do or dream you can, begin it; boldness has genius, power, and magic in it."

I read it over and over and felt its energy light my being.

I knew I could continue to work to make more money to build my lodge, but now that I owned the land, I had been thinking about this creation constantly. Every time I walked from the airstrip to the lodge, I looked up to the mesa, and my whole being lit up with the irresistible pull of my destiny.

That day, when Fabio came into the office, he cocked his head to the side and narrowed his eyes at me, likely because I was nearly levitating with excitement.

"Fabio, it's time," I said.

"Tiempo para qué?" he asked.

"Time for us to build my lodge."

CHAPTER 29

A month later, when the rainy season started, I wrote to Don Michael thanking him for everything he had taught me and the opportunity to work for him. I said that I was headed back to the US and was embarking on a new leg of my path and wouldn't be working for him next season. When I sealed the letter, I felt the importance of the missive. In it my future was shifting, and this represented yet one more commitment to my dream. I was letting go of what had sustained me for nearly a decade. When the next charter flight arrived to take guests from Carate back to San José, I gave the letter to the pilot to pass along to Don Michael.

A few days later, on a charter flight in, I received a return letter from Don Michael. He said he appreciated all the work I'd done for him through the years, and that no matter what, he would always be my friend. He tendered an offer that I found enticing. He wanted me to manage his lodge in Monte Verde. I smiled when I read this. The lodge sat on the edge of the Monte Verde Cloud Forest Reserve, a thriving and fecund home to the ocelot, the colorfully plumed quetzal, and the endangered golden toad. The offer tempted me, but I declined.

I was married to Corcovado.

In May of 1997, Fabio and I flew to Denver, where my dad picked us up at the airport and took us to stay at his apartment. The next night we sat down with him over pizza and discussed our plans. Dad was full of ideas. In recent years he had purchased, renovated, and sold several old homes and apartments, so he had know-how and connections in the building industry.

With childlike enthusiasm, he pulled out a notepad and pen and made a list for us. We would need a cement mixer, lumber, tools, toilets, sinks, faucets, light fixtures, cleaning supplies, linens, towels, and so many more items that, by the end of the evening, filled pages. Supplies like these would be difficult to find in Costa Rica, and exorbitantly expensive. Thus, we would need a truck and some kind of trailer to carry them down through Central America.

Jani came to Denver to pick up Fabio and me, and we drove to Crested Butte, where we house-sat for my old boyfriend Tommy Martinez's sister Pearl and her husband while they vacationed in Hawaii. To earn money, we worked on the house, applying linseed oil to the walls of their expansive log cabin. When they returned, we moved in with Jani and her husband, Tom. They had a new brick house, and we slept in sleeping bags on their wood floor since they hadn't yet bought furniture. I went back to waiting tables at the Paradise Café for breakfast and the Powerhouse for dinner, pulling in lucrative tips.

Fabio continued oiling Pearl's log cabin and doing odd jobs for Jani and Tom. His biggest project at Jani's was to prune towering cottonwoods. Trained by trimming coconut trees in Costa Rica, Fabio shimmied up and hacked off unsightly branches with his trusted machete. He was like a monkey up in the trees hanging from one arm as he worked. Through all our hard work, we quickly saved enough money to buy the equipment and materials we would need to build the lodge.

It was summertime in Colorado, and on our occasional days off I took Fabio hiking in the mountains and swimming at Blue Mesa Reservoir. One day while there, as evening set in, we got chilled because even in summer the water was cold. Using the machete that Fabio kept with him even here, we chopped down some sagebrush and put it into a firepit at a picnic area. We lit the fire and it quickly caught. Too quickly, it turned out.

The sagebrush was so dry that it flared as though doused with lighter fluid. Suddenly it ignited into an inferno, and the wind picked up, lifting one of the bushes, sending it rolling across the picnic area. Fabio grabbed his denim jacket, ran, and threw it over the flaming tumbleweed. I joined him and pitched dirt around it. Finally, the fire died out. I hadn't been back to Colorado for so long, I had forgotten how easily things could burn in a dry year. We were accustomed to the rainforest, where everything was so wet that fires were rare.

I paused to look out across all the dry brush that stretched for miles into forest and felt stunned by what could have happened. If the flames had spread, the whole area could have caught fire, even the forest, and such a disaster would have completely altered the course of our lives. We looked at each other wide-eyed, gleefully relieved to have averted disaster, our hands and faces marked by dirt and soot.

One day I called my mother to tell her I was back. We had barely communicated in the past months because I had been so busy, and because I had found relief in having distance from her and Don, who had so overpowered my childhood. When she answered the phone I could hear the relief in her voice at hearing from me. She invited us to a barbecue at the house in Gunnison. She wanted to meet Fabio and, of course, to see me. We arrived in the evening with a bottle of red wine. Mom immediately hugged me, and she held on much longer than her usual quick embrace. I held on too. It felt so good to be near her, to smell her familiar scent.

And yet, once we let go, we both stepped back, a strange unspoken tension hanging between us. She shook Fabio's hand. "It's nice to meet you," she said.

"It is nice to meet you," he replied, his Spanish accent apparent.

Don stepped into the living room. He took one look at Fabio's hair pulled back in a ponytail and a wisp of disdain crossed his face. But then he zeroed in on me, grasping me in a warm hug. Fabio held out the wine bottle, and Don took it and looked at the label.

"We'll open it now," he said. He smiled and shook Fabio's hand. "Welcome to our home."

We headed out to the backyard, where the river ran. My chest filled with emotion for all the years I had spent in this place, helping to install the lawn, watching the trout and minnows swim, and marveling at the blue herons lifting off the water. Don took his place at the grill, where he uncovered a pan full of steaks and a veggie burger for me, while Mom returned to the kitchen to get the salad and baked potatoes. Fabio nestled in beside me, took my hand, and together we gazed out at the river and mountains.

"Qué bonito," he said in my ear, and the sound of his deep voice brought me back to the present.

We sat on garden chairs at a table and passed the food around. It was all so American—this food, the big house, and the dry Rocky Mountain air—that it felt both strangely foreign and way too familiar. The talk was superficial, as though we were all gingerly tiptoeing through each other's lives. We told them of our plans to gather materials and drive through Central America. They told us how much they enjoyed last winter in Maui, and how they planned to spend every winter there now that they had retired.

Relief at their news settled my heart. I knew they had wanted to spend winters somewhere warm, and I had hoped it wouldn't be Costa Rica because that was my new home. "I'm so glad you found a warm place that you enjoy," I said.

"Yes, we love it there," Mom said, and Don nodded in agreement.

We all sat quietly, and I listened to the river and felt the cool of dusk settling in.

"I heard you're a good, hard worker," Don said to Fabio. "I appreciate that. Just take care of our Lana."

"Yes, of course," Fabio said.

"If there's anything we can do…" Mom said to me as we washed the dishes.

A flutter of fear swirled in my heart, and I glanced back through the living room and saw that Don and Fabio stood on the deck talking. I brought my attention back to the kitchen. "Actually, Mom, no pressure, but I am looking for investors, so if you wanted to—"

"Don would never go for that," she said.

Even though I had little expectation, her quick response felt like a door slamming between us. I didn't press the point. Instead, I helped her load the dishwasher, grateful for our time together.

"Thank you for the lovely evening," I said to them both at the door as we departed. They hugged me, and to my surprise, they hugged Fabio too.

My dad bought a '72 Chevy pickup for us from an old fisherman in Wyoming; Fabio and I drove to Denver to pick it up from him. It sat in the parking lot of Dad's apartment, and I must admit I was a little disappointed when I first saw it. It was black and lime green, with one white door. It looked like it was in the middle of an identity crisis, pieced together from five other vehicles. Dad was determined to sell me on its assets: "It's a standard transmission, which tends to be most reliable, and though the outside is pretty darn ugly, the engine, the chassis, and the tires are all in great working order."

He had another surprise for us: a horse trailer he had bought from a local rancher. It was made to carry two horses, and it, too, he assured us, was completely sound.

I hugged him and thanked him.

When we returned to Crested Butte, we spent what little free time we had sanding the truck by hand. We took it down to its primer coat, and then we used auto spray paint to make it robin's egg blue. We painted the trailer, too, staying with its original cream color. By the time we were done, we had a snazzy duo that would present an upstanding image for all those border crossings ahead of us.

My next task was to teach Fabio to drive. In Carate, he never had an opportunity or need to learn, but now he did. We spent hours on forest roads in the mountains outside Crested Butte jerking along as he grew accustomed to easing up on the clutch after shifting. One time, we nearly ran off the road because his attention stayed too long on the gearshift. Soon he caught on, and he grinned broadly as we sped along the dusty roads.

In September, we gathered a group together at a friend's house in Gunnison to talk about the trip. Nine of us, including Fabio and I, showed up. We sat on couches and chairs and the floor of a big living room and drank beer. I told them about the fun and challenges of driving through Central America. Rebecca, a woman I worked with at the Paradise, was intent on driving down, and my old friend Greg, who I knew from teaching skiing in Crested Butte, also wanted to come. Everyone was excited, but by October, six of us were game to go.

We bought dried beans, dried fruit, trail mix, rice, and a water purifier. We got a cover for the pickup bed and set up a mattress underneath so we could sleep off the ground. We purchased tarps, pans, and cooking utensils. I stuffed almost everything I owned into five army duffel bags. One evening, scanning an atlas, we planned our route.

We were ready.

Late one night, after I finished at the Powerhouse and Fabio had showered away the dirt from his pruning job, I called him over to where I was lying on my sleeping bag with a big piece of paper in front of me. *"Fabio, es tiempo."*

"¿Tiempo para qué?" he asked.

"It's time to make our plan for the lodge," I said.

I had previously sketched a very rough outline for the workers on my land; now we needed to get specific. I drew the boundaries of the land. *"Mira, el rancho grande."* I pointed to a clearing at the center.

He smiled and snuggled in next to me. *"Perfecto."* He smelled of Dr. Bronner's peppermint soap. "Where will the bungalows go?"

"Aquí hay uno," I said, pointing just above the *rancho grande.* *"Aquí hay otro, y otro."* I pointed to various other places on the map.

"Mejor allá," he said, pointing a little farther over for the third one.

"Okay, okay," I said. "Yes, good idea."

I drew in the bungalows, little round houses with thatched roofs, and made winding trails between them and the *rancho grande.* I also drew a trail that went higher, toward the top of the property, where one day I hoped to build a yoga platform, and higher yet, into the primary forest, so the guests could hike with ease to that spectacular place.

Though quiet and not highly educated, Fabio had a keen sense of engineering principles and he knew the rainforest better than most of us know our own bodies. That night, after I fell asleep, he took the plan and drew a series of ditches to drain the rainwater so it wouldn't flood the *rancho grande* or the bungalows. He sketched in where we would use cristobal wood—the floors, pillars, and deck—making them strong and beautiful. And he converted all the measurements from feet to meters, so that our Costa Rican workers would understand.

A few days later, my mom called and asked me to meet her at Jani's house in Gunnison. She didn't say why, but I went. Mom and

I sat on lawn furniture in Jani's yard, which was a bit cold but free from eavesdropping ears.

"Lana, I want to give you some money for your inheritance. I want to see what you can do with it, rather than wait until I'm dead." Her face was softer than usual, her demeanor less guarded.

I sat for a moment and looked at her, sensing that while I'd been away, she had changed, as had I.

She seemed less driven, calmer, her movements more flowing. I had become more accepting of people's differences, their goals and passions, because of my time traveling through Central America and working with such a broad range of people in Costa Rica. My mom valued education and intellect, and she had taught me to do the same. But now I was reaching deeper into my own heart to find an openness and sense of connectedness with the world that she could never really offer me. And yet, that was okay.

"Wow, Mom, thank you."

She handed me a folded check, and when I opened it, my heart beat so hard I felt it pulse in my neck. It was written out to me for $50,000.

I hugged her. "I can't thank you enough, Mom." My voice shook with excitement. "You won't be disappointed. I promise."

The following week, Fabio and I drove to Denver to see my dad. He had great news for us. He'd bought a cement mixer and a tool chest with drawers that held any tool we could imagine, from a hammer to wrenches to screwdrivers and a tape measure. He had also purchased new toilets and sinks for the *rancho grande* and the bungalows.

"Dad, I want to pay you back for all of it," I said.

"No, definitely not," he said, smiling fondly at me. "I just want to help." He immediately launched into more planning. "We'll put the stuff that you won't need right away in a container to ship down to you." At that time Costa Rica, intent on building a tourism industry, was waiving taxes on new goods coming into the country, so this would save us thousands of dollars.

"Thank you so much!" I said, squealing with delight.

We loaded up in Dad's gray Mercedes Benz, me sitting shotgun and Fabio in back, and headed to a Broncos football game. As we drove through the city, Fabio and I marveled at the tall buildings, which seemed so foreign to what we were accustomed to, living on the beach in tents.

Dad turned to me with an excited look on his face. "Lana, how full is your cup?" he asked.

I considered his question. After all our discussions and groundwork over the past months, I knew he was referring not to my happiness cup, but to my project. In my head, I tallied up the check from Mom and the tools and materials Dad had given us, along with "Little Blue" and the horse trailer. I also thought of the hard work Fabio and I had done to put money in the bank.

"I think my cup is a little over half full."

He nodded. "Then you should do it."

His words plucked a deep chord within me. Even though Fabio and I had done all the preparation to begin building the lodge, a part of me had been unable to really fathom it. How could I, a thirty-five-year-old Colorado girl, build a lodge in a foreign country and expect people to come? I could lose everything—my parents' money, my money, everything I had. I could struggle for years and not pull it off. I felt the void of potential failure ahead, as if I was about to cross a deep chasm on a tightrope. *Am I really ready to stake my future on this fantasy?*

To even begin, I had to embrace a whole new view of myself. My mom and dad's belief in me shored up my determination.

I took a deep breath and said, "Yes. I'm ready."

That day, I made the commitment to leap from a cliff into the unknown and to trust that all would be okay. It seemed that every leap I had taken in my life, from attending the leadership conference in high school, to embarking on Operation Raleigh, to heading to Alaska after the Exxon Valdez spill, had taught me the importance of taking risks and following my intuition. I knew I was on the right track.

Over the course of a month, Fabio and I drove with our four friends in two trucks, south through Central America. When we crossed into Costa Rica, we continued driving, over the mountains and through valleys, all the while hoping that Little Blue's brakes, which we fixed in Panajachel, Guatemala, continued to hold. They did just that. Finally one night after eight hours on the road, we arrived in Puerto Jimenez at Fabio's parents' house. It was a small place, so we set up camp outside.

The next day, we left the horse trailer and set out with the truck bed loaded. I had a bold ambition for the day: to get all our gear up onto my land. But the twenty-six-mile drive from Puerto Jimenez to Carate was so muddy and full of potholes my plans quickly changed. After only fifteen minutes of driving, the tires got bogged in a river, and I realized the task was going to be even harder than I had imagined.

While I was at the wheel, everyone got out and pushed the truck. The tires spun in the muddy bottom, splattering everyone. We grew hot, sweaty, and frustrated as we rocked the truck back and forth. Finally the tires gained traction and they whirred out of the muck. Everyone piled back in and we continued.

I'd been in touch with Urbano, the wrangler at the Corcovado Lodge Tent Camp who had become a close friend while I worked there. I told him I needed to buy a horse, so when we arrived in Carate he was there with a beautiful bay who I named Luna because the day I got her, the moon was full.

To my great joy, Urbano also brought four other horses from the camp, along with their pack saddles to carry supplies on the steep forest path to my land. *"Gracías, Urbano. ¡Gracías!"* I couldn't express enough gratitude.

I was also grateful for my experience with horses as we loaded them up with our suitcases, backpacks, sleeping bags, tents, bags of cement, shovels, pickaxes, sledge hammers, and rakes. There was enough left in the truck for a few more loads, so we parked Little Blue under some trees and headed up the valley.

Luna, a strong young mare, was as determined as I was. Immediately, she seemed to grasp what we were doing. She walked so enthusiastically along the trail, I could barely keep up with her. We led the way on the old gold-mining road, while Fabio, Urbano, and my friends Jesse, Greg, Graham, and Rebecca led the other horses.

When we arrived at my land, tears filled my eyes as I was struck by what a stunning mesa it was, with all the fruit trees surrounding the clearing where the lodge would be, and the primary forest towering above. Joselita and Soila and little Hereld greeted us, elated to see us. With great fanfare, they showed us all the work they'd done, planting birds-of-paradise, heliconia, and red bromeliad flowers, along with more fruit trees. They had also cleaned up the land, cutting away brush and vines.

I paced around the property, unable to settle down, my body full of energy. It was a nervous excitement, a mixture of elation at being there and fear of all the unknowns. It was the beginning of our work on the land that I'd dreamed into being. The future felt unmoored, illusory, nearly impossible. I reached out and grabbed hold of a mango tree, its rough bark solid under my fingertips. A toucan soared above the forest canopy, while a grasshopper leapt onto my foot. No, I realized, this was no dream.

This was real.

Urbano, Fabio, Greg, and Jesse took the horses down and brought up two more loads. Meanwhile, Rebecca, Graham, and I erected the tents and Soila prepared dinner. Over the woodstove in the house she cooked pork, beans, and rice, and warmed corn tortillas. We iced beer in the cooler we had brought up on the horses.

Once the last haul was unloaded, we sat on logs around a fire and ate dinner. I swear nothing had ever tasted so good as those tortillas with beans and rice.

After dinner, Urbano readied all the horses except Luna for the trip back to the tent camp. I thanked him so many times, he finally just turned and headed down the trail.

Soon, night settled in and I was full and happy, with the fire crackling, casting a warm glow on the faces of my friends. Fabio took my hand and held it, and I reached over and kissed him, savoring the faint flavor of *frijoles* and *cerveza.*

A screech owl squawked, the sound so loud and close it resonated in my chest. The shriek pulled me away from this harmonious scene, and my mind went to the access road and the challenge it would be to build it; to the lodge foundation, pillars, and roof; and to the bungalows, with their doors and beds and bathrooms. *How will I ever construct a lodge from nothing?* I sensed the dark untamable forest beyond this circle of firelight. But there was something more: a towering force approaching, like a monster wave that was coming to crush me, swallow me whole, chew me up, and spit me out.

I breathed deeply, pushed that thought away, took a swig of beer, and returned to the happy, magical moment in the rainforest with my loved ones.

PART IV

HUMMINGBIRD

RAINBOW OF PROMISE: ACCOMPLISHES THAT
WHICH SEEMS IMPOSSIBLE

CHAPTER 30

I awakened to howler monkeys roaring through the misty dawn, and my mind immediately churned. *Where to start, what to do?* A part of me wanted to snuggle in with Fabio and stay in the peace of this moment, surrounded by the rich cristobal wood covering the walls and floor, but I pulled on my yoga pants and headed out into the day.

I stood in the meadow near the house and imagined the towering roof of the *rancho grande*, its sides open to the breeze. I also imagined its deck, with a view over the forest canopy toward the ocean far below. This day we would stake out the perimeter, and I couldn't wait to embark on the first step of construction.

We had used the horses to bring up everything we had brought with us from Colorado, but now we needed more muscle to build a road so that I could drive Little Blue up, and one day, guests could come too. I rented a tractor with a grading blade driven by a man named Chato, and hired Fabio's dad, Martin, who was a building contractor. He was a clever and determined man who had lived a hard life. In the months ahead, he would be an important presence.

A dilapidated gold-mining road built fifty years ago led through the valley. Chato, Martin, Fabio, and his younger brother Freiman started working at the base of it, plowing it smooth and shoring up weak spots where it crossed the river. It took a few days to get it in shape. The pace slowed when they hit the last quarter mile, a steep incline leading up to the lodge site, where the old road turned into a narrow trail. They cut the brush with machetes so the tractor could grade the passage. Each day, they managed to clear and plow only fifty to one hundred yards. In spite of the challenge of carving a road out of thick forest, I insisted that we avoid cutting down any trees.

In one section, they came to a monstrous fallen ajo tree, the girth of its trunk stretching five feet above the ground. Fortunately, we needed a large piece of wood to act as a bridge above a creek bed, so Martin, Fabio, and Freiman planed one side of it until it was flat, wrapped a chain around it, hooked it up to the tractor, and hauled it over the ravine. It became a graceful crossing, just below where the lodge would be.

After two weeks, the road was complete. Fabio and I rode down the hill on the tractor and drove Little Blue up. As I drove, I marveled at the smoothness of the graded road. When we hit the steep part, I downshifted and Blue strained all the way up to my front door. I turned off the motor and we both jumped out. Fabio ran around the back of the truck, lifted me off the ground, and spun me around. When he set me down, I still felt as though my whole body was floating with joy. Completing the road was a huge accomplishment, and we were on our way to making my dream a reality.

Next Chato plowed the space where the *rancho grande* would be. With the tractor blade, he shoved the dirt off a little cliff at the front, where the deck would hang high above the ground. We were so excited to have a road and to begin the actual construction that we invited all our friends up for a barbecue. We roasted pork and made rice and beans.

Jani and Tom and his two kids, Tessa and Nick, came down from Crested Butte. Urbano joined us, as did Pedro, Chon, and their wives. Families and friends from Carate and Puerto Jimenez also made their way up, so we had a group of about thirty-five. While we feasted and drank beer, the adults played soccer on the graded area that would be the *rancho grande*. The kids used the space in front of the *rancho grande* like a launch pad as they leaped off and flew through the air onto the big pile of soft dirt below, their squeals resonating through the forest.

Jani, Tom, and the kids stayed for ten days, sleeping in a tent and enjoying the dry, warm weather while blizzards pummeled Colorado. Fabio took a day off work to guide them through Corcovado National Park. On another day, they hiked twenty-five miles on an old gold-mining trail across the peninsula from my land to El Tigre and back. The kids were in heaven on the land, where they could play all day outside. Meanwhile, Jani and I did yoga and gardened together. We hiked to the waterfalls and shared stories of our current lives. She was a soothing presence amid all the hard work.

However, as the days went along, I sensed a shift in her. Each day she seemed to grow more remote from me. Toward the end of her stay, she even skipped our morning yoga. Unfortunately, I didn't have time to contemplate this more deeply.

We used Little Blue to haul up more materials. Martin, Fabio, Freiman, and I, along with six workers I had hired from the area, spent a few hours unloading 150 bags of cement, countless concrete blocks, and pipes for the plumbing. We collected downed trees that we would use for the pillars and floors. We also put the Alaskan Sawmill we brought from Colorado to use. It was a portable sawmill with a fifty-inch chainsaw on tracks, so we could make boards from whole logs.

The day before Jani left, she asked me to stop work to talk with her.

"Jani, I'm so busy," I said.

"Please, just for a few minutes."

"Okay, okay." We sat on the little wall facing the broad, staked-out foundation of the *rancho grande*. Having Jani on my land had warmed my heart, but this day I felt wary because her expression was grave.

"Lana, what are you doing?" she asked.

"What do you mean?"

"This is a monstrosity!" she exclaimed. "When we gave you money, we thought we were investing in something modest, a little hotel in the rainforest, but this . . ." She waved her hand toward the cleared land. "I'm sorry, Lana, but it's ridiculous." Her face looked anguished, and in some odd way I could hear her husband's voice in her words.

I was so hurt by her words, I could hardly speak. Yes, it was an ambitious project, but not too massive or outlandish. It was my dream. Finally, I said, "Jani, you can't see my vision for this place, but just wait until it's done. It will be beautiful." I turned away from her, unable to handle her doubt. It was enough to handle my own as I invested every ounce of my energy and spent thousands of dollars every week.

"I just can't believe Mom gave you fifty thousand dollars." She spat the words at my back.

I turned fast. "It's my inheritance, Jani, and Mom believes in this. And what are you talking about? She gave you money even before me." In fact, Mom had given Jani money to fund her Rolfing education.

"I wonder how much she'll believe in this once I tell her what an atrocity it is."

"Go ahead, tell her," I said and walked away. The heat of the insult stayed with me into the evening. It burned in my heart and ignited spite in my mind toward Jani and especially Tom, who I sensed was spearheading this. That night in bed I rolled from my back to my side to my stomach, finally falling asleep. When I awoke at dawn I realized I had to shut the hurt feelings down to get my work done. I would be civil and show Jani that she could not stop me.

The next day, I gave her and Tom perfunctory hugs and had one of the guys take them back to Puerto Jimenez so they could catch the plane to San José. My heart smarted from the tension between us, but I had too much on my hands to worry about it.

As we started building the heart of the lodge, the nine-meter or thirty-foot-tall *rancho grande*, the crew included Martin, Fabio, Freiman, twelve other workers, and me. Once the site was level, we poured the foundation and set the pillars that would support the roof. All of this took weeks because we milled the wood ourselves. At that point, in May, the rainy season was just starting, so each day we raced against the clock. As the season progressed, the rains would make work more and more challenging. For months, we labored long, hard days. We set the pillars in concrete and attached the cross beams. By early July, we were ready to braid on the thatched roof.

The money Fabio and I had earned while working in Crested Butte was already gone, and I'd used a good portion of what my mother had given me as well. Some nights I woke up in a panic, certain that my sister was right. *How could I have been so stupid? I'll never be able to manifest this dream.* I felt overwhelmed by the work that lay ahead and the way money slipped through my fingers a hundred times faster than I thought it would. *What if I run out?*

I squirmed in bed until Fabio took me in his arms and whispered, *"No te preocupes, Lanita. No te preocupes."*

With his warmth and lulling voice, my worry eased.

The roof would be made of palm fronds, which were at least a meter, or three feet, long and very durable, though tricky to work with. They had to be cut three days after the full moon because at that time most of the water resides in the root system of the tree, rather than in the leaves. Harvesting at the right time would make the fronds more durable and increase the concentration of a natural pesticide within them, which prevents insects from devouring the finished roof.

We hurried to complete the framing, so we could get the fronds on before the worst part of the rainy season arrived. As the wet season progressed, a dozen inches might drench the Osa in a single day. Once the leaves were cut we had ten days to braid them onto the roof; if they became too dry, they would lose their elasticity, so braiding would be impossible. If all this was done right, our roof would last eight to ten years.

We brought up the first load and the workers got busy tying on the leaves. It took nearly a month to complete one quarter of the roof, and then it was time to buy more leaves and get them on as fast as possible. We did one side of the building and then started on the other.

The leaves were expensive, and sometimes the workers accidentally dropped them. In the mornings, I always did yoga first thing, and then I came to the *rancho grande* and picked up the fallen leaves so the workers could reuse them. By now we had a crew of fifteen climbing about the rafters because of the short shelf-life of our roofing material. One time, while all the guys were up there working, I bent over and picked up a leaf. To my horror, a coral snake lay coiled underneath. I screamed and jumped back.

There's a saying in the Osa: "Red and yellow kill a fellow, red and black won't attack." This snake definitely had red and yellow stripes. I stood at a safe distance, waiting for movement, but it remained still. For a moment, the fatigue of all the work and pressure, all the pushing to get everything done, weakened me like a viper bite.

The snake still didn't move, and above me a chuckle sounded, and then another, until all the guys were laughing. One, named Javier, laughed especially hard, so I knew that he had placed the dead snake there. I looked up at him and smiled, shaking my head. "You pranksters . . ."

Vilma, my cook at the time, was preparing lunch. I went and had a little chat with her, and we made a plan. When lunch time came, as usual, I served the workers, bringing them each a plate of food as they sat at a long wooden table in the house. When I picked up Javier's plate, Vilma handed me a bottle of tabasco sauce and winked at me. I stealthily poured the hot juice over the *salsa roja con cerdo*, which is pork in a red sauce. Then I stifled a smile as I placed the plate in front of Javier. Busy talking with the others, he was oblivious.

He took one bite and started gasping. His teary eyes grew wide as he fumbled for his water glass. I looked at him and laughed, and then all the guys laughed too.

I always told my employees the golden rule: "Treat people like you want to be treated," and they knew I lived this.

I told him in Spanish, "What goes around, comes around, Javier." Really, though, my heart felt happy knowing that my employees were comfortable enough with me to joke around in that way.

As the workers made progress on the roof, I worked from dawn into the night organizing the project. I bought supplies and food in town and delivered them to the worksite. I decided what we were going to build next, and I made list after list to keep everything moving. We needed nails and pipes and more cement. We needed beans, rice, and tortillas to feed the crew. Everything had to come from many miles away; there was no quick trip to the hardware store. The closest town with stores was Puerto Jimenez, a grueling twenty-five-mile drive, bouncing in and out of holes, negotiating mud, and fording rivers so that the journey took two hours each way. Some of our supply needs required an eight-hour drive all the way to San José and back.

All of it cost a lot of money.

After nine months of this intense work, I looked up one day and saw that the roof was practically done. It was refined and yet rustic, the palm fronds giving texture to its huge expanse. It was a long, pitched roof, with leaves hanging off the edges like natural ruffles. Inside, the *rancho grande* felt like a cathedral, with graceful crossbeams shoring up the lofty structure. The ground level was open, so one could see the forest in every direction. There was really no divide between the inner and the outer. The building's beauty and strength were everything I had envisioned all those years ago when I imagined the centerpiece of my lodge to stand tall and elegantly like the masts of the *Zebu*.

In late October, with the roof almost complete, Hurricane Mitch hit the Caribbean. While it pushed across Costa Rica toward the Osa, Fabio and I were in San José getting Little Blue repaired. I paced around my friend's apartment where we were staying, so nervous I couldn't even sit. Every half hour Fabio and I turned on the TV weather to watch the massive swirl of clouds as the storm gained momentum and moved west. All our hard work could be gone within moments, the expensive palm leaves flying away in the wind, scattering across the forest floor.

If only I were there, I could do something. But I had to admit that I could do nothing. I couldn't fight a hurricane.

When I returned to the Osa, I learned that the workers had continued braiding on the palm leaves until the rain poured so hard they had to stop. I was exhausted from months of work and from worry over the storm. Fortunately, we were spared: the hurricane passed to the north, hitting Honduras, and we only got the tail end, a whiplash of rain.

The rain had almost completely washed out the road between

Carate and my land, so to take up the final load of palm leaves, I rented a tractor. We were in a rush because the hurricane had slowed progress by two weeks and the leaves were already turning brown. The tractor driver, Memo, assured me that he could make it. I also rented a trailer that we loaded with a cement mixer, five big boxes of nails, and food for the crew, along with the huge pile of palm leaves.

I perched on top of the leaves and Martin sat at the back of the trailer as the tractor pulled us along the rutted, rocky road. As I had hoped, the sun came out. Fortunately, I'd worn my bikini top, so I took off my shirt and enjoyed the warmth on my shoulders. Mist rose from the ground, and my exhaustion lifted as well. We crossed the first bridge, and the image came into my mind of myself flying off the trailer and landing on my feet in the creek bed. I had no idea that this was a foreshadowing of what was to come.

We made our way along a cattle pasture, and I was happy because the sun was shining and I was bringing food for the workers. I was returning to my property, and we were going to finish the roof. We started down into a creek bed, rumbling over dips and rocks, when suddenly the tractor's brakes failed. It slid sideways down the muddy bank, dragging the trailer with it. One of the trailer's tires dropped into a hole.

"*Lana, vamos a volcarnos!*" yelled Martin, but even before his warning, I could feel the trailer tipping. While Memo tried to control the speeding tractor, Martin leaped from the trailer. Before I could do anything, it capsized, and I fell, the load rolling around me. I tried to land on my feet, but the weight of the materials crushed me to the ground.

I couldn't breathe. My lungs tried to take in air, but I gaped like a netted fish under the fronds. Their weight pushed me into the earth. Pain ripped through my body, my fingers tingled and curled in, and my mind went blank from shock. The only reason I knew

I was alive was because I could see the light of the sun through a little crack in the leaves, and I could hear Fabio's voice as he tried to find me.

He and Martin pulled away the thatch, and then I saw Fabio's face. I could tell something was terribly wrong because his expression was wide-eyed and grim. I reached my hand up to my face. Blood dripped from my fingers. Pain lashed across my brow and nose, and pounded through my right leg. Fabio helped me stand, but when I took a step, I collapsed. My leg lay twisted beneath me.

Everyone paused as a Range Rover rumbled into the creek toward us. I could barely take in what was happening, my body hurt so much.

"Hey, what's going on? Can I help?" the driver asked.

"*Sí!*" Fabio said. "Can you take her to the clinic?"

"Yep, no worries, mate," he said. "I'll get her there fast."

Fabio lifted me and eased me into the back seat of the Range Rover. I held out my hand to grab him, not wanting to leave him, but I knew he had to stay to get the load and food up to the workers. He closed the door.

The man climbed in behind the wheel and introduced himself as Julian. "Hold tight. We'll be at the clinic before you know it," he said.

I didn't even have the strength to tell him my name.

He turned the Range Rover around, and we climbed out of the creek. Pain shot through my leg with the jostling, and fear gripped my stomach so intensely I put my hand to my mouth to stop myself from vomiting.

A dingo dog panted next to me, and it was some comfort to see his dark eyes and soft fur. His gray and black hair clung to the seat. I reached for a blanket on the floor and pulled it over me, wanting to cover my whole body and even my head. I was mortified to be causing so much trouble for Fabio and my team, and especially this stranger who now drove me along the bumpy road. I hated to be so weak and vulnerable, so I bit my hand to stave off the screams that wanted to come after every bump.

We drove for an hour to Jimenez, Julian talking now and then about his life. He told me he was an Australian magazine model, and that he was building a house in the rainforest. I did note that he was beautiful, with big blue eyes and wavy hair. I did my best to nod but couldn't converse at all, so finally I lay my head back and closed my eyes.

When we finally arrived at the clinic, which was really just an *ebais*, a medical outpost, Julian carried me in and laid me on a bed. The doctor, a stout man with a sweet smile, touched my nose, sending pain through it, and then pressed his fingers to my lip. I learned that my nose was broken in two places, I had a cut on my swollen lip, another under my nose, and yet another across the bridge of my nose. He briefly examined my leg.

"You'll have to go to the hospital in Golfito so they can take X-rays and set this," he said. "But I can stitch up your face."

I closed my eyes and took a deep breath. "Please," I said to him, "do a good job. Don't mess up my face."

He smiled down toward his hands as he prepared the needle and sutures. He worked carefully, cleaning each tear, applying a topical anesthetic, and then stitching me up. I cried while he worked, because I was afraid, and even with the anesthetic, the needle hurt, and my leg never quit throbbing. When he finished, he helped me outside where Fabio's mom, Marielos, waited. She accompanied me to a charter plane that the doctor had arranged to fly me across the Golfo Dulce to Golfito. I appreciated her warm presence during that harsh day.

When we arrived at the hospital, the doctor there, an efficient older man with bushy brows framing dark eyes, took X-rays and determined that I'd broken my leg in four places. The news hit me hard. *Four breaks in my leg.* My legs were so crucial to my life that the idea of losing the strength and agility of one of them sent my mind spinning. *Is the care here adequate? Can they set the leg properly? Will it ever heal?*

Will this be the end of my dream?

He gave me an intravenous pain killer, which numbed me completely and stopped all thought. Once I was thoroughly anesthetized, he set the leg and put on a cast. I was relieved to have the pain stop even for a little while.

That afternoon, Marielos and I returned to the airstrip to take the plane back. I was woozy from the painkiller but made myself stay awake for the ten-minute flight.

She took me to their house, where she prepared a bed for me. Unfortunately, their house had flooded during the hurricane, so when I stepped into the main room, my crutches slurped through an inch of water. She told me that because of the rain, Fabio was stuck at the lodge and would come the next day. He and Martin had loaded the materials back on the trailer and continued on. However, the trailer tipped over two more times before they arrived at the lodge.

The next morning, I wanted to go home but realized I didn't have the strength. I hopped around on crutches, and had bandages wrapped around my whole head with only holes for my eyes, nose, and mouth. I was so weak I had to lie still, with my leg raised.

Mid-morning, there was a knock on the door. Marielos answered it and showed a man into the room. I knew him simply as Gerardo, a bureaucrat from the local government. He was short and dark with glasses, a thick mustache, and dollar signs in his eyes. He had visited me a dozen times in the past months, always greedy for money.

"Ms. Wedmore," he said, "you need another permit." He handed me a piece of paper.

I painfully moved my leg so I could sit facing him. "I paid for all my permits, and you know it." I knew he had heard of my accident and had come at my weakest moment.

"You need to get a permit that costs ten thousand dollars in order to keep going with your construction." He went on and on about how I had only paid for a certain kind of permit, and now I needed to pay more.

I listened and realized he might be right, but I didn't trust him. If I paid him I had no idea where the money would go—likely into his own pocket. I needed more information, and of course, more money.

"No," I said, with all the force I could muster.

"Okay, *entonces*," he said. "You are shut down." He turned and walked out the door.

I sat back, the devastation of his words coursing through my body. *Before it has even opened, my lodge is closed.*

I lifted my leg back onto the pillow and felt tears brimming in my eyes. I didn't let them fall. If I broke down now, I'd sink into a pit of despair so deep I'd never be able to crawl out.

Fabio and Martin arrived in the afternoon. When Fabio walked in the door, his machete strapped to his hip and his eyes looking tenderly at me, I had no choice but to smile. He came to the couch, leaned over, and hugged me. I hugged back, holding on longer than any hug we'd ever had. I told him about Gerardo. His expression turned grave because this was my dream, but it was also his dream. He was so good to me, as were his parents. He sat with me for a while and told me that the work on the lodge had continued, the thatch almost completely on the roof.

When I saw his leg fidgeting from sitting inside for so long, I asked him to go to the bank to withdraw money to pay the employees for their last days of work and to tell me how much remained. I feared finding out the balance but knew I must.

When he returned with the cash, I learned I only had enough left to pay my workers. I buried my face in my hands, but then I pulled them away because it hurt too much to touch the bandages. I was at the bottom of a very dark well: physically, financially, and spiritually broke.

In the coming days, I couldn't bring myself to call my mom and tell her that my dream was crumbling. But I swallowed my pride and called my dad. He was curiously reticent with me and offered no help. I later learned that as promised, Jani had returned home and told him and my mom that the rainforest had affected my judgment and I'd gone wild, like Conrad's character Kurtz in *Heart of Darkness.* She told them I was using their money to build the Taj Mahal, a way too big, way too outlandish structure. They thought I was crazy. Because of this, they would not come see me. In the desolation of physical and emotional pain, a sad mantra developed in my mind: *No one came, no one came . . .*

CHAPTER 31

That night Fabio and I went to bed, and I cried into his shoulder, overwhelmed by pain, uncertainty, and the unbearable helplessness of being injured. I couldn't walk. I couldn't drive a car. I couldn't take care of myself. I couldn't keep my crew on the job, and I may have lost everything I'd worked so hard to achieve.

We were staying in Fabio's family home, which sat along a quiet street near a mangrove forest in the pueblo of Puerto Jimenez. It had two bedrooms and one main room. Fabio and I slept together in a single bed, in a room we shared with his two younger sisters. His parents and youngest brother shared the other bedroom, while his other brother slept in a storage room. Since it was still under construction, the house had concrete block walls that only went halfway up to the tin roof. There was little privacy and it felt as though Fabio and I and his whole family all lived in one room.

In the evenings after dinner, everyone packed into the main room to watch a telenovela. We sat crammed together on a wooden bench that served as a couch. After about a half hour, I fidgeted and my leg ached more acutely from the noise and the cruelty of the relationships on the show, the characters having affairs and yelling at each other. And yet in that house I couldn't escape it, even in our bedroom.

I wanted to scream with frustration. The pain never let up, and I felt like a victim. I *hated* being a victim.

I wanted to be on my land, but the road was so washed out that we couldn't get there. And the rain continued to fall. It pounded like a kettle drum being played on the tin roof and left everything in the house sopped. Water still covered the floor, so I had to hop gingerly from place to place in an attempt to keep my cast dry. And bugs flew in, especially mosquitos, which greedily attacked any exposed skin. I couldn't concentrate to read because there was so much going on in the tiny house.

I was grateful to Marielos and Martin for having me there and taking care of me, but the challenge was wearing me down. Besides the constant pain of my leg and face, my stomach hurt because I was a vegetarian and none of the others were, so I'd been living on fruit, tomatoes, beans, and rice, but even the rice was cooked with animal fat, and the grease made my body ache as though I had the flu. I could barely tolerate being there, but I had no choice.

One night I awoke in the darkness, my leg throbbing. I turned on a flashlight and looked down at my toes. They were green and purple. I panicked, fearing that I might lose my leg, along with everything else that I'd lost. Even though I had been taking pain pills, my leg had continued to hurt relentlessly. I shook Fabio awake. "Something is wrong."

He leaned down and looked closely. "Lana, you have gangrene."

Even though Fabio held me, my body shook with terror. That word, gangrene, was horrifying. I knew I couldn't do anything until morning, so I tried to sleep but couldn't. Crickets chirped and frogs croaked, but even those beautiful sounds didn't calm me.

A quote from Helen Keller that I'd always loved came into my consciousness: "The best and most beautiful things in the world cannot be seen or even touched—they must be felt with the heart." My leg was not as important as my being, I told myself. The notion helped for a moment, but then gruesome images filled my head once again. I could only see my toes. *What must the rest of my leg look like? Green and purple, mangled because it was set improperly?* My mind swirled for hours with the images and thoughts until I bit the sheet to stop myself from screaming.

Finally, dawn lit the sky outside. I got out of bed and hobbled to the main room where I dialed my friend David Kaufman from the language school Conversa, which I had attended when I first came to Costa Rica. He was still a good friend. Since he was so well connected, I thought he might be able to help. I told him I needed a competent doctor, but I didn't have any money. He said one of his best friends was an orthopedic surgeon who could take a look. I gathered what little money I had and bought a bus ticket to San José.

After boarding in Puerto Jimenez, I leaned on my crutches in the aisle because the bus was full. I was traveling alone since we didn't have money for Fabio to come with me. *How will I endure eleven hours of this?* I wondered. After two hours of my leg throbbing and armpits aching from the crutches, a middle-aged farmer, wearing coveralls and a humble smile, stood up and motioned for me to take his seat.

"*Gracías, muchas gracías,*" I said, sitting with such relief I could have cried. I snoozed for a few hours and then stood and offered the seat back. He took it, and we continued alternating for the rest of the trip. When we disembarked, I wanted to hug him I was so grateful, but I restrained myself and merely smiled and said, "*Gracías.*"

My Costa Rican friend Gata picked me up in a taxi at the station in San José and took me to her house. The next morning, she went off to work, and I took a taxi to the doctor.

Dr. Chacon was tall and slender with white hair and the tenderness of a grandpa. He greeted me with a handshake. Using a little electric saw, he cut away my cast, revealing my swollen, purple leg, dusted white with plaster. He gently pressed his fingers to my shin and ankle, which hurt, but I bit back the pain. Next, he took X-rays.

While I awaited the outcome, I fidgeted on the examination table, terrified. I kept banishing from my mind the image of me hobbling around on a pirate's wooden leg. My legs were everything to me, the most cherished part of my body because I relied on them. I had ski raced and bike raced on them, hiked, waterskied, and danced. They were strong and muscular, and they were my future. If one went, how would I ever achieve the dream of my lodge? The ground on my land was rugged, and life in the rainforest was at times unyielding. I needed my greatest strength.

The doctor returned with a slight smile on his lips. "You are so lucky," he said. "Your leg is well set and the bones have fused together correctly." He explained that the break in my tibia was at an angle, which was ideal because the two parts had a lot of area to fuse. "It's not a Swiss watch," he said, "but it is remarkable how it has healed." He also said the three breaks in my ankle were mending well.

"Really?" I said. "You mean I don't have gangrene?"

"You do, but we can take care of that. The cast was too tight, which restricted the blood flow."

As he applied a stockinet and wrapped gauze onto my leg, his face lit up even more. "This is the first time I get to use a fiberglass cast," he said. "You will love it. It's much lighter, and you don't have to worry about getting it wet like you do the plaster kind." With scissors, he jauntily snipped the gauze into sections and laid them over my leg. Then with gloved hands, he pulled the fiberglass strips from a tray of water and applied them on top. Once he had put on two layers, he vigorously smoothed the cast. It felt much better than the previous one, which had been so tight it felt like a tourniquet.

My heart filled with a glow of delight, relief, and gratitude because I would be able to move around Fabio's family home without harming my cast, and I could take a shower without putting a plastic bag over my leg. I shook the doctor's hand and thanked him.

"I will pay when I can," I said.

"I'm just glad I could help you," he said. "I'd do anything for David." He handed me a bottle of antibiotic capsules to cure the infection. I stuffed it in my backpack and hobbled out of his office on crutches, relieved that my leg could breathe again. It felt so much lighter, as though it were really healing now.

On the bus ride back to the Osa, I was able to sit. Amid all the passengers and the air that smelled of garlic breath and diesel fuel, I closed my eyes and tried to sleep, but my mind wouldn't let me. It kept churning with worry and sadness. I dreaded returning to the chaos of Fabio's family home. Plus, I was miserable about having let my fifteen employees go and draining my bank account to zero. A part of me wanted to stay on the bus in limbo because when I hit ground back at my land, I had to come up with a plan, and I had not the slightest idea what it would be.

After staying at Marielos and Martin's house for three weeks, the rain calmed down enough so that Fabio and I could drive Little Blue up to my land. I was overjoyed to be back in the rainforest, hobbling around on my crutches, and sleeping in the quiet of our dry house. Still, the whole project was shut down, and we had no money to move forward with construction, or to pay for more permits, so we simply survived.

Fabio got some guiding work in Corcovado National Park and that brought in enough money to buy food. In his spare time he worked on the roof of bungalow one. I did what yoga I could with my cast and thought about what I wanted in life. *Is this my true journey?* I wondered. *If it is, why has it all gone so wrong?* Up to this point I had experienced life challenges, but I had always been able to rise above them and continue on. Right now, the future I had planned felt absolutely impossible. I tried to listen to my intuition, but my discomfort and fear of failing seemed to cloud my discernment.

The sense of hopelessness expanded whenever I thought of my family. Ever since Jani returned home and told my parents I was wasting their investment, we had barely communicated. And after I broke my leg, none of them reached out or came to help me. I knew that I lived in a remote place and maybe I shouldn't have expected such a visit, but their absence, especially my mother's, hurt my heart.

That's why I was completely surprised when one day, on a visit to Puerto Jimenez, I called Jani and learned that Mom and Don were taking a cruise through the Panama Canal that was going to stop in Costa Rica, and they hoped to come visit. I wanted to see my mom, but I had mixed feelings because of all the tension between us in recent years. I was still on crutches, my bank account was empty, and my lodge might never become a reality. My stepfather had never seen me so defeated. He only knew me as the positive, energetic, and athletic person I had been growing up. It would be a humiliation to have them there.

A couple of days before they were to arrive, Vilma, my cook, and I cleaned the house because I wanted everything looking nice. I still hobbled around on crutches, but I did my best to help her. That afternoon I was wondering where Mom and Don were in the course of their journey, so I went to the deck and looked out. It was almost dusk and very quiet; Fabio, his brother Freiman, and my gardener Surdo were gone repairing the road. I gazed out across the forest to the ocean and saw a ship sailing past less than a mile offshore.

"Vilma," I said. She came to the deck and handed me a glass

of wine. "I wonder if we could call that ship to see if my mom and stepfather are on it." It was only a flash of intuition, but I knew better than to ignore it.

We headed over to the house, me on crutches, her carrying the wine, and I switched on the radio. "Cruise ship, cruise ship that's going north, please copy."

"Yes," a man answered. "This is the Princess Cruise Ship."

I stammered, surprised that I had reached anyone at all, much less the ship right in front of me. "My name is Lana, and I'm on land where I can see you. My mother and father are on a cruise ship going north, and I want to see if they are on your ship."

He paused a moment, and I feared I'd lost him. But then his voice crackled over the radio. "Please wait a few minutes while I find out," he said. "Let's change to channel ten because this one is for emergencies."

"Okay." I changed the channel.

"What are their names?" he asked once we reconnected.

"Dr. Don and Willie Ihrke," I said.

Later I would learn that my mom had spent the day below deck doing laundry, and she was thinking about me all day. When she and Don went up to dinner she saw lights on the land. She said to my stepdad, "I wonder where we are. We must be getting close to Costa Rica."

Don didn't know, but he turned to the first mate at the next table and asked.

"I'm not on duty but I will call right now and see where we are," the first mate said.

"We have a daughter who lives in Costa Rica, and I just want to know if we are close to there," Mom said.

He went to the phone in the restaurant to call the bridge while Mom and Don continued eating.

The first mate returned to Mom's table, his cheeks red with

excitement. "The captain said he has a woman on the radio who is looking for her mom and wants to know if she's on this ship!" He grinned delightedly at them. "What are your names?"

When they told him, he replied, "Your daughter is on the radio. Follow me as quickly as you can!"

The first mate grabbed a ring full of keys and led them up on deck and then through locked door after locked door until they reached the bridge.

Meanwhile, the captain said to me, "We found your mom and dad. They're right here."

My heart beat fast, as I tried to digest this news. Then I heard her voice. "Lana," Mom said.

"Mom, this is amazing." My body filled with goosebumps and tears rushed to the edges of my eyes. "I can't believe you're right there, so close."

"I want to jump ship and swim to you!"

"I want to swim to you too," I replied. My heart felt like a great amphitheater, so open to her. With the sound of her voice, all the anger and uncertainty dissolved.

Before we said anything else, the connection filled with static. We reluctantly said goodbye.

Vilma and I headed back to the deck and looked out at the ocean, where the boat had disappeared behind a mountain. I realized that the ship had only been visible for about seven minutes, and I had seen it. I was grateful I had followed that spark of intuition.

The ship continued north along the Costa Rican shore to Puntarenas, where Mom and Don disembarked and took a bus to San José, and then caught a plane down to Puerto Jimenez. It took them two days to get back to the Osa. I met them at the airport on a sunny afternoon. When they disembarked from the plane, I hobbled over to hug Mom. We embraced, and then she stood back and looked at my face and leg.

"Lana, I'm sorry you've had such a hard time," she said.

Tears filled my eyes. "It's okay, Mom. I'm doing better."

Fabio and Don sat in the front of Little Blue, while Mom and I sat in back on top of sacks of flour, sugar, and beans. The day was clear and warm and I relished sharing the drive up through the valley with my mother.

Once we arrived at the lodge, the day became even brighter. It was summer, so the forest was dry and verdant. Mom and Don wandered around the *rancho grande* truly appreciating it, and my worries about what they would think about my body and the state of the lodge disappeared. We pitched a tent under the roof of bungalow one and they happily slept there.

I awoke the next morning with a sense that Don might be willing to at least help us keep things going until I figured out a plan, so I made a list of what we needed. The most important item was a beginning payment for our permit to operate a lodge in the forest. Also, we needed five sacks of cement, ten kegs of nails, cane for the walls of bungalow one, and more thatch so we could start building the roofs of the other two bungalows. I went to him with the list. I hated asking him for money, sure he would refuse, but I had to try, even if it made me feel like a loser. I couldn't afford to be proud. I needed help, and it was not a comfortable thought. I wasn't really hopeful but was willing to take a chance.

After we ate a breakfast of fruit and *gallo pinto* (beans and rice), I handed him the list. "Can you help us, even a little?" I asked.

He sat back in his chair and read it over. He shook his head and my heart sank. But then he nodded, and my heart rose. He looked across at me. "You've had a rough go, kid," he said. "Yes, I'll help. Will fifteen thousand dollars get you going again?"

"Yes," I said. "That will help so much." Though I knew we needed nearly ten times that amount, it was a start, and right then I had to take whatever I could get.

I jumped up from the table and hugged him, and he hugged me back.

CHAPTER 32

Back when I worked at Corcovado Lodge Tent Camp, we had a guest named Ryan Olson. He was an attractive and innocent computer geek from Minnesota. He first impressed us all when he fixed my boss Don Michael's computer. Soon, Ryan became a good friend of mine and he ended up staying longer than he'd planned. He enjoyed the tent camp and all the fun he was having with me and the staff so much, he never wanted to leave.

One day at the beginning of construction he came walking onto my land. "Oh my gosh, Lana," he said, running to hug me and Fabio. "This is beautiful."

"It's great to see you, Ryan," I said.

He gazed around our little paradise, taking it all in. "I'm staying at Corcovado Lodge Tent Camp. Do you think I could move over here?"

"Sure," I said. "You can be my first unofficial guest."

That night, a handful of our employees, Fabio, and I walked him back to the tent camp under the light of a full moon, talking and telling stories all the way. We left him, and the next day he arrived with his backpack and stayed with us for a week. He became one of my best friends.

That was in early 1998. He returned in 1999. I was happy to see him, but I was also sad because I still wore a cast and our construction was shut down. The *rancho grande* roof was done but the bungalows weren't. After my parents left, we had researched starting building again, but the loan they gave us would barely even cover the cost of our permit, so until we got more money we remained stuck.

I lamented that I couldn't offer Ryan the deluxe stay he deserved. He agreed to join Freiman and Surdo, my gardener, who slept in tents. During this time, Fabio, Vilma, and I lived in the house.

One morning at breakfast at our long table, Ryan had a gleam in his eyes. "Lana," he said. "I'll build you a website."

"Ryan, I don't even know if there's going to be a lodge."

He remained undaunted. "I'll make you a website because the longer you're on the web, the more customers will be able to find you."

"If you want to, I would appreciate that so much, but I cannot pay you. I don't have any money."

"No, no, no. I'll do it as a trade."

"Really?"

"Yeah."

The first thing we did was settle on a name. Somehow through the years the name Luna Lodge had started being a part of my consciousness, but I had never settled on it. Of course, *luna* means moon in Spanish, and I've always revered the moon. It's so powerful and romantic. When I traveled in Australia and missed my family, I would look up at it and know they were seeing the same moon, and it made me feel close to them. And I had named my horse Luna because I got her during a full moon, so that added even more significance. I really didn't even need to decide—the name was just there. When Ryan asked me, I said, "It is called Luna Lodge." I felt the power of saying it like that, as though giving it a name might just make it possible.

He smiled. "That is a fantastic name." When he returned to Minnesota, he built my first website. It was beautiful, with color photos of toucans, the *rancho grande*, and the rainforest in

Corcovado National Park. Ryan continued to keep my site current for seventeen years to come. He continues to visit the lodge every year.

A week later, Fabio brought a gay couple to Luna who he had guided through the park. They had money and were interested in investing. I was so happy to hear this, I said, "I'll make them a cake!"

While I did, Fabio, Freiman, and Ryan took them on a tour of the property. I worked in the kitchen making the cake, which wasn't easy because of my leg. I started from scratch and cooked it over flames in a Dutch oven, a heavy cast-iron pot with a lid. As I stirred the batter, I sang. I knew they would love this beautiful place, that they would want to invest, and my lodge would again be possible.

Suddenly Freiman came racing down the hill and into the house. "Lana, ¡hay una emergencia! It's an emergency!" he yelled.

"¿Qué pasó?"

"I'm so sorry, but I got on a vine and swung across the creek bed like Tarzan, and the guy wanted to try it." He paused, catching his breath.

"¡Digamé!"

"The vine broke and he landed on his wrist."

"Qué lastima," I said. I hobbled outside to see Fabio and Ryan carrying the man down the hill, his partner following. The injured one held his wrist out and moaned in agony. They loaded him in the car, and his partner drove them away, along with my dream of them helping. Fabio and I hugged, both of us feeling completely defeated.

That afternoon we ate the cake with little enjoyment, as though it was laced with disappointment. We never heard from the couple again.

A month later, we learned through a friend about an American businessman who was interested in investing. Apparently, he already owned hotels, mansions, and a yacht. The day of his visit, I put on my nicest sundress and prepared a big pitcher of lemonade. Fabio and Freiman made everything as neat as possible on the building site. This time, even though I still had my cast on, I was going to give the tour in hopes that nothing would go wrong. The man was supposed to arrive mid-morning, so we stood around waiting.

He didn't come.

We had lunch, and he still wasn't here.

As the sun sank below the mountains, we became desperate. Thinking maybe something had gone wrong with his transportation, Fabio and I drove Little Blue into Puerto Jimenez to look for him. We asked around town, and someone told us to check the local saloon. We found him there, his head actually resting on the bar, he was so drunk.

The bartender, who was a friend of ours, said, "Lana, can you pay his bill? He said he couldn't pay it."

"Are you kidding?" I said, incredulous.

"Please," the bartender said.

"No!" We walked out the door.

While Fabio drove us home, I tried to hold steady, but in the silence, a big tear dripped down my cheek. I saw that Fabio's eyes brimmed with tears as well. I reached over and took his hand, and we looked at each other through the prisms of our tears, so defeated we had no words. I sighed as I came to understand how much I had hoped that alcoholic would be our savior.

Back at Luna, I felt drained, my spirit broken. I wanted to work to make my lodge happen, but when I pushed during the day, my leg ached all night so I couldn't sleep. This gnawed at my ability to cope. One afternoon, while trying to help Fabio erect the walls of bungalow one, the frustration intensified until I could have screamed. *This is not the life I want.* In spite of my parents' generosity, my dream of building a lodge seemed unattainable.

Friends occasionally came up to see us, and one of them brought me the book *Conversations with God* by Neale Donald Walsch. In it Walsch told the story of a little white light, and how it wanted so badly to be the Light. God said okay, and He turned off all the lights. The little white light was afraid, doubting itself. *What did God do to me?* he wondered.

He said to God, "You told me I could be the Light."

God said, "Now you are the Light, so shine."

As I lay in a hammock under the *rancho grande*, I contemplated this. In the past, I had struggled with my stepdad's overbearing control and my mom's relentless pushing. Meanwhile my dad told me again and again to follow my truth. Those experiences really affected me. They made me believe that failure wasn't an option—I *had* to succeed. I had to for my parents and everyone involved in this. I realized then that deep within me I believed that I could do this and that I was going to do this. In that moment, I hurt physically, emotionally, and spiritually. I was down in a deep, deep well, but somewhere in my heart I knew that I could climb out. I closed the book and listened to the throbbing life of the forest, which always reminded me of my own strength. I realized that I was that light. I was being called not to rely on others like the gay couple or the alcoholic, but to use my own power, to step in, to know that I could do this.

The next day, I pulled on a pink and white sundress and told Fabio that we had somewhere to go. He drove me down to Puerto Jimenez, where I shuffled on my crutches into the local bank, the same place where I had so happily made my final payment for the land. This day, though, it reminded me of a Wild West bank, with a teller standing behind a barred window. It was freezing cold, the air conditioning blasting on high. It was the only place in town that had air conditioning, so a few local gringos hung out chatting along the far wall. The teller sent me over to a loan officer's desk, where I sat across from a stout little man with pudgy cheeks. I told him I had run out of money and I needed a loan.

He said, *"Sí,"* and nodded his head.

Wow, I thought, *this sure is easy.*

He offered to loan me Costa Rican *colónes* at 32 percent interest.

Thirty-two percent! I had suspected something like this might happen, and so I had done some research. In the US at this time business loans were going for around 9 or 10 percent. "No," I said, "I want a seven-year, dollar loan at nine point seven-five percent, with the first year as a grace period before I start paying it back."

"We have never done a dollar loan," he said, shaking his head as though it was the most impossible request he had ever received.

I sat up taller and cleared my throat. "I would really like a dollar loan because I do not want a *colónes* loan."

"We will have to take this to the San José office," he said.

"Please tell them that this is the standard in the United States right now."

"Bueno," he said. "We will get back to you."

"Gracías." I stood, shook his hand, and turned around to see all the faces in the place, about ten men, peering at me. For a moment I saw what they must have seen: a crippled woman, weak and vulnerable, her face marked with red scars. But I straightened my spine, smiled my brightest smile, and hobbled out.

Fabio guided more tours in the park, and Surdo worked on the lodge grounds. Meanwhile, I did my best to be patient. With little money, we couldn't accomplish much on the property, and if the loan didn't go through we would likely have to abandon the whole project. I did chores around the house, but mostly I focused on resting and on healing my body. I read the *Celestine Prophecy,* finding hope in its message about synchronicity and following your intuition. It affirmed what I sensed in my heart: that the loan would come through, we would resume construction, and my dream would take shape.

One day I looked in my bedroom mirror and saw that the scars on my face were pink rather than the hideous red-maroon they were before. I reached for my crutches but had an impulse to leave them. Even though my leg itched from the cast, it no longer hurt, so I knew the bone had healed. I tested my weight on the cast and it caused no pain. I took a step, and then another. My heart felt light as I hobbled out of the house and toward the *rancho grande*. In that moment, I was free.

Two months after my visit to the bank, a black truck pulled onto the property, and we all stopped what we were doing and watched a man climb out and make his way over to the front of the house. He was medium height and wore a neat business suit.

"*Hola,*" I said, limping up to him.

"*Hola. Eres Lana Wedmore?*"

"*Sí,*" I said.

"*Soy Santiago Montero.*" He explained that he was a vice president from the bank. He rustled in his bag, pulled out a check, and handed it to me. I glanced at it, and then rubbed my eyes and looked harder. The amount was $85,000, and it was made out to me.

I wanted to jump up and down but I restrained myself. "*Gracías, muchas gracías,*" I said. I offered him a fresh-squeezed lemonade, and he accepted. Once I'd served him, we sat on lawn chairs in front of the house and talked. It felt as though the check was burning a hole in my pocket, I was so excited to use the money to pay for the necessary permits and begin full construction. The sun broke out from behind a cloud and lit up the *rancho grande* and the skeletal bungalows behind it, and it all seemed to glow. In that moment I sensed that everything might be okay. I felt like the little light in

Conversations with God that was shining through the darkness.

Two weeks later, an engineer named Rafael Acosta came from San José to help us start the permit process that we needed to complete in order to continue. I paid $10,000 to get a permit from the park service to build and do business in the rainforest reserve. The man who had accosted me at Fabio's family home was trying to extort money, but this Rafael was legitimate. He stayed with us for days and helped me fill out all the paperwork, and he became our friend. It would take three months to get the permit. Once we got it, we would be monitored closely. Rafael and the bankers would come every six months to check on our progress.

While awaiting the permit, we got organized so we could pick up right away where we had left off. We made lists of what we needed to do and what materials we would require. We hired a crew of five workers but told them they had to wait until the permit came. As soon as we received word, we resumed construction. It was May, the rainy season just starting, but that day the sky was blue and the air velvety moist, perfect for building. First we brought up the materials: cement mix, nails and screws, sandpaper, cleaning supplies, and palm thatch.

We had finished the roof of the *rancho grande* but we had two more roofs to build on the bungalows. We started with that, and the five workers steadily focused on the thatch. The bungalows had no walls yet, so Fabio and Freiman worked on those. The bungalows were circular like the homes of the pre-Columbian tribes of Costa Rica. They had open-air bathrooms and charming porches looking out over the rainforest. The walls were made of *caña blanca*, white cane, that ran vertically, creating a unique rustic feel.

As the lodge became more habitable, we hosted our first unofficial guests—besides Ryan. We erected two little pup tents and two army tents under the roof of the *rancho grande*. Friends of friends came to stay, having heard about the lodge through word of mouth. They were thrilled to be camping in the rainforest, hiking to waterfalls, and touring Corcovado National Park with Fabio. We fed them well: fish and fried plantains, rice and beans, and all kinds of organic vegetables from our garden.

A French couple came to stay, slender backpacking hippies. He had a goatee and ruffled hair, while she was blond with striking dark eyes. They stayed a few nights in one of the little pup tents. One morning, in the pale light of dawn the howler monkeys went wild, raising such a ruckus it woke us all up. Later, when the French couple came to breakfast, the man asked, "What was all that noise this morning?"

I told him and his girlfriend it was the howler monkeys, and that they often roared at dawn.

He shook his head, smiling broadly. With a flourish of French accent he said, "My girlfriend thought it was a jaguar, and she jumped right on top of me. So thank you, Lana."

She blushed, and we all laughed.

My heart was elated. This was my greatest desire, to bring wild experiences and joy to people in the rainforest. Even though it was still taking shape, in that moment I once again felt the quivering manifestation of my dream, like a seed just sprouting, its first delicate leaves rising up from the soil.

PART V

MORPHO BUTTERFLY

METAMORPHOSIS: TAKING FLIGHT

CHAPTER 33

We were so determined that we worked ten-hour days to construct the *rancho grande* kitchen, office, restaurant, reception area, and deck, and to complete the bungalows. Once my cast came off, I labored right alongside the guys, only stopping when my leg ached. The work took eight months, and as the year 2000 approached, two bungalows neared completion, and one was ready to go. Unfortunately, it was empty, with no beds, no mattresses, no side tables—none of the comforts that guests expect in a resort.

We worked even more furiously during the run-up to the big Y2K scare. The world feared that since the computers everyone relied on were not programmed for the new millennium they might crash, leaving everyone in a kind of electronic chaos, which some foretold would lead to the end of civilization. We didn't even have time to worry about that, and besides we didn't yet rely on computers for our business, even though we did have a website, thanks to Ryan.

We had no way to communicate with the outside world at the lodge, no phone, no internet, only a marine radio. To receive email I headed east once a week to Puerto Jimenez, where I shared an office with a few other hotels and a few guides. It had a computer, fax machine, and copier. One rainy day in November, I sat down on the rickety black chair in the office and opened my email account. I found a message from my mom filling me in on her trip to Maui with Don and a quick note from Jani saying hi. Jani's was curt, with a residue of the conflict that remained between us. I also opened an email that came in through my website.

It was a note from a woman, Betsy Harper, who had heard about Luna Lodge through one of my old tent-camp guests. Betsy and her husband, Joe, lived in New York City and wanted to come to Luna Lodge for New Year's Eve. I leapt up and did a dance around the office, noting that a couple passing on the street stared at me wide-eyed through the window. I sat down and emailed Betsy back saying, "Yes, please come." I also explained that I would arrange transportation from San José to Carate.

Fortunately, I had a way to get them almost to our front door. A few weeks before, a couple had come walking up our road. They introduced themselves as Lana and Dean Smith. When we shook hands, Lana and I held on a moment longer than usual and locked eyes in acknowledgement of our shared name. I showed them around, and they loved the place. With the roof complete on bungalow number one, but no walls yet, I decided to put a tent in there and invite them to stay.

They were both tan, blond, and fit, with sweet dispositions. That night over dinner, we talked of our adventures traveling, and they told of their life in California and how they came to retire in Costa Rica. Dean was an electrician, while Lana worked as an attorney in a high-powered, all-male law firm. When her health began failing, she went to her doctor, who wrote a prescription not for her, but for Dean. It said, "Take Lana away."

"I followed it to the letter," said Dean. "And so we now live in Atenas and spend most of our days relaxing and exploring." Atenas is an elegant town with a large expat population just west of the capital city of San José. Dean explained further that he generated occasional income with his charter plane.

The next morning, over breakfast, they said how much they

loved staying at the lodge. Spider monkeys swung through the trees right above their bungalow, and at dawn, a toucan, with its yellow and black beak, greeted them as they sat on their porch. Dean said, "We're going to tell everyone we know back in San Diego and in Atenas about this place."

"That's great," I said. "And I'll hire you to fly my guests from San José to Carate."

"Perfect," he said.

That's how I acquired air service to Luna Lodge. I could only hope my other preparations would be as solid.

Shortly after leaving Corcovado Lodge Tent Camp I wrote a letter to some 125 guests who I had gotten to know while working there. In it I told the travelers that I was building my own lodge and wanted their input so I could make it the best accommodations possible. I asked a number of questions about what they liked most about the tent camp and what they liked least.

Amazingly, I received seventy-five responses back. The travelers' comments ranged broadly. They enjoyed being close to nature, but they wanted something cushier, and they wanted en-suite bathrooms, so I was determined to make my bungalows merge with nature rather than shut guests off from it, and to make them comfortable, with private baths. They enjoyed eating in an open-air restaurant, so I did not put walls on the *rancho grande.* They loved hearing the forest sounds at night, so I committed to keeping everything quiet, with no radios or TVs in the rooms, and turning off the generator at 9:00 p.m. They loved eating healthy food that made them feel good so they had energy to play during the days. Those comments shaped my menu. Above all, they wanted to stay longer than the three-day packages offered by the tent camp, so I established an open policy: guests could stay as long as they wanted.

The day my first paying guests were to arrive, I woke at dawn with my mind spinning about all I must do to make their stay perfect. Dean was flying our guests in, and Fabio and I would drive down to Carate to pick them up.

We arrived at the little airstrip and stood in the sunshine as the couple climbed out of the Cessna. They were quintessential New Yorkers, lean, fit, and dressed mostly in black. I wanted to kiss them I was so happy. But I restrained myself and held out my hand to introduce myself to Betsy and Joe. I did give Lana and Dean huge hugs in thanks for flying the guests in.

Fabio had bolted benches in the back of Little Blue, so we loaded in the luggage, settled Betsy and Joe on the bench, and drove up the river valley to the lodge. Fabio drove while I radioed our workers.

"*¿Ya tiene la cama allí?*" I asked Freiman, making sure the bed was set up in the bungalow. Even as we had left that morning, our workers had just started moving the furniture in.

"*Ya, ahora está allí,*" he said. I heaved a sigh of relief.

"Make it up with the nice new sheets," I told him.

"*Sí, ya está hecho,*" he said.

Even with this assurance, I was wary. Would the room be good enough? Would everything be in place? And would the guests judge the way there was only one table in the *rancho grande*, no doors on the kitchen, and no adornments anywhere? I had to let all those details go and trust that everything would turn out just as it should. Fortunately, my leg was getting stronger every day—I still used the crutches when it ached, but most of the time I didn't even think about it. I could now work hard the way I liked.

When we arrived, Fabio took care of the luggage, while I led Betsy and Joe straight to the *rancho grande* deck to see the view of the Pacific. They stood there mesmerized for a good five minutes, and then I led them to their bungalow. As we walked up the path, I looked around at the landscaping that we had worked on for years, with its neat little path winding through the flowers: red ginger, orchids, and birds-of-paradise. Just before we arrived, Freiman popped out the door of the bungalow and flashed me a thumbs up. I took a deep breath and entered.

My heart leapt at the beauty. A king bed, made of teak, adorned the center of the circular space, the vaulted ceiling rising above. A textured yellow bedspread lit up the whole room. Off to the right was the bathroom entry, a doorless arch that led to a garden space with an open-air shower. Off to the left of the main room, a door opened to an intimate porch with two traditional Costa Rican wood and leather rocking chairs perched perfectly so guests could look out at the rainforest. Betsy and Joe followed me on the brief tour, and when I turned to them, their eyes sparkled with delight.

"This is amazing," Betsy said.

"Thank you," I replied. "I will leave you here to get settled. Dinner will be in the *rancho grande*, with drinks starting at six." I left them and walked on air all the way back down to my office, where I sat at my desk and said thanks to the Universe for this gift. Then I remembered, I had a whole night ahead of me, feeding the guests and entertaining them as we brought in the new year. I leapt to my feet and headed to the kitchen to cook dinner, since Vilma was away.

As I entered the kitchen, I was ignited with a purpose to make the experience that evening professional and excellent. Once again, I drew on the power of focusing my energy. As I chopped vegetables, I concentrated on making the pieces a similar size, and I took extra care as I seasoned the chicken and put it in the oven. Everything had to be beautiful and delicious for our guests. There was a sense of shimmering possibility in the air, and I let it fuel my cooking and lace it with love and passion. It was all happening. My dream was real.

I knew I had to be courageous to host my first guests. There were so many people who doubted me—including myself. I needed to refocus my energy so I could override those fears. The guests believed in me and I had to believe in myself. After I finished cooking, I showered and put on a tight red dancing dress, and Fabio wore his best jeans and a blue shirt. I hoped that nothing would go wrong with the food or service. Growing up, my mom had thrown many parties, so I had learned how to set an elegant table, and how to cook for a crowd, skills I honed while working as a cook. I also became good at cleaning up. Tonight, I relied on these skills.

Betsy and Joe entered the *rancho grande*, where I had our one table set. The day before, in Puerto Jimenez I had bought candles, bright orange napkins, and silverware, which adorned the table. I also put a big vase of flowers from the garden in the middle.

We sat, and everyone stayed quiet. The pause was long enough for me to feel the tension throughout my body and hear the pulsing beat of the forest. But then Freiman showed up with a good cabernet. He poured it in the wine glasses, and with the first sip everyone relaxed. We talked and drank and listened to the frogs sing.

"The world is supposed to end tonight, and out here we won't even know it," I said.

Everyone laughed.

"Yes," Joe said. "What a perfect place to be away from all the Y2K craziness. I doubt anything will happen. But the media has hyped it up so much it's easy to believe that everything will collapse at midnight."

"We will keep on running," I said. "The rainforest is strong and never rests."

"We absolutely love our bungalow," Betsy said. "I've never showered in the open air, and wow, it is fabulous."

Joe nodded in agreement.

My heart warmed with her words. I could hardly believe I was sitting there in the *rancho grande* with my very first guests. After all the years of planning and working, my dream had come true. But most of all, I felt grateful that I had followed my intuition: I left my old life and everything I knew to come to Costa Rica. I had invested my all in building this lodge and now, people were enjoying it. What bliss!

We feasted on roasted chicken, potatoes, a Greek salad made with vegetables from our garden, and for dessert sliced mango from our trees. We talked and talked, about their lives in New York, and their work, Joe in finance, and Betsy as a teacher. I told them about how Luna Lodge came to be.

After dinner we broke out champagne and cranked up the music. We danced salsa and then rock and roll to Michael Jackson, the Commodores, and the Eagles. I swayed with Fabio to "Afternoon Delight," and then we switched partners and rocked out with the couple to "Billie Jean." Meanwhile, Freiman and my other two employees hit the floor dancing with each other, and everyone got a glass of champagne.

After hours of dancing, I stood in the middle of the group and clanked a fork on my glass. "Ready! Ten, nine, eight . . ." Everyone joined in as we counted down to midnight. "Four, three, two . . . one!"

We cheered, and Fabio and I kissed, and then everyone hugged everyone else. Then we stopped and looked around, curious to see if some big disaster would hit, like an electric fuse bursting and the lights going out. But of course there was only silence among us and the throbbing sound of the forest, which never sleeps, never stops its exquisite creating.

Joe yelled, "Woohoo!" and we all joined in, happy that nothing had affected our intimate world.

We are safe, I whispered inside myself.

The guests said goodnight and made their way to their bungalow. Fabio and I headed to our house, where we held each other in
bed and fell into a deep sleep.

The next morning, I opened my eyes warily, wondering once
again if the world had blown up or ceased turning, but I only
sensed the life of the forest surrounding us. Without a telephone or
computer we had no way of knowing what was happening. I took
a deep breath, stretched, rolled out of bed, and hoped I'd be able to
meet whatever challenges the day might bring.

CHAPTER 34

In those days—well before TripAdvisor and Yelp existed—hotels relied mostly on word-of-mouth, travel magazines, and guidebooks to draw in customers. Now that the lodge was nearly complete, we faced a new challenge: how to let people know about it. I contemplated this question as we worked putting doors on the kitchen, finishing the walls, decks, and bathrooms of bungalows two and three, and adding final touches such as light fixtures and furniture.

Lana and Dean, the couple who had flown in my first official guests, had already begun spreading the word. A few weeks after their stay, I headed to Jimenez to check my email, and I had two messages from people Lana and Dean knew, requesting reservations. I could hardly believe it. As planned, Dean flew the guests down.

He was an excellent handyman, so he helped in many ways with the lodge, especially with the electrical system, which he checked to make sure it was installed properly. One day he offered to help me haul supplies from San José. I climbed in the Cessna with him and Lana, and we flew up there. We went to PriceSmart to buy necessities for the restaurant such as paper towels, dishwashing soap, and olive oil, and for the guest rooms, toilet paper, tissues, and cleaning supplies. Once we loaded all of it in the plane, it was so full that Dean and I had to leave Lana behind. She didn't mind because she had some shopping of her own to do.

On the way back to Luna, clouds settled in, and we flew above them in the brightest blue sky I had ever seen. My heart soared like the plane; I sensed in that moment that Luna Lodge just might succeed. My intuition had guided me well to that point, and I knew I could continue to trust it.

We started receiving more and more emails through our website, and guests arrived. By this time we had finished the other two bungalows, so we were rocking at full speed. I had so much to do at the lodge that I no longer had time to go all the way to Jimenez to use a computer. We needed internet service at the lodge, so Fabio figured out how we could have a line-of-sight link using radio waves.

Since the lodge was nestled in the forest, though, we couldn't receive service there. Every other day I carried a Yagi antenna, which looks a bit like an old-fashioned TV antenna, about a meter and a half (almost five feet) long with little arms sticking out, way up into the primary rainforest. I also carried a cable and my laptop with the help of one of my workers. We climbed and climbed for about forty-five minutes to reach the highest point on my property, a ridge where Fabio had made me a little half-moon shelf, attached to a tree trunk. While I stood working, an employee stayed to keep me safe. It was a remote area that sat along a mining trail, and miners would pass by occasionally. That was also why I didn't leave the antenna there, so it wouldn't get stolen.

I put my computer on the little shelf, pushed the antenna into the soft ground, checked that the line-of-site was clear across the Golfo Dulce to the town of Golfito, and powered up. By this point I was receiving one or two inquiries about the lodge each day. But on this particular day, I couldn't believe it—the messages just kept coming. There were twenty-five emails. I spent hours answering them, arranging reservations, and I was happy doing it.

A spider monkey who we'd named George swung onto a branch about ten feet above me. "Hi George," I said, happy to see him. He often came around when I was working. Usually, I spent a few moments talking with him, but I was so busy that day I couldn't stop. As I worked, something wet splattered my arm, so I looked up to see that George was peeing. Panicked, I pulled off my T-shirt and threw it on top of the keyboard to protect it. "Darn you, George," I yelled. He was what locals call a *macho*, which meant he thought he was really hot stuff.

I finished the emails despite him, and outlined all the reservations on a piece of paper. Once I finished and started my hike down, the reality hit me: all those reservations meant money. I would finally have enough. I could keep the lodge running. I could buy furniture for the other bungalows and the restaurant. I could purchase deck chairs, and hammocks, and expand the menu. I could pay my workers and maybe even hire a few more. And I could pay back my bank loan. The anxiety that had been weighing on my shoulders dropped away, so that even as I carried all my gear, I felt light as I hiked down the trail.

A few months later, I got an inquiry from a woman in San Francisco. She and her husband wanted to bring three of their four sons to Luna. I was happy to have them because I wanted to cater to families as well as couples.

The day after they arrived, I headed up with one of my workers to check my email while Fabio took the family on a tour through the primary rainforest. They reached a ridge where they could see me in the distance at my little desk, wearing rubber boots, cutoffs, and a tank top, while I typed on the computer.

"What is that?" the mother, Eliza, asked Fabio.

"I'll show you," he said. He led them along a narrow trail that followed the ridge.

As they approached, I looked up from my work.

"What are you doing?" Eliza asked.

"Just answering my email," I said.

She shook her head in disbelief. "I have to write about this."

She explained that she was the editor for one of the most prestigious business technology magazines in the world, *Red Herring*, which was based in San Francisco. It was started in 1993 and flourished during the time of the dot-com boom, with global distribution.

"Our readers are going to love this," she said, as she shot photo after photo of me.

Three months later, I received a large manila envelope with *Red Herring* listed as the return address. I ripped it open and tore through the pages of the magazine to find the story. The photo accompanying the one-page article titled "Wireless in the Rainforest" showed me typing at my little tree desk, next to my antenna. The article explained the technical aspect of our setup, and the way that the internet was truly reaching even the most remote parts of the planet. I was so thrilled I grabbed some scissors and cut out the article so I could frame it and hang it on the wall of the *rancho grande*.

A month later a renowned photographer, Macduff Everton, came to stay because someone in New York had told him about Luna Lodge. He shot for the magazine *Condé Nast Traveler*. I knew that this was my ticket to success. Being in those pages would launch my lodge into the international travel world. I prepared his bungalow myself, making sure everything was perfect, and I oversaw his meals and his activities, tweaking anything that wasn't the highest quality.

Over dinner, Macduff told Fabio and me that he had traveled around the world three times and crossed the Greenwich Meridian twenty-six times shooting photos for magazines. "In all those travels, I have seen the rainforest from a plane and from down within it, but I have never seen a view of the rainforest like this," he said, waving his hand out toward the canopy where the eye follows the green to the Pacific Ocean. "It's spectacular."

I smiled at him. That was why I built Luna Lodge where I did.

The next day he departed for New York, his camera full of vivid photos. I was hopeful about the article but knew that nothing was certain.

I used the intensity of my anticipation to prepare for a holiday. *Semana Santa*, the Latin American celebration of Easter week, had begun. On Good Friday, we hosted a feast. We cooked baked *dorado* (mahi-mahi) and decorated everything with Easter colors. As I prepared for the party, I was more agitated than usual. I knocked over a chair, dropped silverware, and became confused about what else needed to be done. My intuition told me that something was coming, something big and challenging.

On this Good Friday, my bungalows were full of guests who wanted to go down to the beach and watch the sunset. We headed down, and it was worth the trip, because the sky glowed orange, with pink stripes. When we returned, I climbed out of the truck, and as always, observed that my house built of cristobal wood that I so loved just wasn't in the right place. It was the first thing you saw when you drove up to the lodge, when really the spectacular *rancho grande* should have been first. This had troubled me for the four months since we opened, but I had been unable to solve the problem.

During our Good Friday celebration we all sat around the big table and talked of the holiday and what it meant. We had five guests, along with Fabio's mom, Marielos, and all his brothers and sisters. Vilma's boyfriend had come down from San José, and her son Maicol was there, too, though not at the table with us that evening.

Maicol was seven years old, and he was beautiful, with skin the color of Kalamata olives. He exuded kindness, had a bright smile, and was curious about everything. In fact, Macduff, the *Condé Nast* photographer, was so impressed with him that he included him in many of the photos he shot.

My rottweiler named Balto also hung around enjoying the company. He generally slept in the house under the step up to my bedroom, but suddenly he was at the edge of the *rancho grande* barking incessantly. Usually, he was like a teddy bear, sweet and quiet. That night he wouldn't stop his loud, deep barking.

We were just about to start dancing, so everyone got up from the table, still talking and enjoying the tasty chardonnay we served with the fish.

Suddenly from the kitchen, Vilma yelled, "*¡Encendio!* Fire!" She ran past us toward the house, and we all followed her. I smelled the sharp scent of smoke immediately. Fabio turned off all the lights so we could see if the flames were moving toward the *rancho grande*, and then rushed to the water tank where he filled two buckets to throw on the fire. Usually the wind blew from the south, but I hoped today was different, so the flames wouldn't ignite the crispy, dry thatch of the lodge.

Shoving those thoughts aside, I joined Vilma at the door of the house. To our dismay, we saw her son, little Maicol, huddled on the bed in Vilma's room, surrounded by flames, his face wet with tears. I realized that Balto, who was still barking, was trying to alert us. When Maicol saw us, he leapt up and ran through the flames into his mother's arms. We took him to the *rancho grande*, where we wrapped him in a wet sheet.

I used the radio to call our neighbors and tell them we had a fire, but it was so late only one of them answered.

"Please, can you help us?" I said. "Radio Puerto Jimenez and see if anyone can come!"

I had never been in a fire. Fabio's family, however, had lost two houses to fires, so Fabio continued in full action. He stationed one of the guests at the corner of the *rancho grande* to alert us if the flames jumped over there. Then he got more buckets of water from the tank and doused the fire. Meanwhile, my mind churned about what I could do for Maicol.

The country of Japan had just donated a new four-by-four Red Cross truck to Puerto Jimenez. I radioed again to see if the Red Cross would come, and they said they were on their way. I also learned that there was a doctor in one of the nearby hotels. I called there on the radio, and the hotel owner ran to get him. When the doctor introduced himself, I told him that Maicol's knee, part of his face, and his hand were burned bright red. He told me to put a sheet on him and put him in cold water, which we had already done. Next we were to blow cool air over his skin. While everyone else passed buckets hand-to-hand from our water tank in an attempt to put out the fire, Vilma, Fabio's siblings, and I fanned Maicol with magazines. Tears streamed down his burned face, but he made little noise. Clearly, he was in shock.

I feared for his life.

As I fanned Maicol and saw that he might be okay, I realized the magnitude of the fire. I could lose everything I'd worked so hard to build. I had insurance on the lodge, but not the house. Still, I feared most for the lodge. If it burned, I wouldn't have money to rebuild even with the insurance, and I didn't have the energy to go through all of that effort again.

Everything we owned except my laptop was in the burning house—our money, our clothes, my jewelry, letters, and photos were all in there. The only thing I truly needed to retrieve was a Guatemalan bag. I had stuffed our cash in it, $500 worth, along with our passports and other important papers.

I left Maicol in good hands and went to the house. The flames completely engulfed Vilma's bedroom and the kitchen, but they were just heading into Fabio's and my room. I took a deep breath, ran inside, and grabbed the bag. As I ran back out, I paused to seize two plastic trash cans that held all our sheets and towels. The ceiling was covered with a plastic sheet we had installed to stop the soot that built from our stove from falling on us. As I pulled the trash cans across the floor, a piece of burning plastic the size of a Frisbee dropped and barely missed my face. I let go of the cans and sprinted out.

Later I figured out the likely cause of the blaze: to accommodate all the people sleeping in the house, we had many mattresses on the floor. Over the past twenty years, it had been waxed with petroleum, so it was prime to ignite. When a breeze blew in an open window, it must have knocked over a burning candle, setting fire to the floor and mattresses. Maicol had been on his mattress, and when the floor turned to an inferno, he had jumped up on the bed, but it was also burning.

Once the fire was under control, Fabio loaded Maicol and Vilma up in Little Blue and drove them toward Puerto Jimenez. My pilot friend, Alvaro, intended to fly Maicol and Vilma to San José so they could go to a full hospital. En route to Jimenez, Fabio met up with the Red Cross truck. The medics transferred Maicol to their vehicle and drove him and Vilma the rest of the way to the plane. Word of what had happened spread through the community, and locals arrived at the airstrip, where they shone their headlights on the runway, so the plane could take off safely.

When Fabio returned he reported that Maicol was on his way, and we all sighed with relief. The lodge guests wandered off to bed, while I arranged places for the others to sleep in a shed on the property. Exhausted and covered with soot, Fabio and I stood at the edge of the *rancho grande* on a little concrete bench. What was left of the house still smoldered, and when I looked over at the ruins, I cried, all the tension finally releasing from me. Fabio sat there, stoic, his hands clenched in his lap.

"Where there's fire, there's got to be water," I said, and I wasn't even sure what I meant. But my intuition told me that one day, in the spot where the remains of the house stood, I would build a swimming pool for our guests. I felt skeptical about this vision; it seemed nearly impossible with the ruins of my house still smoldering. However, I knew that my intuition tended to steer me well, so I tucked the idea into a little compartment of my mind while I focused on the present moment.

As tired and sad as I was, I was grateful to be sitting under the *rancho grande*. It and the bungalows had not burned—the wind had blown in our favor.

The next day, after a restless night trying to sleep on the concrete floor of the *rancho grande*, I put on a black bra, a pair of Fabio's underwear that had been in the Guatemalan bag, and my rubber boots. These were now my work clothes since my only remaining clothing was the dress I had been wearing when the fire started. While we cleaned up the ruins of the house, people started arriving: goldminers, friends from Puerto Jimenez, and hotel owners from the beaches. They brought clothes and towels and bedding. Their generosity so touched me that tears streamed down my soot-blackened face.

Fabio and I sorted through the few things in the house that hadn't burned: some dishes, a book, a chair. Then he set fire to the rest of what remained well away from the *rancho grande*. I put pieces of charred wood in a wheelbarrow, wheeled them over, and threw them on. It felt like a sacrifice, a part of my heart burning up with the remains of the house I so loved. A piece of black plastic went poof right in front of me, disintegrating completely.

Okay, I understand, I said to myself. *My house was in the wrong place and it needed to go. I wouldn't have gotten rid of it. I wouldn't have burned it down. Now the lodge is better without it.* I decided this experience must be divine will.

In the coming months, Fabio and I slept in the shed on the property. Before this, the employees had used it to eat and socialize. Now, we were simply grateful for this shelter from the weather and for the gifts that had come. Friends and people we didn't even know donated so many clothes that I gave some away to the gold miners. I still didn't have any jewelry or other fine things, but I didn't really want anything. My life felt pure and simple. It was a rebirth.

Oddly, many guests we had in the coming months had also endured a house fire. One couple had built a million-dollar home in Southern California, and it burned in a forest fire that same year. It was good for me to talk with these people. It felt like it was healing the loss. A few months later, the guest from California who had lost her house sent me a superb blue dress with a flouncy skirt, and a necklace with a blue heart surrounded by pearls. I cherished these.

The real gift was that Maicol was okay. He had a dark maroon spot on his cheek and blistered skin on the back of his hand, but he was alive and home with his family.

In May, just when the rainy season was starting, I received a package. I opened it to find two copies of *Condé Nast Traveler*. The cover, in bold letters, shouted that this issue published "The Gold List: The World's Best Places to Stay." I flipped through the pages, searching, searching, but not finding anything about the lodge. I saw articles about elegant hotels in New York, Geneva, and Paris, but nothing on Luna. Disappointed and confused, I perused the ads in the back of the magazine. Finally, I came to the inside back cover, a monthly column I was familiar with called "Room with a View." My heart leapt with joy.

There, filling three-quarters of the page, was a photo of the porch, rocking chairs, and view of the rainforest from bungalow one, that I'd named the Honeymoon Suite. Below it, the text read:

"Early risers will awaken to the symphony of some 400 bird species emanating from the leafy canopy below. Like them, your bungalow has an expansive, bird's-eye view of Corcovado National Park, whose lush rainforest ranks as one of the most biologically diverse places on earth . . ."

It went on to talk about the abundant wildlife in Corcovado. I read it over and over. My heart filled with a feeling I hardly recognized: a warm, glorious relief. Tears welled in my eyes, and I wanted to shout to the treetops: *I made something, and people think it's good. I worked hard to create this place, and people love it.* I cried and laughed and then I sat down, all my energy dissipating into a relaxed sense that finally everything was going to be fine. I could stop fighting and simply enjoy life.

That magazine had a worldwide distribution of more than a half-million readers. My lodge, pictured in my imagination that day fifteen years ago aboard the *Zebu*—and since then fought with every fiber of my being to manifest—had launched onto the world stage.

CHAPTER 35

Every experience in my journey has led to this life of hosting guests and friends at Luna Lodge. I love the way it feeds me and others. My family roots in the rough ranching country of South Dakota, my experience of a loving but overbearing stepfather and a mother who pushed me to always do my best, as well as the unconditional support from my father, all taught me to work hard and believe in myself and follow my own dreams. The opportunities I had as a kid thanks to my parents and my hometown of Gunnison, Colorado, the hiking, biking, river-running, horseback riding, and skiing, as well as building our house—all of it has created a highly textured tapestry that continues to weave richness into my day-to-day life of running a lodge.

My life has been full of love for fabulous men. My sailing adventure with Tommy Martinez gave me my first sense of true freedom. During my trips to Alaska with Cole I learned about love and about relentlessly following my own path rather than the one set by a man in my life. And of course my years of building and running the lodge with Fabio helped me come to know both the rainforest and my own inner self more deeply. The courage of these men to live fearlessly has helped me do the same. In a similar way, the women in my life—Jani, my mother, and close friends all over the world—have taught me to be nurturing and loving, traits our world today needs so desperately.

My time in the forest has helped me embark upon new endeavors. I am now a certified Forest Bathing guide. I take guests and others on journeys into the forest so they can experience the quiet and love with which everything and everyone is imbued. When we learn to tune in to the quiet inside, our whole lives become more harmonious.

I have also become a Reiki Master, so when visitors come, I am able to offer them the healing power of that flow from the rainforest, often with remarkable results.

My adventure with Operation Raleigh and time at Cape York in Australia taught me so much about how to tap into my own inner strength. There were times on the *Zebu* that were so physically and emotionally challenging that I didn't know if I could make it through. I had to reach deep inside to navigate them, and I was always able to do it. That inner strength is there within each of us. The more we believe in it, and use it, the stronger it becomes.

During my employment with Costa Rica Expeditions, I learned every detail about hosting guests and running a remote lodge. I changed beds, cooked meals, ordered food and supplies, managed reservations, recruited and supervised the staff, handled customer complaints, queries, and relations, made and followed a budget, and kept the books. I had the opportunity to do it all—and that knowledge and understanding helped me be successful and a better employer. My goal now is to be empathetic with my employees. Often we all work very hard, but I've learned to manage people with love rather than force. It's easy when everyone is stressed to switch over to a forceful attitude, to push and push, but this usually creates discord. My goal is to supervise with kindness, with praise, to respect my employees the way I want to be respected. This helps them respect me.

The years of labor and the uncertainty of building a lodge in the rainforest was the richest experience of my life. And I see this as a universal truth. When we are most pressed, we become the most open to seeing ourselves, our lives, and others in a new light.

This certainly happened to me after I broke my leg and ran out of money to build the lodge. That's when I read about the little light that had to own its brightness and take action on its own behalf. It is so easy to get into a pattern of relying on others—and blaming them when we don't get what we want. Now I do my best to always turn that pointed finger back at myself, to look at my part and take responsibility for changing what I can. When I finally surrendered getting help for the lodge from the gay couple and the alcoholic, and even my family—though my family did help quite a bit—I became responsible for my destiny, and that is so powerful. Taking charge is a beautiful thing.

Above all of these lessons, the greatest one of all was the way the whole journey taught me to trust my intuition, my true, deep knowing. We can all come to know our inner knowledge by listening to it. It has taken years for me to really learn to pause and listen. I have made many detours, each one showing me what I didn't want. Today, my intuition is my most important guide. And my greatest joy comes from helping others listen to their intuition.

That part of me, and you, is connected to a much larger and more knowing power. My whole journey has taught me to trust that there is a power much stronger and wiser than I am, orchestrating everything. The more I learn to turn inside, the more it enriches my life. These days I do my best to channel that love, whether through my hands as I do Reiki, or in the forest, when I guide my guests through Forest Bathing meditations.

Most of all, though, I do it in my everyday interaction with my guests when I greet them with a smile at breakfast, help guide their plans for the day, and dance with them after dinner. I do the same with my family and community. This creates harmony within and without. I can be love in the world, and from that, amazing things always happen, so that I spend my days in a constant state of appreciative wonder, always ready for the next adventure.

FINAL PART

WHITE HAWK

AWAKENING THE VISIONARY WITHIN:
MESSENGER AND PROTECTOR

EPILOGUE

Early one morning in 2001, I was doing yoga on the deck at the front of the *rancho grande*, soaking in the view across the rainforest canopy to the Pacific. I wore a one-piece cheetah-print yoga outfit that brought out the wildness in me. I challenged myself, holding some of the toughest poses such as crow and headstand for longer than usual. When I finished, I lay on the deck in *savasana*, or corpse pose. On that warm, dry summer day, the forest teemed with life all around me.

I was exhausted from continuing to build up the lodge and tending to guests who at that point arrived in a pretty steady flow. I relaxed for a while with my eyes closed. Suddenly a shadow crossed over the top of me. It blocked the sun on my eyelids for just an instant. I opened my eyes to see a white hawk floating above me. It was magnificent, big and strong, and the whitest white one could imagine, with long wings and a fan tail edged in black. I sat up and watched it make its way toward the ocean, soaring and circling on the updrafts.

I felt its presence in my heart, a loving fullness, as though when its shadow had crossed my body, we united in spirit. Ever since then, the hawk has visited me during crucial moments and guided me. Many important truths have come through his presence. He reminds me to believe in my own strength and to realize that I am much more than this physical body. When I hear his call, *hee-EE-ah, hee-EE-ah,* or when I see him, I know that everything is going to be all right.

Several years later, I was climbing up the winding path to teach yoga on the 1,600-square-foot yoga platform we built in 2003. Nestled on top of large wooden pylons, it cantilevers out over the steep hillside high above the treetops and the *rancho grande*. I looked across the forest canopy to the azure Pacific, but even that view did not quell my worries. I was concerned about money and my reservation bookings and my relationship with Jani and my dad, which continued to be strained.

Once I prepared for class, my five students and I sat on our mats to start some breathing exercises. I sensed the hawk, so I looked over my shoulder. At first I only saw puffy white clouds, but then he flew in front of the platform. He circled for a few moments, his powerful body soaring carefree on the updrafts. I paused to soak in his beauty and grace.

When I turned back to my class, my body and mind felt relaxed, and I continued in this centered state throughout the hour of yoga. After we rolled up our mats, I said to my friend, "I sense that he's still around." We descended a few steps leading down from the platform, and suddenly there he was, flying across the canopy in front of us. My heart soared even higher. *He is here because I truly need him.*

At times he urges me to pay attention to circumstances I need to see in the world around me. One of those is the state of the natural environment here. Though the Osa Peninsula continues to be a remote place, it is gaining in popularity for travelers and businesses. The nature here feels the impact of that. Commercial farming enterprises purchase land at prices that entice the locals to give up their homes. Then the businesses plant species that aren't indigenous, which thrive and spread into the rainforest, harming the intricate ecological balance. Businesses also remove crucial habitat and migration corridors. This forces animals to flee or become accustomed to humans, endangering their survival. Some nights I awaken terrified for the future of the ocean, trees, and creatures here.

The white hawk's presence has inspired my next life goal: to create a foundation to save as much rainforest in the area as possible. In 2007, I initiated this endeavor and named it the White Hawk Foundation. At its center sits Corcovado National Park. As a national park Corcovado is protected from logging and mining, and acts as a safe haven for many threatened species.

The White Hawk Foundation dovetails with this initiative. The foundation had a good start after television producer David Weddle and his wife Risa came to Luna from California. David was co-executive producer of the hit series *CSI: Crime Scene Investigation.* He and Risa so loved Luna Lodge and Corcovado that they stayed in touch and one day offered to hold a fundraiser for the foundation in Malibu, California. I flew up for the occasion, attended by the glitterati of Hollywood. It was a great success, raising thousands of dollars. Notable film producer Tom Shadyac came and donated generously, as did many others.

The foundation helps spread the word about the importance of protecting nature and purchases crucial parcels of land bordering Corcovado to keep the park safe from exploitation. At this writing, the foundation has bought four hundred acres adjacent to Corcovado. Our goal is to acquire 1,250 acres and more. This land will act as a buffer zone to prevent the park from becoming an island where species suffer because they are trapped in an isolated space.

Meanwhile, Luna Lodge has matured. On our sixty acres of primary and secondary forest, we use hydro-electric and solar power to generate almost all of the electricity, creating as little impact on the environment as possible. We have eight bungalows, seven tent dwellings on elevated decks, and three more traditional rooms. We have had visitors from 130 countries and have been recommended in many publications, including the *New York Times*, *Condé Nast Traveler*, *Travel and Leisure*, *Yoga Journal*, and CNN.com. I regularly host retreats for guests who come to deepen their yoga and spiritual practice. I also put on seminars for the community, empowering local girls to make positive life choices.

After thirty-eight years here, I am still deeply in love with Costa Rica and especially the rainforest. The earth's rainforests are the very breath of the planet, perfectly symbiotic with all living creatures. These shrinking islands of green are home to more than half of the world's species of plants and animals. They produce 40 percent of the earth's oxygen, and they absorb carbon dioxide, reducing the planet's greenhouse gas levels.

We need these wild places not only for our physical survival, but for what they can teach us about living with love. The rainforest has taught me many things. While in my younger years I was pulled about by my passions, my steadfast devotion to the rainforest taught me the value of fidelity to my mate and my life's dreams. It has also taught me to be responsible for my actions since they have a "butterfly effect" in my life—even small changes can lead to large consequences down the road. For instance, when I dedicate myself to listen ever more closely to my intuition, suddenly a whole new way of living opens up.

In the rainforest, this is especially visible. Loss of one species triggers a destructive domino effect for the entire ecosystem. In a similar way, positive personal decisions made by individuals, such as using sustainable power and protecting land from exploitation, have a globally curative effect. My new objective is to show people the positive potential of this butterfly effect.

Some days I look around at this magnificent lodge nestled in the forest and I can hardly believe that it is real, that my dream actually came true. Now, I am bringing the same determined passion that created Luna Lodge to the goal of healing what the Inca's called *Pachamama*—Mother Earth. I'm doing it one tree at time, and I invite you to join me.

ABOUT THE AUTHORS

Lana Wedmore

Lana Wedmore has lived a life of unrelenting adventure, eschewing convention and embracing the unknown. She is a dynamic speaker and natural inspirer, who has worked in Costa Rica tourism for thirty years. She set up a program to save sea turtles and the White Hawk Foundation to preserve parcels  of rainforest. Most recently, she was elected Vice President of the Wellness Association, which works hand-in-hand with the Costa Rica Institute of Tourism to help businesses provide wellness activities such as meditation and yoga to travelers. She also helped plan and build the first bamboo sustainable school in Costa Rica. Lana is a certified shaman, Reiki Master, and yoga instructor.

Lesley S. King

Lesley S. King has traveled the world writing for *The New York Times*, *Audubon* magazine, United Airlines *Hemispheres* magazine, and the Frommer's and Dummies guides. She is the author of more than a dozen books.

OTHER BOOKS BY LANA WEDMORE

Restore Your Balance in Just Ten Minutes a Day.

Do you ever wake up feeling stiff and sore? Do you sit at a desk all day and lack the energy to get up and move? Do you know you need exercise but you can't find the time? Then *Yoga for Connecting, Mind, Body, and Soul* is for you. In ten minutes a day, this book will help you: 1) Restore your body's energy 2) Refresh your mental state 3) Rediscover your soul.

Your health is your most important asset. Whether you're dealing with anxiety, lower back pain, or jet lag from a busy travel schedule, there is healing for you in these pages—regardless of your age or ability.

With step-by-step instructions and photographs for each exercise, the movements in this book can be done in a chair, hotel room, or even your own bed before you put your feet on the ground. It's never too late to find your balance and fitness. Come join us!

Releases in October 2020.